MONKEYS ON THE ROAD

ONE FAMILY'S VANLIFE ADVENTURE SOUTH IN SEARCH OF A SIMPLER LIFE

MARY HOLLENDONER

First edition

ISBN: 978-1-7379436-2-4

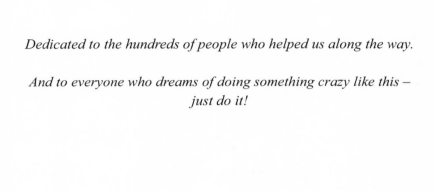

Dedicated to the hundreds of people who helped us along the way.

And to everyone who dreams of doing something crazy like this –
just do it!

Every tomorrow ought not to resemble every yesterday.
- Beryl Markham, *West with the Night*

CONTENTS

NOTE

All events in this book are true and happened to the author between 2017 and 2021. Some names have been changed to protect the privacy of those depicted. Dialogue has been re-created from memory.

To see photos of our adventures along the way, and for an interactive map of our route, go to www.monkeysontheroad.com

USA

1

THE BEGINNING

I climb up into the passenger seat of our big white van and click my seat belt with trembling hands. My heart is pounding like a drum in my chest. I take a deep breath and turn to look at my husband, John, in the driver's seat. His grin is enormous, with just a touch of nervousness around his eyes, as he turns the key in the ignition. I don't know whether to laugh or cry... I think I do both.

Are we really going to drive thirty thousand miles across 20 countries? Will we make it? What will we do next?

Our six-year-old daughter, Lilly, simply looks out the window and says, "Okay, let's drive to Mexico." Like it's just another day!

On top of the excitement and nerves, I also feel relief. Relief to finally be on our way, after years of intense planning and preparation. It's like I've been standing at the top of a cliff, anxiously waiting to jump into a beautiful pool below me, and am finally free to just do it and stop worrying. But then again, the free-fall is the most terrifying part of the jump.

Only two weeks ago I was getting cold feet. John and I had already quit our jobs, rented out our house, and missed enrollment for the next year of Lilly's public school. But I was obsessively reading the news from Mexico, getting more and more concerned.

Highest number of homicides in 20 years! Mass graves discovered next to the road! Decapitated heads found in a cooler! Tourists poisoned at resorts! Are we completely insane to drive into this country with our little girl? I marked the dangerous areas on a large map of Mexico, assuring myself that we could weave a path around them.

But then, along came an abnormally strong set of hurricanes, hitting Mexico on both sides of the country. I don't want to imagine hunkering down in our little van, arms wrapped around Lilly in futile protection, while a hurricane bats us around. So I convinced myself hurricanes could be avoided by keeping a close eye on the forecasts.

And finally, only one week before we planned to cross the border, there was an 8.2 magnitude earthquake with epicenter in southern Mexico! It was the largest earthquake to hit Mexico in a *century*. Is someone trying to tell us something?

What if Lilly gets seriously hurt, or kidnapped by Mexican drug lords? Or we have a car crash, or the van is stolen? Or what if we survive the trip but then we can't find jobs when we return to the US? Or, one of us gets cancer and we can't get US health insurance? There are 101 reasons not to do this trip, and I started thinking about all of them.

Ultimately, I turned to logic and probabilities – yes, it is possible that any of those things happen to us, but it's more likely they won't. The most likely outcome is that we'll grow old and hope to have lived the lives we wanted. So we made the uncomfortably exciting choice to leave our safe path and venture into the unknown.

I remind myself of this as I turn around to check Lilly is buckled correctly into her car seat. For the third time.

We finally bump down the driveway away from our home, memories flooding past our windows, as the neighbors wave and cheer us on. My head is swimming with the to-do lists from the past few months, but at this point, it no longer matters what we forgot to do or pack or research. We are driving to South America! No turning back!

One mile down the road, I sheepishly turn to John, "I left all of our food in the fridge back at the house."

And thus begins our journey of 30,000 miles. With a U-turn.

2

THE REAL BEGINNING

I t seemed like I had it all. A loving husband and healthy, happy daughter. A fancy job at a hot tech company. A big house in a friendly neighborhood. How could I possibly complain?

But there was a nagging voice in the back of my mind telling me this was not how I wanted to spend another decade of my life. Impressive jobs come with a lot of stress, and mine was no exception. My day was spent running from problem to problem, barely finding the time to eat and often returning home headachey and short-tempered. In the evenings, I tried to focus on my daughter but always had one eye on my work phone, my brain still processing the day's unresolved issues. Heartburn often kept me from sleeping at night, and eventually my body protested with an allergic reaction of red hives, which my doctor couldn't attribute to anything besides stress.

I've always had a strong relationship with John, but we didn't get enough quality time together, usually discussing child care logistics or other life admin in our rare moments alone. I desperately craved more time with him and our daughter Lilly, but it felt like life was flying by at top speed. It's already Christmas again? Lilly is turning five already?! If we didn't change our lifestyle, it seemed like I would blink and Lilly would be 18! We only have one child, and after three miscarriages we've decided not to have any more, so our time with her feels precious.

So John and I started to brainstorm how to make a significant change in our lives. We first considered moving to a smaller town in the mountains to make outdoor adventures more accessible and live in a community of like-minded people. Year after year we discussed this option, but the timing was always wrong for one of us to leave our career behind... I was ready but John had just gotten his start-up funded, then John was ready but I had just accepted a promotion at work, then I was ready but John had just sold his start-up and was contract-bound.

Finally, the stars aligned for both of us to leave our jobs at the same time. By this point, we felt so burned-out that we wanted a significant break before settling down in a new location. Simply moving our life to a new town didn't feel like enough – same life, different backdrop. So, we spent countless hours discussing ideas for a mega-adventure. I read dozens of books by people who'd pulled the trigger on a big life change – from the NY exec who quit her job to start an organic farm in Vermont to the young couple who sailed around the world after a weekend sailing class – I felt inspired by these real people who weren't famous or wealthy but had done such unique and risky things.

Initially we were both drawn to the idea of a physical challenge trip. Before Lilly was born, every vacation and weekend had revolved around physical adventure, usually rock climbing. John and I have both been climbing-obsessed "monkeys" since before we met. We come from very different backgrounds, but our love for rock climbing in Yosemite is what brought us together.

John is a self-proclaimed redneck from rural Washington state. He worked as a wildland firefighter for 10 years, spending months camping out in the wilderness every summer digging fire line and cutting down burning trees. He then used his tree experience and rope skills to land a job caring for the giant trees in Yosemite – the world capital of rock climbing. I'm a city girl from central London, England and had rarely even laid eyes on a tent when, by dumb luck, I got into a rural university in New Hampshire and discovered my love of the outdoors. I then worked in consulting for a few years, saving money and adventuring on weekends, until I managed to get accepted on the Search and Rescue team in Yosemite and moved there full-time.

So Yosemite is where John and I met and where we were married three years later. When we decided we should get "real" jobs and move to San Francisco, we continued to retreat to Yosemite on weekends. When we decided to have a child, I kept climbing there until the week before Lilly was born, wearing a special harness to fit around my enormous belly as I waddled my way up the rock. But when we made the decision to quit our jobs, Lilly was only five years old – still too young for big vertical adventures – so we thought beyond climbing.

I'd done some bike touring in the past and I'd long been intrigued by the idea of bicycling the length of the Americas. We did a two-week test trip pulling Lilly in a trailer, but realized she would get bored sitting for so many hours a day, plus I didn't like the idea of her bouncing along behind me on a one-lane road in the mountains of Ecuador. Ultimately, we were so enamored by the idea of traveling from our home all the way to the bottom of the world without ever getting on an airplane that we stuck with the idea, but, by van instead of bike. (And maybe our lazy, middle-aged bodies were glad to use Lilly as an excuse for traveling the more comfortable, easy way!)

We let this seed of an idea take root in the back of our minds, nurturing it over the following year. I put up huge maps of Central and South America on our bedroom wall as a constant reminder of our audacious plan. I created spreadsheets galore to analyze our likely expenses and our savings, and I painstakingly tracked our spending to get serious about a budget to maximize the time we could travel. Then I tackled homeschooling legalities and guessed my way into inventing a curriculum, researched border crossings and insurance for the van in a dozen-plus countries, figured out health insurance, read up on current events in each country... the to-do list was endless, but thrilling.

Meanwhile, John obsessively researched the right vehicle to buy. He decided on a 20-year-old Ford E350 diesel van, due to its apparently unbreakable engine. It was a gargantuan task to gut the van and build it out. Learning everything from online videos, he created an electrical system with solar panels on the roof and batteries to power lights and a fridge; as well as a plumbing system with a water tank, sink and filtration for drinking and washing. He constructed wooden cabinets for storage, installed a heater and a fan, and built a small table for homeschooling in the back. Evenings and weekends for most of a year, John toiled away in our driveway until he had created the perfect little home for three. Lilly immediately named it Vancito. (The suffix -*cito* in Spanish means *small* but is also often added to names as a sign of affection.)

While consumed with the logistics of making the trip happen, it was easy to push away thoughts of what we'll do after. We tell most people that we're doing a one-year road trip, but we both know that we're looking for more than that.

I secretly hope we'll discover some idyllic mountain town with a fascinating foreign culture but like-minded adventurous people, with a low cost of living but opportunities for interesting jobs, where we can live happily ever after raising Lilly as a bilingual child in a great local school. But I also recognize the foolishness of pinning my hopes on a mystical perfect location. I know that I thrive on change, and part of me wonders if I want this to be more than a one-off trip... maybe I want travel to *be* my life. I hesitate to admit that to all but my closest friends, knowing that most think we are crazy to be putting our successful lives on pause even for one year, so they would never understand the idea that this could be a permanent change. Or maybe this trip will maximize my change-o-meter and I'll be ready to settle down afterwards?

So we reassure our parents and work colleagues, and perhaps ourselves, that we'll likely return in a year to plug back into the rat race, all the while hoping it won't happen, and we set off into the unknown. Three "monkeys" on the road to the end of the world...

3

LESSONS LEARNED IN THE FIRST 24 HOURS

I f the first night is any indication of the rest of our trip, we should turn around now.

The drive itself is beautiful and nostalgic. We don't leave home until late in the day, so we end up driving through Yosemite during the magic sunset hour. The alpenglow paints the familiar peaks orange, highlighting every detail on the granite faces in front of me. We stop briefly for a photo at the lake where we were married ten years prior, and I cement my last memories of Yosemite, pushing away the doubts that creep into my mind. Can we ever find a more beautiful place than this?

We find a deserted spot at the end of a dirt road on the shore of Mono Lake, just outside of Yosemite, and set up our camp for the first of hundreds of times. It's a process that soon becomes second nature to us, but at this point is new and confusing. We pull down our folding table and chairs from the roof and set them up next to the van, along with our portable camping stove, to make the outdoor kitchen. Then we raise the roof of the van from the inside, which unfolds tent fabric to open up an extra three feet of space, allowing us to stand comfortably inside. There are movable panels around chest-height that create an "upstairs" bed platform for sleeping, or can be stacked together to give us room to walk around inside. Finally, we spin the two passenger chairs around 180° to face backwards, making a living room area. Hey presto, it's a house!

John and I are exhausted from the intense last few days of packing and preparation, but Lilly is so excited that she keeps leaping back and forth between her bed and our bed. The cold finally draws her into her sleeping bag and we all fall asleep.

It is a freezing night, literally – my water bottle freezes solid. Not long after I fall asleep, Lilly wakes up crying from the cold so we pull her into bed with us. That makes three bodies attempting to sleep in a space only a few inches wider than a single bed. As much as I love being close to my family, I tend to prefer sleeping without a knee denting my spine and my face pressed into a tent window zipper.

A couple hours of fitful sleep later, I am re-awoken by strange scuttling noises, and see John fiddling with his headlamp. He shines a light down and we both peer over the edge of our bed. Caught by surprise in the sudden beam of light is a cute little white mouse. For a split second, I see his red eyes looking up at us from the depths of our trash can, and then he vanishes under our bed. We start discussing traps or enticements to get the mouse out, but our half-asleep brains can't process such a tricky problem, so we just take the trash outside and fall back asleep, promising ourselves we'll solve it in the morning.

What feels like only moments after I fall asleep for the third time, I awake with a start at the sound of an engine approaching. Beams of light shine in through our windshield and bounce eerily around the fabric of our tent. I am not at all used to this idea of sleeping in a public place in the middle of the wilderness, so the arrival of a stranger in the night is intimidating. I push aside thoughts of theft or assault, and unzip my window and peer out. A beaten-up old car parks nearby. I wonder if I should go find the can of bear spray that is our only weapon, but I don't want to take my eyes off the vehicle. There is some movement and a headlamp beam flickers around. I watch as long as my weary eyes let me but eventually fall asleep again.

Dawn comes too soon, and I curse the bright sunlight for waking me so early. I feel the warm rays of the sun heating up our tent and I reluctantly open my bleary eyes. My groggy brain remembers where I am and turns on in a flash.

Did the mouse eat all our food?

Has the mystery person outside stolen our camp chairs?

And, is Lilly frozen to death in her sleeping bag?

I turn to face John so I can throw these concerns at him. I see one eye peering out at me from under his sleeping bag. It does not look like a happy, well-rested eye, so I leave it alone and climb out of bed. Lilly is buried so far into her sleeping bag that I can't see her. In a motion that is to become a regular habit on this trip when we reach colder climates, I poke the pile of fluff to elicit sufficient movement to confirm life. Yes, being a mother makes you weird.

I open the door to check on our various belongings strewn around outside and see a figure wrapped in a sleeping bag lying in the dirt. He sits up and greets me when he hears my door open, "I think I have frostbite, could you take a look at my foot?"

And that's the first of hundreds of chance meetings that form the true backbone of this story.

Seventy-one-year-old Joe had been camping up in the mountains by himself. The cold front caught him by surprise, so he'd hiked out in the night to his car, driving only a short way before seeing our van and deciding he was too tired to continue.

"I haven't slept under a roof since April," he assures us. (It's now late September.) He explains that he only sleeps in his home during winters, and isn't going to let this cold front stop him adventuring outdoors for another couple of months. It's so inspiring to meet someone of his age who can hike into the high Sierra by himself, sleep outside, wake up and plan his next trip. *Wow*, I think, *can I be like Joe when I grow up?*

He tells me that he hasn't been able to feel his toes for almost 24 hours. I gingerly peel back a white, cotton sock from a wrinkled, leathery leg. The foot underneath appears almost white in color, and is swollen hard to the touch. I dig out my wilderness medicine notebook from our first aid kit, (didn't think I'd be using it less than 24 hours into the trip), and try to compare photos and descriptions. "If it's badly frostbitten then you should leave it frozen and get to a hospital. If not, just let it warm up and it'll be fine." But how to tell the difference? I'm no expert and there's no cell reception to do more research.

We invite Joe to share our breakfast, glad now that we splurged on *four* plates instead of only three when we packed the van. Yes, those are the kinds of big decisions you make when you have a tiny home! He is grateful for the scrambled eggs and coffee, but he won't listen to my advice to go to the hospital. It's the typical US problem – he doesn't have insurance so can't risk getting slapped with a crippling bill. He simply puts his shoe on and drives away. Ironically, after we cross the border to enter the "developing" world, no one we meet worries about health care costs.

I think about Joe over the next few days, wondering what became of him. He wrote down our blog website but he didn't even own a cell phone, so I don't expect to ever hear from him. It is our first experience of having a personal encounter with someone whom we'll likely never see again. Welcome to vanlife – this is going to happen to us hundreds more times.

We watch Joe drive away down the dirt road back to the highway, then look around at our new home in disbelief. This time yesterday we were normal people in a normal house. Now, just 24 hours later, we are living – sleeping, cooking, homeschooling – on a wide, sandy beach in front of a glassy lake, with nobody in sight. It feels surreal. Are we really doing this?!

I sit at our fold-up table outside, guiding Lilly through her reading lessons, while I watch seagulls cruise over the mirror-like water in front of me. John stands barefoot in the sand at our stove, preparing lunch. We explore the limestone tufa formations, noticing osprey nests balanced on top of the larger ones, for a break between reading and math classes. I could get used to this.

Except for the not-sleeping-all-night part.

Postscript: A couple weeks later I got a mysterious message via our blog's Contact Us page. It was from a nurse who was treating a patient who'd asked her to send us a message. He wanted to let us know that his toes were damaged but he was going to be ok. She assumed we must be his family since we were the only people he was contacting. At that point we were well into Mexico. I responded asking if we could help in any way, but never heard back.

I like to imagine I'll be as tough and adventurous as Joe when I am in my 70s. But I hope not as alone.

Lessons learned during our first few days of vanlife:

1. Make slow, careful movements inside our tiny home. We've moved from a 2,000 square feet house to a 70 square feet van. Consequently, in the first few weeks we are constantly stubbing our toes, hitting our heads, and banging our knees.
2. Sleep without moving. John and I have slept hanging from rock faces in Yosemite and in small tents on the ground, but for most of our 15 years together we've slept in a queen-sized bed. This barely-larger-than-a-single-bed thing is going to take some getting used to. I wake up with an aching back the first few weeks, but my body soon adjusts.
3. You don't need more than three shirts! I loved selling/giving/throwing away most of our belongings in preparation for this trip. Now we each have only one drawer for clothes, and we know the location of every little thing in the van. If we don't use it regularly, it's gone. I love the feeling of having less, and using every single thing we have.
4. We have a great kid along for this crazy ride. Lilly's bed is basically just a shelf, barely wider and longer than she is, and we only let her bring a small handful of her favorite toys along. But the first morning she woke up and said with a big grin on her face, "I don't want to go home, I want to sleep in the van again!" I'd call that success.

MEXICO

We drove 4,250 miles over 11 weeks in Mexico.
September to December, 2017.

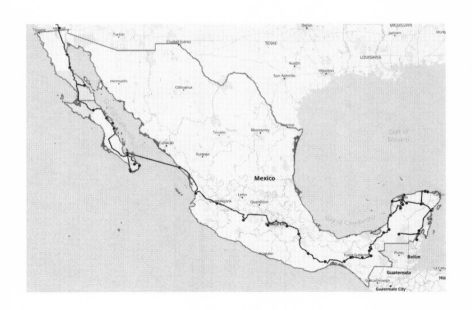

4

WELCOME TO MEXICO

We turn south and head for the border, with a few stops on the way to visit friends and explore the spine of jagged peaks that line the highway in the Eastern Sierra.

Crossing the border feels momentous. I've been to Mexico several times, even entered via land borders before, but I've always returned within days. This time, as I explain with great enthusiasm to the border guard, we will not be returning to the US – we'll be exiting Mexico on the other end of the country into Belize! He's not impressed, and simply stamps our passports for a standard six-month visa.

The guards searching the vehicles have much more enthusiasm for their work. We watch as the cars in front of us are entered by multiple men – trunks opened, back seats tipped down, engine examined – and we initiate a performance that we are to repeat dozens of times over the next three years:

Step 1: John smiles broadly from the driver's seat and cries, "Buenos dias" to the approaching police officer, whose face is fluctuating between distrust and curiosity. We have about ten seconds before he makes up his mind whether we are friend or foe.

Step 2: Lilly leans over John's shoulder to smile at the police officer through the window and shout, "Hola!"
Step 3: John reclines back in the driver's seat and I lean over to talk in Spanish. I tell the police officer about our trip and ask for recommendations of where to camp safely that night.
Step 4: Police officer peers briefly over John's shoulder into the back of the van at Lilly and waves us on, "Buen viaje."

Aspiring drug smugglers take note: if you have a small child and can learn to speak Spanish, you could have a successful career.

A moment later, we're driving through the town of Mexicali. I can't believe we are really here! For the first of a dozen times to come, I am reminded of the power of this man-made line in the sand. People are suddenly shorter and darker skinned, there is a vibrant feeling of life and color and noise all around us, and of course everything is in Spanish. We focus on the basics – find an ATM to get local currency (pesos) and then get far away from the border area before looking for a place to camp.

Our excitement and feeling of freedom is overwhelming. We had planned to go to a pay campsite for our first night in Mexico to get our bearings, but the web of dirt roads by the coast is irresistible. I zoom in on Google maps satellite photos and search for a break in the hillside of cactus that could get us out to the ocean. I trace a faint line with my finger on the screen that seems to reach all the way to the ocean from the highway. Let's try it!

A couple of failed attempts later, we arrive at a wide open beach with nobody in sight. The dirt road we've been following ends when it reaches the sand, but we see myriad tracks that extend out closer to the water. John states the obvious, "I bet we could drive the van closer to the water to camp for the night."

I heartily agree.

We confirm that we're still above the high tide line, then John shifts into 4WD to follow one of the tracks into the sand. We get about 20 feet before the tires start spinning helplessly. We try backing up and get stuck again.

I hop out and look at the van. "Yup, it's stuck," I helpfully shout to John. What would he do without me?

Lilly climbs out and starts playing in the warm sand as the sun starts to set around us. It's a novel feeling to carry our entire home with us – we have food and shelter and the equipment to get ourselves unstuck, so there's no sense of urgency.

I dig a track in front of and behind each wheel and John makes a little forward progress by rolling back and forth in the space I've dug. We repeat the process a dozen times until we're finally back onto harder sand. It's now dark and I call Lilly over as we set up camp for the night. She's barefoot of course, and we don't find her flip-flops until the next morning. My raised-on-a-farm husband looks at all our tracks, smiles and says, "Damn, it feels good to be a redneck."

We sleep warm in our beds that night, listening to nature's sound machine of endless crashing waves.

In the morning, I peek out of my window to discover the ocean has disappeared! The tide has gone out and it's now a quarter mile from the van to the water's edge. It's an endless playground for Lilly – tide pools to catch hermit crabs, sand islands to run between, and knee-deep warm water to splash in. We walk far down the beach to explore and find an enormous, dead turtle. I sit next to him on the warm, wet sand, studying this interesting body that I've never seen so close before, thinking about how he ended up here.

By late morning we've finished Lilly's school lessons for the day and it's high tide. Lilly is absolutely delighted to be playing in the shallow, warm ocean – she can't stop jumping and laughing as she splashes in the water. And John declares, "I'm not going to wear a shirt again until 2018." But we need to get moving if we're going to find another safe place to camp before dark tonight.

That's when I have a revelation. We don't *have* to move on today. We don't *need* to get further south every day. We're not in a hurry anymore!

After 10 years of Silicon Valley living, it's strange not to have a deadline or a goal. Yes, we're going to Argentina, but it's not a race, it doesn't even matter if we don't get there. This is our experience, now. It's not about rushing to the next place.

So, we stay another night. And then another. No list of tourist sights to check off. Just a deserted beach with our little family and no other humans for miles. Delighted by passing dolphins, surprised by visiting stingrays, entertained by hundreds of hermit crabs. Taking our time to cook good food and not feeling impatient with homeschooling. Listening to Lilly's imaginative stories, drawing and coloring with her, reading her story after story. It's so rare for us to have time to just be together. And it's so liberating to travel in a van so we don't have to commit to any schedule – we only leave when we run out of water and food.

Mexico swoops down from the US like a backwards J, but on the west side of the country is the 760 mile-long Baja peninsula reaching down into the Pacific ocean. We're driving down the east coast of this peninsula, rather than the Pacific side, hence enjoying calm water and sunrises rather than big waves and sunsets.

About a third of the way down Baja, we decide it's time for our first shower since crossing the border. We've been "wild camping" so far, meaning that we just park in the middle of nowhere for the night, so there are no facilities like bathrooms. It does feel slightly unnerving to set up our beds and kitchen out in the public thoroughfare, with no idea of who might pass by, but it's worth it to camp in such beautiful locations.

We cruise down a roller coaster hill into the little village of Bahia de Los Angeles and pay for a *palapa* (open shade structure) on the sand with shared bathrooms. Our palapa neighbors are also overlanders, Canadian Brad and Argentine Viky driving from Canada to Argentina with their two-year-old son. They suggest that we join them the next day on a boat trip to see the largest fish on Earth – whale sharks – so we sign up for the $30 tour.

The next morning, we pile into a small motor boat with three other couples, including our new overlanding friends, and bounce over the small waves into the calm bay. Cutting the engine, the driver points to a floppy dark fin rising out of the water ahead of us. Not the stiff, gray, shiny fin from horror movies, but still very clearly the fin of an enormous shark. I have barely enough time to register the immense dark shape lurking in the water beneath the fin, when the driver shouts, "Go!" and I leap off the boat.

In the two seconds that my eyes are closed while I jump into the water and right myself, my imagination goes wild. The shark has approached and opened its jaws wide to devour me whole, and when I open my eyes, my last sight on this Earth will be its teeth. And, John will have recorded the whole incident on his camera.

I open my eyes to see the fin rising out of the waves at the height of my face just a few feet away, and swim toward it, against every instinct. Appearing out of the depths of the ocean is an endless fish body, with a huge shark tail waving at the top. I have to swim fast to catch up to his head, but then I cruise through the water accompanying this enormous, gentle creature. I don't know if he even notices or cares that I'm there, but, for a few precious moments, I am right alongside him as we travel together, in parallel, through the warm ocean.

I study his enormous oval mouth, his oddly small eye, his deep gills, his patterned and scarred body. I keep kicking to stay alongside him, experiencing this crazy sensation of travelling like a giant fish through the endless ocean, never looking ahead of me, only to my left to watch this incredible body as it moves effortlessly through the water. Eventually I'm so out of breath from trying to keep up that I stop kicking and watch him disappear into the distance. Wow!

On an adrenaline high, we stop to snorkel in a peaceful bay on the way back to shore. We spy hundreds of open clam shells on the ocean floor, but none that still house their original residents. John dives to the bottom and scrabbles with his fingers in the coarse, brown sand. He surfaces with a triumphant smile and a heavy, sealed, pair of clamshells in his hand. The rest of us join in and it doesn't take long before we have a full bag.

The ten of us from the boat trip cook a feast for dinner that night. We boil ocean water in a big pot to cook the clams, and fry butter and garlic with mushrooms for a dip. I didn't think too much of the clams, but John ate several dozen. The next morning, arising with the sun over the calm waters, he was running to the toilet clutching his belly. He spent most of the day there. Maybe eating shellfish that you dug out of the sand with your toes and then cooked in seawater isn't the best idea?

Your picture postcard beach view is palm trees and sunset. Here, we have neither. Instead, we get the magic of a full moon rising over a calm, still ocean. An entirely new experience for me.

As luck would have it, we hit the peak full moon while camped here with our new friends. One by one, we stop talking and stare in amazement as an enormous yellow-orange ball crests the horizon. It seems to fill half the sky. And the color is such a strong yellow-orange, nothing like the usual white I usually see. How can that possibly be our moon?

Its reflection on the calm ocean in front of us grows longer and brighter as the moon rises higher. Unlike the moon itself, its reflection is totally white. It paints clear, shimmering, white ripples on the distant ocean, in a triangular shape narrowing toward the sandy shore where I'm sitting, like it's pointing at us. As it gets higher into the sky, the whole beach starts to light up as if it were day. I can see my long shadow gradually get shorter and shorter as if the sun were rising overhead. It's so bright we can walk around with no flashlights and easily see the path between the rocks, even in bare feet. I can clearly see Lilly's face as she sits playing in the sand next to me.

My favorite part of this spectacle is that 12 hours later, I'm sitting in the same spot on the sand, again watching an orange ball cresting the same horizon in almost exactly the same location. But, this time it's the sun. I've always preferred west-facing coasts for sunset-watching, but I'm learning a thing or two about the beauty of moon- and sun-rise.

Heading south from our whale shark camp, we inch our way down the coast from one remote beach to the next, never traveling more than a few dozen miles each day. At each wild camp, the ocean is so still and clear that we can stand in the shallows and see colorful fish swarming our ankles. They bump into my feet when I stand still. When I dive down into them, they don't even swim away from me. It really feels like we've jumped into a giant aquarium.

Unsurprisingly, southern Baja is where Lilly has her snorkeling breakthrough, so we all get to swim together marveling at the fish, rather than one of us babysitting Lilly while the other snorkels alone. It's wonderful to hear her muffled cries of wonder through the snorkel and see her excited splashes as she points out fish in this magical underwater world for the first time.

Between the wide open sandy beaches with their infinite wild camping opportunities, and the web of dirt roads where we rarely see another car, Baja is the perfect introduction to overlanding for us newbies. We learn to pay attention to our four key systems: water, food, toilet, and trash. As the water and food levels diminish, conversely our toilet and trash fill up. The food effectively moves from the fridge to the toilet, with a short detour inside of our bodies. It's such a simple equation that I never paid attention to while living in a city, but now it dictates when we need to move on.

The other surprising change in our lifestyle is that we now sleep and wake with the sun. When the sun sets, we eat dinner and read books and tuck into bed. We sleep with all the windows open, and wake up to a fuzzy orange glow across the horizon. I watch through the window as the light rays gradually stretch their way across the glassy water, eventually reaching all the way to the sand where we are parked. The seagulls start their loud chorus of calling to each other as soon as the sun touches the shore where they are sleeping, and it's impossible to sleep through them. What a change from waking up bleary-eyed to a beeping alarm clock.

We haven't been overlanding very long, but I'm already enamored by the freedom of this low-cost, simple lifestyle, and am determined to figure out how to maintain it.

5

IN SEARCH OF TURTLES

O ver the past two weeks, we've slept every night on a deserted beach with only crabs and birds for company. Now we're driving into the city of La Paz, with its 250,000 people, at the southern tip of the Baja peninsula. My senses are stimulated in new ways as I'm surrounded by crowds of people, hear music drifting out of restaurant windows, and admire colorful murals on the sides of buildings. Even though I don't typically love cities, I am invigorated by frequent and significant changes like this.

La Paz is situated in a large bay within the Gulf of Mexico – that same calm, warm body of water where we've been camping all the way down Baja. We enjoy strolling along the pedestrian path that follows the coastal road for a couple of miles. Look to your right to appreciate the ocean with its diving pelicans and seal heads peeking curiously out of the water; but turn to the left and you see traffic, restaurants, and night clubs with music blaring and people spilling out onto the street. What an intriguing juxtaposition of images. During the daytime, the city is dead because of the stifling heat that leaves you unwilling to move a single bone in your body. But at night-time it comes alive with people walking, biking, roller blading, eating out and dancing in bars.

I'm lucky to have an old friend from college living here in La Paz, so we enjoy having a local show us around her adopted city and welcome us into her home. Vanlife is not conducive to city dwelling, and we're grateful to have a safe place to store our home on wheels while we explore the city on foot.

Cecilia's life revolves around the ocean. She spends most of her days working at a sustainable fishing non-profit, and after work she goes stand-up paddle boarding a few blocks away in the ocean, regularly seeing dolphins and seals. I'll never forget the image of her standing on her board with an enormous smile on her face and her two dogs at her feet as she paddled across the bay – what an incredible way to unwind after work! These are the healthy work-life balance examples I need in my life.

Over dinner at Cecilia's house one evening, a friend of hers mentions a non-profit group that runs a turtle sanctuary and accepts volunteers by the day. It's chance conversations like this that lead to some of our best travel experiences, and we are ready to move on from the big smoke anyway, so, down yet another bumpy dirt road we go...

Asupmatoma is just one small building on the sand, with three mobile homes behind it where the volunteers live, plus miles and miles of sandy beach with thousands of turtle eggs buried beneath.

The volunteers patrol the beach 24 hours a day. They look for tracks that they recognize as those of a mother turtle. When they find them, they examine the direction of the tracks and figure out where she walked up, where she paused, and where she walked back to the water. Then they use a stick to poke around in the sand looking for a soft spot which would indicate a nest. Then they dig down and, if they find eggs, move them to their hatchery for safety.

We walk over to the hatchery and one of the biologists, Monica, lifts a protective box off a nest that she expects might be ready to hatch. She gently pushes some sand away, and... little gray heads start poking out! She gently places the first turtle into Lilly's cupped hands, then keeps digging to pull out more turtles. I can't believe the seemingly endless supply of turtles from the sand. Monica's helper is rapidly counting, as turtles are wriggling out, and ultimately notes down the total of 108 for this nest. Lilly happily cradles her newborn turtle, while listening intently to Monica's explanation of the turtles' life cycle, and interrupting to ask many questions.

At first I was horrified that they'd steal the eggs from the mother turtle. But apparently the mother lays her eggs and heads right back into the ocean, never to return – so the eggs are on their own. On the beach there are coyotes looking for a quick meal, as well as poachers who collect the eggs to sell as a delicacy for local people to eat. If the eggs are left in their natural nest, only 20-30% will hatch into baby turtles, compared to 80-90% of the eggs that are moved to the hatchery.

"Never buy or eat turtle eggs!" Monica preaches. We all nod confidently that we'd never dream of such a thing, blissfully unaware that in two weeks we will find ourselves sitting at a generous family's breakfast table in front of a bowl of turtle eggs!

After watching the babies emerge from the sand, we help send them on their way into the ocean. Monica draws a line in the sand between us and the ocean. She walks around with a bucket full of wriggling baby turtles, stopping to let each of us reach in and pick up a handful. We carefully set the turtles on "their" side of the line, and point them in the direction of the ocean. It's intimidating to see these tiny creatures walking bravely into the same surf that John and I had not dared to swim in the night before when we camped here – the waves on this Pacific side of Baja are enormous.

Suddenly, a rogue wave crashes up to us, reaching knee-height. "Do not move your feet!" warns Monica, as baby turtles swirl around our ankles in danger of being trampled, and I grab Lilly's arm as she falls over.

As the wave recedes, we notice a crab slink out of its hole, run over to a baby turtle, and start whacking it with its claw. We all shriek, torn between obeying, "Don't cross the line," and saving this little turtle. Monica runs over to separate them and fills in the crab's hole with sand. A few moments later, we see another crab run over to another turtle and this time successfully grab it and drag it back to its hole in its claws. My heart's in my throat as I see the crab tugging the turtle down into the hole, which isn't quite large enough to fit the turtle's shell, when Monica comes to the rescue again.

Yesterday, Lilly was playing on the sand with the crabs, personifying them, pointing out imagined mothers and fathers and children, and building them houses out of sand. Today, she's watching them attempt to kidnap and eat helpless newborn turtles. I can almost see the neurons making new connections in her six-year-old brain as she tries to process this shocking information. Back in the van later that evening she explains to us, as if trying to rationalize with herself, that turtles need to be protected but also crabs need to eat.

We camp out with the Asupmatoma employees on their beach that night, swapping stories and learning more about their work. The people are smart and dedicated, working literally day and night to help these turtles' chance of survival. For us, it's just one day of many on the beach, but we leave feeling educated and inspired. I think we'll declare it Lilly's first science class of the school year, and I hope it'll stick with her far longer than any textbook.

* * *

Down here at the southern tip of the Baja peninsula we have two options for continuing south. One is to return back north almost to the US border and then turn right to drive through mainland Mexico – but that region is renowned for its drug activity. So we decide to take the second option: an overnight ferry across the bay.

We spend a hectic afternoon back in La Paz dealing with customs, measuring the van, and buying ferry tickets. There are two ferry companies to get from Baja to the mainland – the expensive passenger ferry that has private sleeping cabins and a swimming pool, and the cheaper truckers' ferry with... well, truckers. Since we're trying to travel as long as possible without working, guess which one we take?

Driving into the belly of the beast is like a giant game of Tetris – the men working on the boat direct the vehicles to maximize every nook and cranny of space on the ferry. Vancito is packaged like a sardine between giant semi-truck trailers that run their engines all night, resulting in a deafening noise surrounding us as we try to sleep. The exhaust of the ferry is only a few feet away, emitting such a strong diesel smell that I sleep with a sheet pressed over my nose and try to take shallow breaths. At some point in the night Lilly climbs into our bed, crying that she can't sleep.

We are relieved when the sun peeks over the horizon and we join the hundreds of truckers on the upper deck of the ferry to watch Mazatlan come into view. I realize that Lilly and I, and our friend Viky, are the only females on the entire boat! We wait hours for the giant Tetris game to be reversed, and are finally able to roll down the ramp into mainland Mexico – our first taste of true Mexico.

Geographical note: I was confused to see signs in Baja written "Baja California" instead of "Baja Mexico." I distinctly remember crossing the border from the US into Mexico!

Here's what I learned: Back when California was part of Mexico 200 years ago, "California" comprised Baja plus what we now know as California. To differentiate the north and south, they were called "Alta California" (upper) and "Baja California" (lower). I guess we dropped the "Alta" when we took California from Mexico, but the "Baja" name just stuck. (Lilly asks me if this means she can be Mexican, because she was born in California.)

6

MIDNIGHT EVACUATION
FROM THE TOP OF A VOLCANO

A rriving on the mainland is sensory overload after three weeks cruising down the empty Baja peninsula. Suddenly there are so many people and so much noise. People try to sell us all kinds of things on the side of the road – tamales, plastic toys, dried shrimp, maps. The landscape changes from brown to green, and we see fields of the blue-green spiky agave plant that is used to make tequila and mezcal. The wonderful news is that fresh fruit and vegetables are readily available here – back in Baja, food has to be shipped from the mainland, so it was hard to find fresh food in the little shops we typically frequented there.

In the small city of Patzcuaro, we stop at a farm on a hill to ask about parking for the night – no more easy wild camping on the beach for us. We are pointed to a large grassy field out back full of donkeys, horses, turkeys, doves, chickens... make yourselves at home! It's a novelty to weave my way between animals, nudging aside fur and feathers left and right, each time I walk to the bathroom, and there's a hilarious cacophony of squawks and bays and gobbles all day and night.

Lilly loves having pets for a few days. The donkey comes within arm's-length of our fold-up table when we're sitting outside doing school every morning, making it even harder than usual for Lilly to concentrate on her math problems. And despite my warnings about approaching strange animals, Lilly wraps her arms around his neck to give him good morning and goodnight hugs every day. I guess we made the right choice getting those rabies shots before we left the US!

Although we've been in Mexico now almost a month, we've only been in the deserts of Baja with very limited food options. So in Patzcuaro, we enjoy walking through the city streets marveling at the variety of fresh food and talking to the different vendors. People here make something at home in the morning, carry it to the town square, set up their folding table with some paper plates, and sell to passersby until they run out. Simple as that. Tacos, tostadas, ceviche, and many things we've never seen before. We decide to entirely boycott restaurants – far better to enjoy multiple small dishes at the different food stands which each come with their own cultural experience.

We stop in the main square where two girls approach Lilly and invite her to play. She's initially shy but I persuade her to go with them. I have no idea how much she understands as the girls chatter away at her in Spanish, but they play together happily racing around the plaza, and give each other big hugs when the other family leaves. We also stop at a hardware store because John wants to buy an axe – he's unable to give any explanation for needing one, but swears it will fit under his seat and thus take up no space, so I don't argue. Lilly meanwhile, bored, opens and closes the various door latches that are on display.

As we walk home to the van at the farm that evening, it gets dark very quickly. Outside of the town center there are no street lights and the narrow village streets are pitch black. They are also full of life – families outside talking, food vendors calling, dogs barking from the open flat roofs of houses – it's a friendly walk home in the warm evening air.

But once at the entrance to the farm, we see that the giant black entrance gate leading to the driveway is locked. The fence on either side is barbed wire. The 12-foot-high gate has nothing to climb on, even for us seasoned climber monkeys. We bang on the door and shout, but the restaurant is a ten minute walk away from the gate, so no one can hear us.

Then I notice the rain gutter opening under the gate. It's tiny, but, could Lilly possibly squeeze underneath?

I shine my phone light into the gutter and encourage her to try. She says it's too scary, but eventually I convince her to lie flat on her tummy and wriggle through to the other side. Maybe not the best parenting move, but what else can we do? I pass her the phone light and she disappears. I'm sure she'll drop my phone, fall over in the dark, and start crying helplessly. But, to my surprise, CLICK, the door opens.

"Mama! It was just like the lock I was playing with in the store with Papa!" she cries out proudly. Unbelievable.

On our way south, we detour to Volcan Nevado de Toluca where you can hike up into the dormant crater. Arriving at the little village at the base of the volcano it is immediately obvious that we are in a different climate – the people are dressed in big woolen shawls and coats, and the women have long black hair as if to keep them warm.

We don't notice the altitude change at first because we're driving, but we both get headaches as we drive up higher. I had glanced at the altitude in our guidebook, but it hadn't registered to me because it was listed in meters. I finally look up the conversion and realize that we are going to be sleeping higher than we've ever slept before (13,600 feet), and the summit will be the highest we've ever been (15,500 feet).

We park at the road's end, just one mile from the crater. What an intense change from sea level where we've been the last month. It is bone-chillingly cold, the air is so thin that we are gasping for breath just setting up the van camp, and the views are magnificent. It feels thrilling and outrageous to be camping here. For the first time, we cook indoors and we use the heater. Lilly flatly refuses to get out of the van at all because it's so cold. My headache is getting worse but I ignore it and go to sleep early.

I wake up at midnight with serious trouble breathing. I lie in bed concentrating hard on taking long, deep breaths to try to get oxygen into my body and fall back asleep, but I can't. I climb down out of bed to grab the trash can because I'm sure I'm about to vomit. My heart is beating way too fast. John joins me and says he hasn't been able to sleep either, but he only has a headache.

We discuss whether we should go down. The key is to figure out whether I'm getting worse or better. I feel really awful but I'm sure I should be able to breathe myself better. After all, I've been this high on several mountains in the US before and never had trouble, what is different this time? Maybe because we drove here from sea level and are sleeping the night here, whereas previously I've climbed to this elevation under my own leg-power and turned around at the summit.

Around 1:30 a.m. my lips and face start tingling. My vision gets blurry and then everything goes dark. My head feels giddy and I feel like I'm about to black out.

"We're going down now!" states John, as I recount these latest developments. In retrospect, I was obviously getting worse, but I wanted so much to summit the volcano the next morning that I was in denial.

We swear by the overlanding motto, *Never drive in the dark*. Whether it's bandits or stray animals or simply a giant hole in the road, driving in the dark is never a good idea. But I suppose if your wife is about to lose consciousness from lack of oxygen, you make an exception.

So we pack up the van and carry Lilly fast asleep from her bed into her car seat, still inside of her sleeping bag. I slump in my seat and John drives into the pitch black darkness at 2 a.m. on the twisty volcano road. It's our first time driving in the dark in Mexico. We drive 10 km, descending about one thousand feet, and park at the entrance gate. I immediately feel better and we all sleep until late morning.

I feel so disappointed that we were just one mile from an amazing summit, from getting higher than either of us has ever been before, and we had to turn back because of my uncooperative body. But looking back on it the next morning, it was clearly the right decision. I felt like my body was completely shutting down. I guess that's what lack of oxygen does to you.

Looking on the bright side, we learned a valuable lesson for when we get to the mountains in South America – we need to ascend more slowly. And, I learned what true altitude sickness feels like.

7

DANCING WITH SKELETONS
(DIA DE MUERTOS)

T he crowds are densely packed around us in the warm night. There's no distinguishing between street and sidewalk, save for when an errant car foolishly tries to drive through the mob of bodies, and we slowly part to allow it through. All around us are smiling faces covered in the black and white and red face paint of the colorful Mexican skeleton.

Out of nowhere, a group of people plant themselves in the center of the street and pull various instruments out of their cases. The crowd, as if of one mind, stops moving and surrounds the group, smiling expectantly. Trumpets start blaring in that upbeat stereotypical Mexican tune, and everyone starts whooping and dancing to the jolly beat. Casting my eyes above the crowd, I see five enormous skeleton figurines lifted high into the air, bouncing with the music. I hold Lilly tight in my arms as we are swept into the spontaneous parade, twirling and dancing together with the musicians and puppeteers. I look at Lilly's face, only inches away from mine – it's painted solid white with large black circles around her eyes, and is adorned with red sparkles and glitter. She shrieks in delight, "Mama, we are IN the parade!"

. . .

Dia de Muertos is one of the biggest festivals of the year in Mexico, and the city of Oaxaca has one of the biggest celebrations in the country, so we're delighted when we find a room to rent with safe parking for the van right in the heart of the festivities. I've long heard about this tradition, but don't really know anything about it besides skeleton paint and crazy costumes, so I'm excited to learn more.

Dia de Muertos means Day of the Dead, but this is not a dark, spooky or sad time. In my culture, we have a negative association with the deceased – fear and grief. The Day of the Dead seems to be an attempt to remember our loved ones in a more uplifting way. Mexicans consider this a time for their dearly departed to return to visit, so it is treated like a family reunion and celebration.

On the morning of November 1st, we walk cautiously through the *panteon* (cemetery). I'm concerned we might be imposing on personal grieving moments, but we find it awash with color and music. People spend the day "visiting" their deceased loved ones at the grave sites. They install speakers to play music, bring food and drinks for a picnic, and surround the grave chatting together like it's a family reunion. I've never seen a cemetery like this!

The deceased are also expected to return to their homes to visit, so every family builds an altar to welcome that person home. Typically the altar includes photos of the deceased and samples of their favorite food and drink. So you see a photo of Grandpa Juan surrounded by bottles of beer and a plate of doughnuts! And on the ground in front of him is an intricate design of a flower or skull or a favorite saint, entirely created by hand from rice, corn, beans, and seeds. From the simplest house with just a taped-up photo and some tortillas, to a fancy hotel with a roped-off spectacle of larger-than-life framed photos and extravagant meals – everyone has an altar.

Of course, Dia de Muertos is also an excuse for a big street party. Walking downtown on our first evening of the celebration is an amazing sensory overload. There are spontaneous parades in the middle of the street blocking traffic, live music blaring out from trumpets or beating out of drums, make-up artists on every corner painting faces like the dead, and mouth-watering smells from food stands on every corner of every street. I love the energy!

The parades have no police escort, no barriers, no warnings. They just appear in a street while cars are attempting to drive down it. One time we see several dozen people in tribal native attire thumping drums and building an altar with burning incense in the center of the road. Another time it's a more somber affair with men in black suits carrying an enormous statue of the Virgin Mary out of a church. Or there's the more traditional parade of dozens of men playing trumpets and carrying enormous skeleton puppet figures.

Each time, the crowd fills every inch of space around the music and we'll be in a spontaneous street concert. They'll play music for perhaps 10 minutes, then, by some unspoken signal, they stop in unison and continue progressing down the road. The crowd moves with them and the cars can finally drive by. Usually we let ourselves float along with the momentum of the crowd, but sometimes we are drawn into the procession itself, turning the tables on our perspective – now looking out into the throngs of people on the sidewalks watching *us* go by, and being filmed by a sea of phone cameras.

When we tire of the street party chaos, we evacuate onto a side street for a break. We duck into a completely empty nightclub to buy a mezcal cocktail, and Lilly and I take over the empty dance floor for a few minutes. Another time, I lean against a window of an art gallery for a rest, but the window slides open to reveal a smiling face who promptly invites us in for a tour. At midnight one evening, I notice a line of large tables and see a sign "Chocolate and Bread tasting" – two of my favorite foods home-made here and handed out freely, yum.

After we tire of the evening festivities late at night, we slowly walk home, stopping for snacks from the many delicious food stands on the way. Pork tacos, mystery soup (*pozole*), and jello never tasted so good as after a long day of walking and dancing around the city. Generally, the food in Oaxaca is fantastic. We always eat at the little tables on the side of the road which are generally run by a woman selling whatever she cooked that morning at home – so delicious!

Long after midnight, with Lilly passed out asleep on John's shoulder, we get back to the little room we rented in a family's house near the center of town. We wake Lilly up just long enough to scrub the paint off her face, and we all fall asleep to the sound of the continuing parades outside, accompanied by the occasional BANG of a firecracker.

Such a different experience from desolate beaches or volcanoes or small towns. I am starting to learn that constant change is the essence of vanlife, and I love it.

8

TRAPPED BY AN ANGRY MOB THEN
WELCOMED BY STRANGERS

We've only experienced friendliness from Mexican strangers so far on this trip. Maybe it's because we have a cute little girl with us, or because I speak Spanish, but more likely it is simply that Mexicans are genuinely kind and welcoming. A smile and a wave from people on the street as we drive past, locals always happy to help us find our way in a new town, a friendly pat on Lilly's head as an older woman walks past her on the street – we start to assume this kind of welcome is normal.

Until it's not.

Driving east out of Oaxaca, we are feeling high on life after four days of socializing and partying at the Day of the Dead festival. As we approach a toll booth, we can see a large crowd of people blocking the road in front of us. I scan my eyes over the group, expecting to see families selling water, snacks, and local handicrafts like we typically see at any slow-down on a road in Mexico.

This crowd looks different. Mostly younger men, many drinking out of dark bottles, all of them idle. I feel my body tense.

"Don't stop," I state needlessly to John, who I know has already drawn the same conclusion and has his eyes set on the toll booth about a hundred feet past the crowd. We both reach for the door lock button at the same time, and roll up our windows. John attempts to creep the van forward through the throng, pretending to ignore them.

Bad idea. People start to crowd in front of the van, shouting at us. Worse, I hear pounding echoing on the van walls behind me. We are being surrounded. Lilly looks up quizzically from her book at the sudden thumping on the wall next to her head. My mind starts racing through escape scenarios.

John revs the engine of the van, partly to scare people back and partly to advance a few more inches. In response, the angry yells escalate and the crowd tightens around us. Now I feel the van rocking to and fro as people are pushing on our walls. I see no path out of here except for driving into a mass of humans, an option which John briefly voices but does not initiate.

Realizing we have no other option, John reluctantly rolls down his window. Immediately, an angry young man demands money, aggressively reaching one hand into the van trying to intimidate us. John asks why, who are you, and where is the toll booth operator? I can't get a word in from the passenger seat, and watch helplessly as they shout incomprehensibly at each other, language barrier and testosterone working together to quickly escalate the tension.

A movement in front of our windshield catches my eye. A teenage boy is standing directly in front of John and staring angrily at him. Another joins him. They are both staggering slightly as if drunk, and I realize they are holding large rocks. I feel my heart race. The boys hold up their rocks and start banging them together in a threatening manner, alternately motioning at John as if to invite him to a fight.

I feel a dreadful certainty in my gut that if someone smashes our windshield and tries to force their way in, John will be pushing his foot on the gas pedal, no matter what's in front of us.

I scan the crowd for help, looking for someone in charge. Or at least for someone who's not young, male, and drunk – that is a deadly combination. There's no police presence, no toll booth operator, but I make eye contact with an older man who's watching from a safe distance. I take a deep breath to calm my nerves and roll down my window to gesture him over. I speak overly-slowly in Spanish, as if

I'm having to think hard about how to form the sentences, "I'm sorry we don't speak good Spanish and we're confused because we usually pay at the toll booth but that young man is asking for money outside of the toll booth could you please explain it to me, sir?"

You can almost see the tension dissipating in ripples starting from the older man and spreading wider through the crowd, as my message gets passed along. It's as if the whole crowd breathes a sigh of relief.

The older gentleman explains that they have been given permission to take over the toll booth for one day to raise money for their community, which we are driving through, that was destroyed in the earthquake. He tells me that some people died, many homes were destroyed, and the kids can't go to school because the classroom was knocked down. They are asking for a 50 peso donation to help rebuild the town, and I immediately reach for my wallet. His story could be a complete fabrication, but it's an easy escape from our situation. Before I can fish out the money, however, a police car pulls up behind us with its lights flashing, and the crowd opens a path and waves us on. As we pull away, the man I'd been talking to drops a printed note through my window onto my lap. It gives the same explanation about the local community working together to raise money and rebuild their village. I don't think his story is a fabrication.

It shook us up. Partly because of one scary moment that could have escalated to a bad conclusion. But also because we had not contributed an insignificant amount of money to a worthy cause because we assumed the worst about the people in front of us.

We talked endlessly about it on the drive that day. How would *we* act if we lost our home in an earthquake, and then rich foreigners driving by refused to donate a tiny sum of money to us? We fluctuated between frustration that they'd started out so aggressively, and guilt that we hadn't tried harder to understand the situation, and ended up simply vowing to be more aware of the plight of people around us when making snap judgments in future.

* * *

From the angry mob, right into the hands of the most welcoming experience of our trip to date. This lifestyle really smacks you with opposing ends of the spectrum of emotions.

Distracted by our bad experience that afternoon, we don't realize how late it's getting until I see the sun setting behind us. I spy a lake on the map which will probably make for a decent wild camp for the night, so we pull off the highway. We pass through a village and drive to the end of a dirt road where it dead-ends at the lake. Its small, sandy beach is crowded with locals. Music is blaring out of the loudspeakers on a little three-wheeled taxi, several families are sitting on the sand watching their kids swim, and a lady is selling snacks and *horchata* (rice drink) on a fold-up table. We are craving peace and solitude after our stressful afternoon, so we park the van on the side of the dirt road and hope that everyone will leave soon so we can set up camp.

Within minutes, two girls around the same age as Lilly approach her, "Quieres jugar?" (Do you want to play?) Lilly gets shy and hides behind me. It takes a lot of encouragement, but eventually she joins them. I stay close watching them build sand castles using plastic cups from the horchata-seller and dig tunnels to the lake with sticks.

Once the sun has set and other families start to pack up and leave, the older of the two girls approaches me, "Mama says to go sit nearer to them." So John and I join the circle of grown-ups laughing and chatting next to the horchata table. The camaraderie is obvious and strong between all of them – constant joking, friendly teasing, much laughter and story-telling. They keep calling each other by nicknames like *gordo* (fattie), or *guero* to the palest of the group.

The snack-selling lady, whose name is Edu, prepares *chicharrones* (deep fried pork skin) with various mysterious toppings and hands one to each of us. The three young men hand out beers. Someone produces a bag of tamales and gives us each one. Seeing Lilly hungrily devour her tamal, two of the young men get up and hop on their motorcycles, "We'll get some more," and disappear into the night. Turns out that Edu's mama makes these tamales, and one of the young men is engaged to Edu's daughter, so he's going to his grandmother-in-law-to-be's house to get more.

Lilly wants to take her new friends to play at her "house," so we give everyone a tour of the van. We adults then return to the lakeside to chat, the parents leaving their kids in the van with stern instructions, "Don't touch anything!" This seems to be the turning point in the night where we are completely accepted as part of the group. Something about the fact that we are trusting their kids alone in our home, builds trust among us quickly.

While we are at the van, I grab a bottle of home-made mystery booze we bought from a small restaurant before Oaxaca and try to pour cups for everyone, but instead I'm drawn into a drinking game with the men. They all laugh uproariously, but good-naturedly, as the older man in the group tries to make me drink a shot of liquor for every cup I pass out. And when my bottle is empty, the same two young men from the tamales-mission go on a beer-run into town.

It feels just like a typical night out with friends. But, we are with complete strangers, speaking a foreign language, on the outskirts of a tiny village that isn't even marked on our map, in the middle of the night. Sometimes you just have to trust in the kindness of strangers.

Finally, at 1 a.m. the three young men drive home, informing us that they will return in the morning to bring us more tamales. The family packs up their wares to leave as well. The mother in the family, Edu, turns to me, looking concerned, "You're going to sleep here?"

I nod.

She turns to her husband and they exchange glances, holding an unspoken conversation in a single moment. She turns back to me and states simply, "Come home with us."

I resist, stating we don't want to inconvenience them. She insists. They point out that it's the last day of the Dia de Muertos holiday so there's a chance drunk people may come by in the middle of the night, and they'd feel better knowing Lilly was safely sleeping at their house. When she frames it in the context of Lilly's safety, of course I gratefully accept the offer.

So, for the second time in one week, we break the cardinal rule, *Never drive in the dark*.

We pack up and follow the three-wheeled taxi into the darkness,

42

turning left onto one of the small dirt pathways that lead up into the village. Edu's husband wakes up his neighbor to tell him to move his taxi so that our van can fit in, and John backs up into the narrowest of driveways, waking up the entire neighborhood with our loud engine.

Lilly is fast asleep on the front seat while we meet the neighbors, who are all part of the same family. We are introduced to Edu's sister. The grandma comes out to ask if we liked her tamales. Edu shows us the bathroom in the house and says to come in any time while they are sleeping. We set up our beds and fall asleep in the front yard of our new friends' house, surrounded by chickens, roosters, dogs, and an extended family who has welcomed us as their own.

The next morning is hot and still. The houses are packed together, allowing no breeze to squeeze through. I see the grandpa asleep in a hammock, and Edu and her husband asleep in a bed by the front door. I assume they choose to sleep outside due to the heat. In the morning daylight I also notice they seem to have their entire kitchen outside, even the refrigerator.

Once everyone is awake, I comment how much I love the outdoor kitchen set-up. She admits it is less of a chosen design and more about safety. They are all terrified of another earthquake striking their town and collapsing the house on them while they are inside, so they've mostly moved outside. She points to the large cracks through the walls, supports, and roof of the house. They can't afford to repair the damage, which increases the danger of a future tremor destroying the place. They all get somber for a moment as they recall how terrifying it was to feel the earth heaving violently under their feet for almost a full minute.

Kids, however, don't seem to notice the serious stuff. Lilly plays with Edu's daughter and niece for hours. She is taken to all the neighboring houses, each owned by someone else in the extended family, while we hang out with the parents making breakfast. It always takes a leap of faith for me to let Lilly disappear with strangers on this trip, but in this instance I feel pretty good about it.

Edu insists we stay for breakfast, and she and her husband scurry around the outdoor kitchen cooking, intermittently sending one of the kids to another house to get various ingredients or to borrow an extra chair. We all sit down at the table, and Edu sets a bowl in front of Lilly – it's an entire fish with eyes and tail still attached. *There's no way she's going to eat that for breakfast,* I think, *and I don't want to offend this kind family.* But, she surprises me and eats it all with not a single negative comment.

They also bring out a bowl of small, wrinkled, white eggs. I'm hesitant to ask what they are, since I'm pretty sure I know the answer...

"Tortugas." (Turtles)

Now we find ourselves in a moral quandary.

Only two weeks ago we were at the turtle preserve in Baja talking to the scientists who are trying valiantly to save the turtles. They have guards stationed at the hatching areas trying to stop poachers stealing the eggs and selling them for food. They taught us that one of the biggest reasons for turtle numbers dwindling is that villagers eat the eggs. They made us all promise never to eat turtle eggs.

And now we're sitting outside an earthquake-damaged house at the humble kitchen table of an incredibly kind family who is generously sharing this delicacy with us.

All eyes look upon us expectantly. Edu tears back part of the top of the egg to squeeze some lime and salt over it, and hands it to Lilly. She prepares another, this time with the addition of hot sauce, and hands it to John. He smiles half-heartedly and looks at me, as if to say, "What am I supposed to do?" They both say it's delicious. I am the rude one who declines.

After our fish soup and turtle egg breakfast (never thought I'd be writing that sentence!), Edu starts soaking rice for the horchata drink that she'll make the following morning. She makes it fresh every morning early before going down to the lake to sell it. She has a simple milling machine that grinds the rice with a hand crank, which she also uses to crush corn into chicken feed or to make tortillas. She makes a small batch of horchata that morning for us, and insists that we take a bottle with us for the road.

When we are packing up to leave, I notice that someone has left a plate with three more of grandma's tamales on our kitchen table in the van. Edu also packages up some cured mango that she makes and gives it to us for a snack. Then she sends her daughter into the house for a framed photo of the town church and insists we take it with us to remember them. That is just too much and we refuse, saying we might break it. So then she starts to pull the photo out of the frame to give us – this ancient photo that they could never replace! We take a photo of it and she is satisfied. Phew.

We feel conflicted by the obvious discrepancy in wealth between us and them, contrasted by who is giving to whom. We brought out the food we had that could go with the breakfast but it's not much. I want to leave Edu money – after all, her profession is selling food and drink, so it would be natural to pay for it – but when I pull her aside and mention that we'd love to contribute some money for everything, she very firmly brushes the idea away, with such conviction that I do not bring it up again.

Finally in the afternoon we head out. Our family escorts us to the edge of town to ensure we don't get lost. The mum, dad, and two girls all pile into the three-wheeled taxi, waving and smiling as we follow along behind. They stop at a market and motion for us to wait. Edu runs in and comes back out with her sister who wants to say goodbye and hug Lilly. Then we finally are on our way.

Maybe I'm getting soft in my old age, but I am teary-eyed when we drive away. I am astonished at their generosity. They have so little. Their house is literally falling down. They sell rice drink for a living. Yet they shared everything they had.

As we were all hugging each other farewell, in a feeble attempt at a thank-you, I offered up, "If you ever come to the US you have a place to stay." But they laughed good-naturedly at my offer, making jokes about hiding in the trunk of a car to sneak across the border. I asked if we might mail them something in future, but they didn't know their own address, suggesting we could write, "Edu, near the church" and the town name on the envelope.

So, how do we repay them? We can't. And they have no expectation that we will.

John and I have long conversations about it on the drive out, under-scored by our recent experience with the angry mob at the toll booth, and decide we should try to be more generous, generally, on our trip. This turns out to be a timely moment for a pay-it-forward experience, as we are about to enter one of the poorest parts of Mexico.

9

MAYAN VILLAGES OF CHIAPAS

I n just one week, I've almost suffocated on top of a volcano, we've partied with thousands of people in the streets of Oaxaca, the van was almost stoned by an angry mob, and we've experienced overwhelming generosity from a local family.

Overland travel puts you out there in myriad experiences, and our first week on mainland Mexico was no exception.

Leaving our Jalapa family – as they have thenceforth been known, named after the town where we met them – we see obvious earthquake damage everywhere we go. Stopping to buy fruit or ask for directions, I chat to the local people and hear variations of the same story: Kids cannot go to school because the school buildings are too badly damaged. Adults don't know if their houses are safe to sleep in, but they can't afford repairs. Communities are working together to reconstruct some semblance of water, sewer, and electricity. Everyone says that the government is not helping, yet they are all hearing about foreign countries donating money that isn't reaching them.

All this destruction, combined with our Jalapa family generosity and angry mob misunderstanding, leaves us wanting to do something more than just sightsee.

Through the travelers' grapevine we hear about an organization here in Chiapas that's accepting volunteers to teach English. It's a school that provides housing and food for children who are unable to live at home, whether due to poverty or danger in their own family. We pull into the parking lot late in the afternoon, and Lilly jumps out and runs to the playground. Her shyness with new kids is slowly diminishing, and we hardly see her during our stay there.

The kids explain that they only go to school one day per week, each age group taking a turn using the limited school infrastructure that remains after the earthquake. They have no idea how long it will be until everything gets rebuilt. I talk to some of the visiting mothers, who miss their children desperately but are so grateful there is a safe place for them to live. It's hard to put myself in their shoes and imagine sending Lilly away to live at a school because I'm unable to provide a safe home for her.

John and I prepare English classes and put together an educational slideshow of our trip to share with the kids, but we can't find anyone in charge to help integrate us into the school day. Our lessons often end up as one-on-one conversations with any child we can find who is interested, and we don't feel like we are really helping. John tries to talk to someone about helping repair the playground, but can't find anyone to coordinate with or to ask about borrowing some tools. So we only stay for three days and then move on. I can't blame them for not trying to accommodate every random passing do-gooder, but I leave with a stronger desire to get involved somewhere else.

We stop briefly in the colorful town of San Cristobal de las Casas, but are reminded that cities and large vans are not a good mix. We're looking for a place to camp, so I hop out of the van to ask a hotel about a parking space. John says he'll drive around the block while I investigate, but immediately finds himself on a narrow one-way road with a wall to his left and cars parked along the right. He continues hesitantly until he gets to a spot where the parked cars are so close that he can't fit through, then pauses, uncertain what to do. There's a line of traffic behind him, making it impossible to back out, and at that very moment Lilly announces that she has to poop urgently and cannot wait another minute! She climbs down from her car seat and pulls out our porta-toilet while John reluctantly decides he has no other option but to edge forwards. Our tall tires start to rub against the solid wall on his left and the car on his right, squealing as if in protest, and our engine revs louder as the van struggles to make way. As he starts to press harder on the gas pedal, Lilly shouts from the back of the van, "I need some toilet paper!" John briefly takes his hands off the wheel to throw some back to her, trying to ignore the smell coming from behind him, then gingerly depresses the gas pedal again. Suddenly – POP – the parked car to his right bounces over a couple of inches from the force of the van's tires pushing against it, and he is free!

Once out, he calls me and calmly states that he will *not* be returning to the hotel where he left me. We eventually find a spot on the edge of town to park. And to empty our toilet.

Driving north out of the city the next day is a fascinating study in rural life. The streets feel much more alive than back in the US. We crawl along on small roads through village after village, seeing hundreds of makeshift houses perched on the edge of the road, getting a five-second glimpse into so many lives around us...

A woman hanging out her family's clothes to dry on a line.

A group of men pouring concrete together to build a floor for a neighbor.

A line of uniformed kids walking home from school with no adults.

A man welding on the side of the road with no eye protection.

It's like watching an endless reel of video snippets showing lifestyles of rural people. Invariably at each house, from the sound of our engine approaching, all the faces turn to stare at us with a mixture of curiosity and apprehension in their eyes. The moment I wave and shout *hola*, those same faces brighten with broad smiles and we hear a chorus of *buenos dias* and *holas* in response. Kids prod each other to look at the foreigners driving by, and giggle when we shout a greeting.

It's a social drive because we're moving at a snail's pace with the windows down. The road is full of potholes, people, animals, and lots of unmarked speed bumps. It's such a different experience to go slowly on these small roads with our windows open, than to drive fast on the toll roads with the air conditioning blasting. Sure, it's less comfortable, but we see so much more.

Whenever we stop and talk to someone, I notice a strange accent. Eventually I ask someone about it and am astonished to learn that Spanish is the second language here! Mayan is the mother tongue. Some of them do not speak Spanish well at all, and they have to ask a neighbor to help when we talk to them. The clothing is also different from what we've been seeing so far in Mexico – women are wearing black dresses with colorful flowers embroidered on them, or long, black, furry skirts.

It seems that everyone is selling something. We stop at one house that sells bananas, another house has eggs and milk, another has roast chickens. One enterprising household sells jugs of diesel. I hop out of the van when we see baskets of fruit that we don't recognize and I ask the girl what they are. "Aguacate," (avocado) she replies. They are green, but the resemblance to avocados stops there – they are small, perfectly round and rock hard. She sees my look of disbelief and grabs one between her two palms and squishes, making the hard shell crack open like a nut. Inside is a perfectly ripe avocado, which she hands me to taste. I buy 6 for 10 pesos (about 50 cents US).

We do enjoy two impressive tourist sights – both waterfalls – while driving through the state of Chiapas.

We arrive in the late afternoon at Misol-Ha waterfall and set up camp in the parking lot. I walk around to locate the flattest and most private area, and then John maneuvers Vancito in while I do my air traffic control guiding. There's another overlanding couple performing the same dance with their truck, so once we are all set up, we join forces for an evening expedition to the falls.

A path has been carved into the stone cliff passing behind the waterfall, giving tourists a unique perspective of the falls from behind. It is even more unique to walk behind the water in the pitch dark! We turn off our headlamps and stand behind the 115 feet free-falling shower, experiencing only the thundering sound and wet spray without the visual cue for our eyes.

Continuing up the trail past the falls, we find an entrance to a cave and step inside. By the light of our headlamps, we see water reflecting below us and hesitantly climb down until we're standing in ankle-deep water. As we continue further into the dark cave, the water gets deeper and deeper until it almost reaches our waists. Lilly climbs up onto John's back to avoid having to swim, so she is the first to notice the dozens of bats swinging by their toenails not even five feet above us! I've never seen bats so close – they are surprisingly cute little buggers. Lilly is thrilled because she's just watched a show all about bats, so she enthusiastically educates us adults on their eating and sleeping habits.

Nearby, we visit Agua Azul (literally, Blue Water), which may be the most beautiful waterfall I've ever visited. We arrive at the end of the day, and I walk out to the end of the wooden boardwalk, climb over the barrier, and jump into the water. I have the huge pools entirely to myself.

It is surreal to swim in such bright blue colored water. The chalky powder suspension makes it feel like I'm in some magical blue glittering potion. I half expect to see some smoke spiral out of the water and a wizard appear in front of me. I breaststroke my way across the pool watching my arms glisten under the intense blue water. The sunset light reddens around me and I hear loud cries from hundreds of black birds flying in and out of a cave behind the falls as I swim closer. The drippy-looking, chalky white limestone cliffs all add to the wild and unique look of the falls.

The next day we are surrounded by tour buses and large groups of loud people and it's an entirely different experience. We don't even get in the water because it's so crowded and noisy. Both of these waterfall visits remind us of one of the huge benefits of vanlife – visiting popular places when no one else is there.

In this part of Mexico we are seeing many more signs of poverty. Most families are living in barely thrown-together shelters with dirt floors and no running water, trying to earn money in any way they can. It's all about self-employment out here – there's no employer providing any kind of income security. Everyone we see is an entrepreneur, selling whatever they can to make ends meet, or trying to live off their own land. Our impression is that these people are determined, hard-working, and family-oriented.

It's eye-opening to realize that we have more luxuries (clothes, books, toys) and even basic life essentials (electricity, internet, propane stove) in our little temporary van home than many people here do in their permanent house. Our family and friends think we are roughing it on this trip, but we have a clean, dry home and enough money to buy any supplies we need. We are living in relative luxury, and it's uncomfortably obvious how privileged we are as we drive through this area.

Our main topic of conversation in the van becomes poverty and what to do about it. I doubt it's a standard homeschooling lesson for six-year-olds, but Lilly is getting an earful. Ultimately, we decide to give money to people who are trying to do something, like the disabled man at the traffic light trying to entertain with a hoop, or kids trying to sell anything. But for people simply begging, we give food instead of money. Every new face at our window prompts a quick family discussion, then Lilly runs into the back of the van for some food or I hand John some coins.

What hits me the hardest is seeing so many kids of Lilly's age out working by themselves. Kids who should be in school are standing in the middle of a road trying to sell food, or wash your windshield, or simply beg for money. Some of these resourceful kids are really hustling – we come across several groups who hold a string across the road so we are forced to stop the van. One little girl, barely taller than Lilly, climbed up onto our front left tire, holding onto John's open window for balance, so he could not drive away without causing her to fall off.

I can never pass a child, particularly a girl Lilly's age, without giving something, so we end up buying whatever the kids are selling. Mini bananas, peeled oranges, fried mystery things, unrecognizable nuts. We start saving our coins so that we can give them to the kids we come across, resulting in many bags of mysterious foods piled up in the front seats of the van.

One morning, I'm sitting in the van with Lilly doing math school at our little table, with all the doors open. A girl about Lilly's age walks up, trying to sell us bananas. The contrast is uncomfortably striking. The girl is standing barefoot outside the van in the dirt parking lot. She leans over our six pairs of shoes that are strewn about on the ground (flip-flops and sneakers each), and boldly places a bunch of bananas on the table next to Lilly's piles of textbooks and art supplies. She's by herself, carrying a heavy bucket full of bananas, trying to earn 50 cents per bunch. I buy more bananas than we can possibly eat.

The following day, I go to a little store and see a girl, shorter than Lilly, carrying a baby in a sling on her hip. She's buying groceries, handing over money, counting her change. I would never send my six-year-old out by herself to the local store, with or without a baby on her hip! But some parents don't have the luxury of making that choice.

The parents here don't love their kids any less than we love ours, they just lean on each other more. In some ways that can be good. The kids here are so mature and responsible. It makes us think that we underestimate kids' capabilities in our country and that we baby them too much. John and I talk a lot about it but decide that travelling through Mexico with no friends or family nearby is not the right time to start encouraging Lilly to go off doing things by herself.

It's not a ground-breaking discovery that we have an easier life than most people on this planet, but it's a good reminder – one that we should all get every once in a while.

10

HOWLING TREE MONSTERS AMIDST ANCIENT MAYAN RUINS

We head north from Chiapas toward the Yucatan, which you can envision as the tip of the backwards J that is Mexico. This area is sometimes referred to as the Egypt of the Americas due to the number of ancient ruins sprinkled around, dating back 2,500 years. John adores the history and adventure of exploring these ruins, while I am usually more impressed by the unique creatures and trees that we find while wandering deep into the jungle to remote sites. After visiting Uxmal, Chichen Itza, Tulum, Palenque, Calakmul, Tonina, as well as Tikal in Guatemala, our two favorites are Tonina and Calakmul.

Tonina is not really on the standard tourist path, being in Chiapas instead of the more popular Yucatan, so there isn't a single other person there when we arrive. There are no barriers preventing entrance to anything and we find endless tunnels, pyramids, and even a labyrinth. The steps up some of the temples are so narrow that only the ball of my foot can fit on each one. It's like tip-toeing up a series of short ledges with no railing, in order to climb up the side of a skyscraper for a couple of stories. I am nervous watching my little girl climb up, and balancing myself back down again is even harder. We are a rock climbing family, but I would usually have Lilly on a rope at this height!

Some of the more popular ruins are more developed and better restored than Tonina, but much of their areas are roped off from visitor exploration and they are crowded with people. While at these locations, we try to use the crowds to fuel our imagination of what it was like at its heyday, full of residents and peddlers and worshippers.

Calakmul is a 200 km detour from the nearest city, hidden in thick jungle near the Guatemalan border. You feel like Indiana Jones as you wander through the dense foliage "discovering" seemingly untouched pyramids of rock. It was in use from 550 BC to 900 AD, and, at its peak in the late first century, there were fifty thousand people living there! The city where we lived in California has seventy thousand people, and an enormous amount of infrastructure – it's hard to imagine that this dense jungle and piles of rock buildings were able to sustain almost the same number of people over 2,000 years ago.

What really wows me is that the rulers here also governed other towns that were 100 km away. They had no means of communication besides word-of-mouth, and the only way to travel was *on foot*. (Horses didn't come here until the Spanish arrived in the 1500s.) From what I gathered from chatting to folks who work here, they reckon people would walk up to 50 km in a day when traveling with information between towns for their leaders.

The views from the top of the great pyramid are fantastic. I enjoy a meditative moment sitting alone 150 feet up on a rock pedestal built 2,000 years ago, looking out over the vast expanse of jungle, unbroken except for an occasional stone pyramid peeking up through the trees. It's an incredibly peaceful and awe-inspiring place to sit and think about life all those years ago. Some governing leader used to sit right here and shout commands to people around him: Feed me! Carry me! Wipe my bum!

One structure we see at almost every ruin is the ball court. I don't know how archaeologists pretend to know anything about a 2,000-year-old game, but they claim it was played with a rubber ball, two teams, and one or two hoops about head-height for scoring goals. And

– the oddest rule in the game – you could only touch the ball with your hip, knee, or elbow. No head, feet or hands!

After seeing many of these ancient ball courts in person and trying to imagine what they were used for, we have the great luck to see a re-enactment one evening in Merida. The players assemble in the street under the imposing shadow of the city's large, dark, stone church. The team on our side wear body paint markings and a stone snake figure wrapped around their head with the mouth and tongue pointing out toward the opposing team.

It's a wacky game! As the ball careens toward a player, you expect him to kick or hit it, but no. The player throws his body onto the ground, into the path of the incoming ball, and thrusts one hip toward it, giving it a loving tap, back toward the other side. It's then received similarly by the players on the other team, all the while wearing intimi-dating war paints and horns. It's a comical sight, but it helps to complete the picture in my mind the next time I'm standing in the ancient ruins of a ball court, imagining the sights and sounds of the game 2,000 years ago.

While John and Lilly climb yet another pyramid, I sit down in some shade offered by an ancient structure behind me, and just watch the world go by for a few minutes. A young white couple filming each other while climbing the tall steps. A Mexican family dragging their toddler around by the hand. The ever present hawkers trying to get anyone's attention.

A teenage boy catches my eye. He's looking at his phone in that peculiar way that can only mean he's taking a selfie. Angling this way and that, pouting his lips to get the right jawline view, looking down his long cheek bones into the camera lens. It strikes me how different his facial features are compared to the faces we see emblazoned on billboard advertisements on the side of the road, or printed on food packaging in stores here. Those faces are always white skin with the flat bone structure that I have. I'd already noticed that the people portrayed on TV or in advertisements here do not look like the people who actually live here. Now I notice it more intimately, while watching this boy trying to get the "right" look in his selfie phone view to share online.

Eventually I stand up and climb the stone stairs behind me. When I reach the top, I see an image carved in stone from thousands of years ago. I'm looking at the teenage boy. Those same features – strong jaw, long curved nose, deep set eyes. This is the face that was admired thousands of years ago. This was the face copied by artists and etched permanently into stone for temple visitors to see as the image of perfection. I wonder if that boy will climb these stairs and feel proud to see the reflection of his strong physical features in these carvings?

Spending all this time in the jungle, I've discovered my new favorite alarm clock – howler monkeys. Our first encounter with these impressive little creatures is while camping in the jungle near Calakmul ruins. At bedtime on our first evening there, I'm cuddled up with Lilly in our sleeping bags reading her a story about dragons, when suddenly a deep roaring sound echoes in the trees all around us. Lilly starts bouncing up and down in our bed shrieking, "Howler monkeys!" They make a great soundtrack to my story-telling about dragons fighting bad guys.

It's shocking that a furry little creature, barely knee-high to me, weighing in around 15lbs, can make such a terrifyingly loud sound. They make the loudest noise of any other land creature – yes, louder than lions or elephants! When you are camped in a remote jungle with only a canvas tent protecting you from the darkness outside, and you hear their roaring echoing all around you, it is certainly reminiscent of a horror movie soundtrack.

I'll never forget one evening walking alone down a narrow path through the trees to get to a bathroom from the van. I could only see the small circle of light from my flashlight bouncing on the ground in front of me, when suddenly the deafening roaring started above me. In the periphery of my flashlight beam I saw the branches of the trees moving around from some unseen force. Sticks and leaves started falling around me from above. If I hadn't seen the little guys in daylight earlier, I'd have probably peed my pants while sprinting back to the van.

Another, much less fun, aspect of spending so much time in a jungle setting is the constant bug bites. One memorable night, parked at a campground outside of Palenque, Lilly woke up in the middle of the night crying.

"What's wrong?" John asked, half asleep.

"I need a fork," she demanded.

"Why do you need a fork in the middle of the night?" I asked, not sure if she was perhaps dreaming.

"To scratch my bites!" she replied.

Fair enough. I climbed downstairs and passed her up a fork.

11

SWIMMING IN METEOR HOLES, AND
FINAL DAYS IN MEXICO

The story goes something like this: 65 million years ago, a meteor crashed into Earth in this area of the Yucatan. It killed all the dinosaurs, but also created thousands of deep underground sinkholes along the circumference of the crater impact zone in an arc across the Yucatan Peninsula. Over time, these sinkholes filled with fresh water from deep within the earth, creating some of the most unique swimming areas I've seen. These are *cenotes*.

Some cenotes are totally buried underground, approachable only via dark tunnels. Some cenotes have been entirely opened to the sky after years of erosion, thus appearing more like a normal lake or lagoon surrounded by cliffs. The most interesting are those still mostly underground but with enough erosion over the years to have created a skylight opening to let the sun in. We visit ten cenotes while traveling across the Yucatan, and see all types.

Our favorite visit is to Kankirixche, near Homun. We drive down a dirt road, through a tiny village, down another dirt road, and find a little parking area. Two men live there in a rickety house and say we can camp for $1 each. I look around but see nothing but jungle surrounding us, so I ask if there is a trail to get to the cenote. The man points to the top of a ladder poking out of a small hole about 50 feet away.

"That's the cenote?" I prepare to be mightily unimpressed, but dutifully walk over to peer through the hole.

A rickety bamboo ladder leads down into a large, underground, glistening swimming pool. The afternoon sunlight highlights the center of the pool all the way down to the rocky bottom. It's absolutely gorgeous! We quickly pay our $1 and change into bathing suits. It's incredible to swim from the cool, dark water into the warm, bright patch of sun and out the other side. The juxtaposition of crystal clear blue water surrounded by dirty, drippy, brown cave is quite striking.

A handful of people come and go during the day on a taxi cenote tour, but by about 4 p.m. we have the whole place to ourselves. After dinner at the van, we put back on our wet bathing suits and bring our flashlights to climb down the ladder in the night. Once the three of us are at the bottom, we turn off our lights and swim in the pitch darkness together, with just a tiny glow of light provided by the sliver of moon low in the sky through the hole up above. It is spooky and wild to swim in that water with no sense of sight. I am so impressed that Lilly jumps in and swims with us, but she never lets go of me.

The water in every cenote is incredibly clear. It feels magical to swim underneath and see so clearly, like you're floating in space far above the ground, looking down and around you at caves and stalagmites. It is deceptively clear, throwing off your depth perception when you jump in – they appear to be much shallower than they are, because you can see the bottom so clearly from above. More than once, I've jumped in and got water up my nose because I hit the water higher than I'd expected.

Some cenotes have platforms of different heights to jump from, and others have tarzan swings of varying lengths – we have hours of fun leaping and swinging at these pools. Another is more of a spelunking experience: at the end of a long walk through a muddy tunnel, dodging stalactites and stalagmites by the light of our headlamp, we discover a clear pool where we go swimming in the pitch blackness.

There are thousands of cenotes sprinkled around the Yucatan like part of a scavenger hunt, waiting to be discovered. It's wonderful to camp in our van right next to them, giving us private evening and morning visiting rights to these unique swimming holes. They are definitely a highlight of our time in Mexico.

* * *

We manage one last wild camping experience before leaving Mexico, at the remote salt lakes near the northern coast of the Yucatan. What a unique location! We drive along a single-lane dirt track that sits precariously on a narrow spit of land rising just barely above sea level. We're hemmed in by the ocean on our left, and a series of colorful lagoons on our right.

Want to watch the sunrise over the ocean? Turn your head to the left.

Want to see wild pink flamingos walking through a lagoon? Turn your head to the right. Let's hope climate change doesn't happen overnight, or Vancito will become a submarine!

We find a spot to park about equidistant between the ocean and the lagoon. It's a unique experience to cook dinner at the van, watching the sunset light reflect on the bright pink flamingo bodies in the lake in front of us, while also hearing the ocean behind me. Lying in bed in the van that night, my eyes see the moon reflecting on calm, still water; but my ears hear loud crashing of ocean waves. What a wild place to camp.

In the early morning I discover that the flamingos have walked over to the edge of the lagoon where we are parked. From so close up, I now see that they are huge – probably hip-height on me. I creep out of the van, while Lilly and John are still asleep, to get closer.

I walk down one of the spits of land jutting into the lagoon and sit reading my book as the sun rises behind me. There's a frequent honking noise coming from all around me, like from geese or ducks – I guess that's the sound flamingos make. Every once in a while, a pelican flies in and lands amongst the flamingos, as if to remind me that the ocean is right behind me, and why am I sitting over here ignoring it?

The ground beneath me is slightly sticky, almost like wet clay. It must form the floor of the entire lagoon, as I can see the flamingos walking all the way across. They walk very deliberately and delicately, like they might fall over at any moment on their skinny legs. And, their knees bend backwards! When I see some walking on dry land in front of me I realize what they remind me of – women teetering around in high heels.

Their flying is no less comical. They start by making a running motion with their feet still touching the water, so it looks like they're running on the surface of the water like a character out of a cartoon. Eventually they get airborne and flap across the sky looking like a Gonzo muppet nose attached to a straight arrow.

We notice that the smaller flamingos are white, and later learn that they are *all* born white, but after eating nothing but little pink larvae for a few years, they turn pink. The living incarnation of "You are what you eat." Apparently, they eat for 12 hours a day, then sleep and do it again. What a life.

* * *

Our final days in Mexico include a wonderful week with friends visiting from California, upgrading Vancito's suspension thanks to aforementioned friends carrying 200 lbs of steel on the airplane in their luggage, and Lilly crashing her bicycle into a parked motorcycle – an entire construction crew of concerned Mexican fathers came running toward her screams; she was fine.

Looking back over these first three months of our vanlife experiment, what stands out the most to me is the quality time with John and Lilly – we are together 24 hours a day, every day! In the evenings we sit in the van together drawing, reading, playing music – all things I never had time for back in California. Lilly will ask a simple question like, "Why does that family live in a mud house?" and it'll prompt a long discussion about the differences we see around us. It's intriguing getting to know my own daughter and husband so much better – having debates about poverty and education, snuggling in a tiny bed in the dark reading, figuring out a new town in a foreign language together – I feel closer to them than I ever have.

Camped on the shore of the idyllic multi-colored lake Bacalar on our final night, I recall how concerned I was in the weeks before leaving the US. The news was full of scary stories of crime and natural disaster. Then we crossed the border and I was nervous the first few times we set up camp in a public area – what if a bad guy comes to our van in the night? But we've managed 4,250 miles over three months without running into bad guys.

Night after night, we've set out our beds and turned off the lights to sleep, protected only by the walls of our vehicle and a faith in humanity. And morning after morning, we've been greeted with smiles from the local people and enjoyed a front row seat to wilderness landscapes. The worst injury any of us sustained was when I got into a hammock that wasn't attached properly and I fell on my bum. Yup, the deadly Mexican hammock – you'll see it in the next US government travel advisory.

Mexico has been a great introduction to overlanding outside of the US. We are ready for Central America.

Baja beach camping

Homeschool on the beach

Mainland farm camp

Dia de Muertos in Oaxaca

Jungle girl

Swimming in a cenote

The road fell off!

BELIZE

We drove 370 miles over 3 weeks in Belize.
December, 2017 to January, 2018.

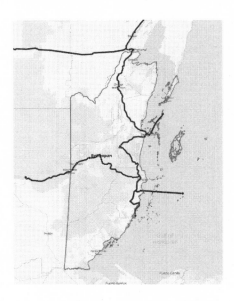

12

DEFIANTLY DIFFERENT BELIZE

W hy is this tiny, 70-mile-wide country so different from the rest of Latin America? I'm astonished at the sudden mix of cultures, languages, and races that I see co-existing around me, after the prior three months of homogeneity in Mexico.

Walking through town I see tall, black people speaking Creole and cooking Caribbean food. They are wearing colorful clothes and their hair is often in dreadlocks. We no longer hear jolly Mexican trumpets blaring out of every radio station, but instead Bob Marley and other reggae tunes with lots of drumming.

But then I walk into a fruit market and find families of Mayans who look like the people we've been seeing the past three months in Mexico. They speak Spanish and/or Mayan and sell food that looks more Mexican.

Next I enter a grocery store and notice that it's owned by Chinese people. They don't speak much English *or* Spanish, and appear to be somewhat segregated. Every grocery store we see in this country is owned by Chinese people, and this appears to be a point of some disgruntlement with the local Belizeans.

Leaving the grocery store, I see a horse-drawn buggy pull up and a group of blonde-haired, blue-eyed, white-skinned, German-speaking Mennonites climb out! There are several Mennonite colonies scattered across Belize. They live very independently, but are the providers of most of Belize's fruit and vegetables.

So much diversity in such a tiny country!

The primary language seems to be Creole, although most Belizeans switch seamlessly between Creole, English, and Spanish. I was stunned when we crossed the border from Mexico and the border patrol man spoke to us in perfect English. He said we had to pay for a van fumigation, which turned out to be a sprinkling of water onto our windshield as we drove under an arch, so I handed him some Mexican pesos. He handed me some change, and I glanced down to see Queen Elizabeth of England looking up at me! I couldn't Belize it!

Yup, this place was a British colony until 1981, and I see evidence of it everywhere we go. I spent the first 18 years of my life in London, England, followed by 20+ years in the US, so I get some unexpected childhood reminders as I explore Belize. My favorite English chocolate bars are for sale in all the grocery stores – we couldn't buy those in Mexico (or the US) so we'll be chocolate smugglers into Guatemala. Signs are in English, and speed limits are in mph instead of kmph. There are even meat pies for sale in lots of shops, and good cheese available. Yup, it feels like home. Well, except for the permanent 80 degree weather and the Creole language everywhere. And, lucky for us, they switched over to driving on the right-hand-side of the road back in the '60s.

The food, however, is decidedly not English. And, it's a welcome change after three months of the same Mexican meals. Yes, you think you adore Mexican food, but try eating it every meal for three months and I promise you'll be begging for vegetables. Here I'm eating curries and fresh fish, with coconut flavors and Creole spices – delicious.

Most tourists come to Belize to visit one of the islands on the reef – it's the second largest in the world after the Great Barrier Reef in Australia. We went first to Caye Caulker, which was a fun, but busy, touristy island. It is full of restaurants, bars, tour operators, and music, but has a very relaxed vibe. There are no cars, and most people get around by bicycle, so the pace of life is slow. We fed tarpon, saw a seahorse in the wild, and swam in the midst of a nurse shark feeding frenzy, with stingrays rubbing my ankles like house cats.

But we want a more wild and remote island experience while in Belize. So, after much searching, we find a reef with simple lodgings that has space for us over Christmas week – Glover's Atoll "Resort."

Ha! I can't type that word without laughing out loud.

No electricity, no plumbing. You haul water in a bucket from the well and wash your dishes in a bowl – but only if you've remembered to bring your own soap and sponge, otherwise you're scrubbing your frying pan with sand. Bathroom facilities are a shared composting outhouse and cold water outdoor shower. We sleep in a semi-open, thatched cabin on stilts that provides little protection from wind or rain (of which there is a lot) and cook our meals standing in the sand at an outdoor stovetop, dodging sand flies and hermit crabs.

But, we're on a gorgeous palm-tree covered island out in the middle of the reef. There's no town, no hotel, no one else on the island besides the few other backpackers who came on our same boat. We walk a few steps from our simple hut directly into the coral reef for amazing snorkeling, surrounded by every color of fish you can imagine. We use our inflatable kayak daily, go scuba diving, climb palm trees, swim and fish.

It's paradise, but definitely Robinson Crusoe style.

As remote as we are, a present for Lilly does appear in our hut on Christmas morning. She runs outside and points out reindeer footprints in the sand, and swears she heard noises in the night. It's our first Christmas of the van trip and she seems happy with just a couple of small gifts, and a day spent snorkeling in the ocean just steps from our little hut.

The underwater visibility is amazing. I float around and see fish with electric blue trim along their edges, jellyfish smaller than my hand, a school of 20 squid wiggling by, parrotfish, and puffer fish. I'm distracted momentarily by a jellyfish who's too close for comfort, when from the corner of my eye something much larger than everything else appears. My heart jumps and I inhale sharply through my snorkel as a dark shape, longer than I am tall, approaches. I remind myself that nurse sharks aren't too dangerous and I try to calmly watch him, tall tail fin waving back and forth as he swims right by me and disappears.

It's captivating to swim through this underwater ecosystem, uninvited but tolerated by the inhabitants. A silent observer of an entirely different world thriving right in front of us, yet I so rarely see it in my normal life.

When not in the water, we try our hands at becoming hunter-gatherers. There's something very satisfying about finding your own food, and I don't just mean finding the right aisle in the supermarket.

My daily contribution is coconuts. It feels like I'm in some sort of strongman contest as I manhandle a 15-foot-long heavy bamboo pole to reach up into the branches of a palm tree, and knock at a coconut repeatedly until it falls down. Then I use the handle-less machete blade, that is thoughtfully left out for us guests, to try and whack off the tip of the coconut without losing all the liquid, or my fingers. That's just to get a sweet drink from a green coconut. Trickier is getting into the brown coconuts for the white meat inside. First, I work off the tough sinewy hair with a metal spike, which is 10 minutes of sweat and occasionally blood and tears for me. Then I bounce the machete against the nut repeatedly, nature mocking the steel blade with a meek "ping" noise, until eventually it cracks open. Lastly I grind out the coconut meat inside with yet another scary-looking rusty tool. I'm pretty sure it's a net negative calorie experience!

As for John, he's enjoying trying to get us fish each day, whether by fishing line, harpoon gun, or his bare hands. Yes, bare hands... The day we arrived, he met another tourist who had brought special lobster-grabbing gloves he'd bought online – I kid you not. So the two of them kayaked out and took turns free-diving down trying to pry a lobster from under the coral to bring home for our dinner. The local guys who lived on the island were quite amused. (No lobsters were harmed that day.)

Just as exciting, but more productive, are John's harpoon fishing adventures. We meet a lovely Swede called Anders, as obsessed by fishing as we are by climbing, who invites John to join him one morning. John returns to me and Lilly later that afternoon, raving about the primal experience: You swim around on the surface until you spot a fish below, then take a deep breath and kick down to the level of the fish. Now hold your breath while you slowly stalk it under water, and eventually fire when you get close enough. Definitely the kind of activity for getting in touch with your inner caveman.

Whenever they return from fishing, John and Anders stand in the shallow water alongside the boat and clean their fish, cutting directly onto the wooden dock as if it were a kitchen cutting board. This activity always invites an eager audience of nurse sharks and stingrays, who swim around John's and Anders' ankles begging for scraps. This is Lilly's favorite part of the fishing trip – she picks out which shark looks hungriest and tries to toss fish heads to it, shrieking in delight if "her" shark manages to leap over the others to catch the morsel.

My freshest food experience ever is the afternoon that John returns from deep sea fishing with a tuna. One of the islanders pulls a knife out of his pocket and cuts it up into slices, tossing the excess to the splashing horde of sharks around the dock and handing us the good parts in a plastic bag. We carry it the few steps to our cabins, where Anders produces a bottle of soy sauce. I'm a little dubious, but I reach into the plastic bag to grab a piece of tuna – that I've just seen cut from the fish on the dock – dip it into some soy sauce and drop it right into my mouth! First sushi since we left California, and it's delicious.

John strong-arming a bamboo pole to knock down coconuts

GUATEMALA

We drove 620 miles over 8 weeks in Guatemala.
January to February, 2018.

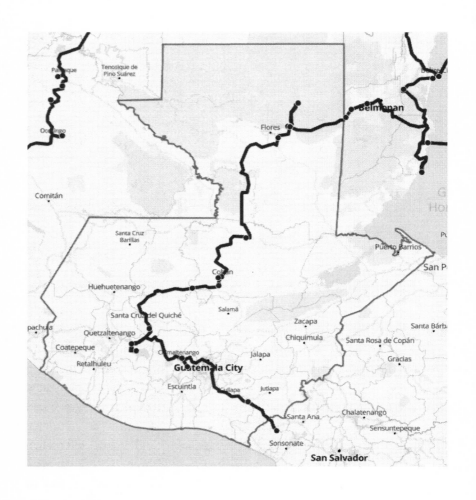

13

VOLUNTEERING WITH LOCAL KIDS

W e walk across an invisible line in the dirt and suddenly everyone is speaking Spanish again. Country borders are such a bizarre concept when you experience them up close and on foot. New currency, new language, new skin color, new food – they all change in a matter of 100 feet. It seems so arbitrary and yet so precisely defined along this man-made line.

The Guatemala/Belize border is under dispute due to Guatemala's long-standing claim over Belize. The maps we see while in Guatemala show either no border at all, with Belize simply included as part of Guatemala, or a dotted-line border labeled "undefined." It's an especially strange idea to us after experiencing a very defined customs, passport control, and vehicle import at that "undefined" border.

Ever since our attempt to volunteer, not very successfully, at the children's home in Mexico, I've been looking for another opportunity, and we find one in the small town of El Remate just 40 miles from the Belize border. We meet a Canadian woman, Anne, who moved here 20 years ago and has been improving healthcare and education in the community ever since. She's an inspiration – modest, generous, hard-working, and loved by everyone in the town.

Anne started out with just a tarp stretched from the side of her little rental house to create a space for providing basic medical services to the locals. Over the years she earned the trust of the community, gathered donations internationally, and motivated volunteers to come help. Her organization, Ix-Canaan, has grown substantially since those early days. She currently has a fully built-out medical clinic, dentist office, computer lab, and library. Additionally, she provides English classes in the library whenever there are volunteers available – that's where we come in.

We meet Anne on Friday, spend the weekend creating lesson plans, and show up Monday morning at the library for our first day on the job.

It is surprisingly difficult to teach a group of kids when, 1) you never know how many will show up, 2) they speak varying levels of English, 3) they range in age from 4 to 18 years, 4) more kids keep arriving throughout your lesson as the word spreads around town! John and I prepare lesson plans in the evenings, but usually have to adapt on the fly depending on which kids show up each day.

I am so impressed by the focus and diligence of these kids, voluntarily joining an after-school lesson when they could be outside playing. I'll never forget the intense concentration in the face of seven-year-old Ivania, leaning toward me, staring at my mouth trying to imitate the sounds I'm making, "My nah-meh ees Ivania" over and over. She's one of the few kids who comes every day to class, carrying her little notebook and pen, learning more quickly than the teenagers are. But it strikes me that she can work harder than I ever did, study more than I ever did, and still not have the same opportunities for success that I had.

Meanwhile, Lilly is making fast friends with the girls who come every day to play at the playground. The first few days she stays close to me or John during class, feeling shy and clingy, but after a few days she begins to feel right at home and we hardly see her all afternoon. The only downside of Lilly's new friendships is the arrival of some unwanted guests – head lice! Multiple eye-burning shampoo treatments and many hours of bug squishing later, she and I manage to evict our new tenants, never to be seen again.

By the end of the first week, we can't walk anywhere without running into our students. The older kids shyly greet us in halting English and introduce us to their parents, the younger kids run up and hug Lilly and ask her to play. I'll stop to buy a banana smoothie at a little road-side fruit stand, and there's Mateo grinning at me from behind his mother's back as she works the blender.

Our daily commute to school becomes something of a Pied Piper act. As we walk along the dirt roads, my regular students flag us down and walk alongside us. Lilly's favorite playmates run out and hug her, then they skip together up the hill. A mother whom I've never seen before calls out from her front door asking me to take her son with us, and a little boy runs over to join our group. It's lovely to feel part of a welcoming community, even just temporarily.

Lilly becomes particularly close to an eight-year-old girl, Diana. We usually stop at her house in the morning to pick her up on our way to the library, and bring her home afterwards, so she and Lilly spend a lot of time together.

Diana and her grandma, Rita, live in a very simple house along the main road. They have four walls around one bedroom with a dirt floor and a hanging lightbulb, then an outdoor fireplace under a corrugated iron sheet to use as a kitchen, and chickens and an outhouse behind the house with a bucket setup for bathing. Lilly doesn't even register that this is so different from what she's used to back in California. She and Diana play hide and seek in the dark house, or make up games with sticks and dirt, or chase the chickens around outside for hours.

The first evening that Lilly and I stop by to visit, we find Rita rolling out corn dough on a large, flat stone to make tortillas. She greets us warmly and sends Diana out to buy bread down the street. Diana takes Lilly by the hand and they walk out together, my eyes nervously following as they walk down the road. I realize this is the first time that Lilly has gone out without an adult! I decide to trust in eight-year-old Diana, and in this small town where everyone knows everyone, and turn back to talk to Rita.

Rita sets a pot of water in her open fire to warm it up for coffee, and I hesitantly ask where the water comes from. "*El chorro*," she says

– the faucet outside distributing water from the lake. I watch carefully but see that she doesn't boil the water before adding some coffee powder and serving me a cup. I take one sip of the lukewarm, brown liquid and then pretend to look for Lilly outside while I surreptitiously pour most of it out in the dirt. These are the kind of tricky social situations I haven't quite figured out yet.

(Ironically, this town *is* the first place John and I get food poisoning, but it's not from the tap water, it's from a fried fish meal at a tourist restaurant in town.)

The next morning, Lilly and I walk out to buy bananas and we see Diana walking down the street by herself carrying a basket of tortillas, selling them to local restaurants. We walk with her back to her house where Rita is making more tortillas, handing stacks to Diana and telling her which store to deliver which stack and how much money she needs to get from each. Lilly and I accompany her on her deliveries, and I'm so impressed at her keeping track of all the different customers and the money. She's only one year older than Lilly! I point out this difference in responsibility level to Lilly later that day – her only chores are drying dishes and making her bed – but I don't know if it resonates.

When the deliveries are complete that afternoon, I ask Rita if she knows where I can buy chicken, since the only meat we see for sale here looks very old and dodgy. She leads me out behind her house where there are several chickens running around and asks me which one I want! This is not a question I have ever been asked before, and I have no idea how to answer it. But the next morning, Diana shows up at our van with a freshly killed and plucked chicken in a plastic bag.

Later that week, Anne asks if I can work with Diana on her Spanish reading and writing. So at her house that evening, we read some of her school text books together while I help her sound out words. I talk to Rita afterward about Diana's homework and explain how she might be able to help her more, by reading to her before bed or checking her writing assignments. She is not responding very enthusiastically to my suggestions, and our conversation starts to feel awkward until I finally figure it out... Rita cannot read! I am gobsmacked.

Imagine how different your school experience would have been if your parents had not been able to even *read* your homework assignment, never mind actually help you with it.

Rita shows me the list of school supplies that Diana needs for the new year. (The school year starts in January here.) She can't read the list, and can't afford to buy the materials. So Diana and Lilly and I go on a shopping trip together the next day. I'm amazed at how specific the requirements are – "One 80-page notebook with double spacing and covered with red paper for Spanish class," – and there are a dozen more notebook descriptions like this. Anne has told me that part of the grade for a class is dependent on having the right materials for that class, so maybe, in a tiny way, we can give Diana a little leg up on school this year.

One of our last evenings together, Rita and I sit together on the two plastic chairs in her kitchen and chat while the girls play outside. It is dark but for the light cast by the streetlight outside the house, so I can't see her face, but it's easy to follow her slow, deliberate Spanish. She asks about my life and our trip. Then she tells me about her family situation raising Diana as if she were her mother, lowering her voice when she talks about Diana's mother moving to the city to try to earn money for them.

She explains that life in Guatemala is so much better now than when she was a child during the civil war. She mentions the "bad times," which I hadn't wanted to ask her about. She tells me that her father, her brothers, and most of her sisters were killed. She describes hiding in their house every evening after dark, feeling terrified at the sound of anyone approaching outside, never knowing if someone would come for her the way they came for her father and brothers. Her mother and one sister escaped to Mexico, and then returned many years later. I listen quietly and she concludes by stating simply, "It was a terrible time."

What civil war? A brief history: Guatemala was run by conservative military dictators for decades. Left-wing guerillas, prompted by the extreme poverty that was being ignored by the government, started fighting the military forces. Through the 70s and 80s, the government waged war against its people, commanding executions and abductions. Some 200,000 civilians were killed or "disappeared." The military led massacres of entire villages of indigenous Mayan people. In recent years, some of those leaders are now being tried for genocide by the Guatemalan government. (End of history lesson.)

It's incredible to me that such terrible things happened in our lifetime here in Guatemala, and yet the people appear to be so optimistic and happy. I suppose when you've lived through something that awful, perhaps you are more grateful for a safe and simple life. It speaks volumes to the strength and determination of the people of this country.

* * *

John and I were really torn about staying or leaving El Remate. We felt like we'd started putting down some roots and building a community for the first time since leaving California. Anne talked to us about teaching in the local public school, instead of at her library after school, which was very appealing since we'd have a fixed classroom of kids. She also said we could enroll Lilly in the same school, which would be a great experience for her to learn Spanish and become more independent. Ultimately, we couldn't find a comfortable long-term living situation, plus we haven't got more than 30 minutes from the Belize border yet, so we decide to explore the country further before settling down.

14

RAINY CENTRAL GUATEMALA

We camp in a parking lot in the middle of a big city, in the rain. By the side of a road across from a hotel, in a muddy dirt field. At a restaurant on the side of a highway with semi-trucks passing all night, in the drizzle. Outside of a remote village at the bottom of a dirt road... in the mud.

Yes, you're noticing a common theme – Guatemala does not have great camping sites, and we could not escape the rain.

Rain + vanlife = not fun.

Our "house" is tiny but we have an infinitely large back yard... except when it's cold and raining. So we look at weather forecasts and decide to beeline south across the country to escape the rain, having just a few adventures along the way.

We drive several kilometers down an impressively steep dirt road and set up camp at the bottom of a river canyon. Lilly and I tiptoe our way through the mud to the outhouse nearby, where we come across a woman with two kids. They are walking barefoot and balancing large baskets on their heads, full of the clothes they have just washed in the river, while we are wearing our fancy hiking sandals yet are slipping and sliding all over the place. I start chatting to them to learn about their tiny village across the river, but receive only smiles in response.

After some confusion and charades, I finally figure out they don't speak Spanish! I am speechless.

Local people start to gather around us like at a new roadside attraction, but all we can do is smile. It reminds me of when John and I backpacked across Africa and struggled to communicate with anyone. It makes such a difference when you can have real conversations and make connections with people.

Finally, an older gentleman joins us who speaks some Spanish. He leads Lilly and me across a narrow, rickety bridge spanning a river about 75 feet below to reach the tiny village on the other side. He steps nimbly over the many missing wooden slats, and I eye Lilly nervously as she jumps over the large gaps, following behind him. He explains that this is a community of families who share a shop and a school, and run tours to the local caves for income. The group of houses is tucked into the base of a steep canyon, with the only exit being that rickety bridge and then the steep dirt road out. Talk about being isolated.

I ask if the kids learn Spanish at school, but he shakes his head. I'm amazed. "How can your kids ever live somewhere else than this village if they don't speak Spanish?" I ask.

"They cannot," he simply responds.

Lilly and I walk around a little but we are unable to communicate with anyone, and there is nowhere to go. As we return back over the terrifying bridge, I notice a young girl washing her family's clothes in the river far below. *That is what she's going to do every day for the rest of her life,* I think to myself.

That evening John and I debate the merits of kids being taught Spanish to enable them to move out of their community if they choose to do so, versus the importance of continuing traditions. I do not know the right answer, but I feel very grateful for the opportunities enabled me by speaking English and Spanish. Most places we go we find that the people speak their native Mayan language *plus* Spanish. But this village is an exception, frozen in time.

* * *

We try to drive into the city of Chichicastenango via the main road, but it appears that the market takes priority over driving on weekends. John eases the van around a tight left turn, and there, straight ahead of us, is a market in full swing. The street is filled with stands selling fruit, clothes, kitchenware, anything you can think of. The stalls are crowding into the already-narrow street, metal posts sticking out with fabric flapping to provide shade, leaving a narrow, weaving obstacle course for a giant foreign van.

My first instinct is, "Turn around!" but there is already another car behind us. John edges forward. Stall owners pull their tables out of the way, barely glancing at us, like this is an entirely normal occurrence on market day. We are so close that if I reach my hand out the window, I could pick up a trinket or two. I try to smile calmly and wave at people, as if I'm in a parade, rather than just an idiot tourist who took a wrong turn. It seems like we're going to make it through, when a man walks up and starts talking to John through the window. He's saying we hit his car. I recall nothing of the sort, but John acquiesces it's possible we scraped something without feeling it.

"What? You hit someone's car and didn't even stop?" I scold John.

"There are so many dents on his truck, I'm sure we made no difference," he tries to defend himself. "Anyway, we are driving slower than walking pace, I knew he'd come talk to us if it's a problem."

We pull over as soon as we're through the market, a crowd of people now surrounding us, eager to watch the drama unfold. The man takes us back to his pick-up truck, which is indeed so covered in dents and dent-filler that it's impossible to tell what the original color of the vehicle was. He points to a dent that may be newer than the rest, about an inch in size, and says that we made it. We return to our van and there is indeed some red paint on the ladder on our van, so we admit fault and offer to pay. He first asks for Q4000 (about $500)! We laugh out loud, having recently paid a welder Q50 to repair a part of our van, and offer to go with him to a body shop to pay directly for the damage. It's obvious he has no interest in actually fixing the dent, so we eventually agree on Q170 and part ways amicably.

The market is far more enjoyable when we return the next day, on foot. We squeeze our way through a sea of red-clothed bodies, none of which reaches higher than my shoulders. Looking down, all I see is black hair and red shawls. John and I stand out like beacons high above everyone else, but Lilly is just short enough to be submerged in the flow of humans. I hear her cry out for us as she gets caught up in the crowd and can't catch up. Looking back, I see John reach into the river of bodies and pluck Lilly out of it, to join him at shoulder-height above everyone else.

What a colorful place! Every female seems to be wearing some shade of red, and is carrying a baby on her back in a similarly brightly colored shawl. The *corte* is the big wrap-around calf-length skirt, and the *huipil* is the blouse. Both are very colorful, with different colors and designs to indicate which town you are from, like a Scottish kilt identifies you with a family clan. Even the youngest of girls wear this outfit – it is incredibly cute to see a tiny girl toddling along with the perfect formal dress on. The men, however, mostly wear jeans and t-shirts.

This is the first part of Guatemala where most of the women we see are wearing traditional local clothes. Subsequently, it is the norm everywhere we go until we arrive in the city of Antigua.

* * *

Our favorite camp spot on this section of the trip is at a coffee co-op. It's a community of several hundred families who plant, harvest, wash, dry and sell coffee beans. And, they turn out to be incredibly welcoming to random van families passing through.

We arrive in the afternoon and they invite us in for a coffee (of course), even giving one to Lilly (who liked it, after adding much milk and sugar). We sit around a table all drinking coffee together answering their questions about our trip, and asking our own questions about their community. They deliver cups of coffee to the van, even in the pouring rain under umbrellas, multiple times during our stay. On a hot, sunny afternoon, they bring frozen coffee on a stick. Whenever we attempt to thank and pay them for their hospitality, they shake their heads and say they are "honored" to host us.

A señora walks us down the hill in the evening to show us the daily routine of the people delivering the beans they picked that day, which will be measured and recorded so each family gets their appropriate payment. Each family has their own plot of land where they grow their beans. They harvest the beans by hand, put them in a sack, and carry it on their head that same day to the machines that wash and dry them. The co-op buys the beans from the individuals, keeping 5% for co-op costs (eg. the machines), and works with a federation which roasts and grinds the beans to be sold all over the world.

The co-op was started by the grandparents of the people we met. It was originally owned by Germans, but they were kicked out of the country during WW2. The locals bought the land from the government with a government loan, and now have been running it for three generations. They all seem very proud of their lifestyle and profession. Most of the associates we meet are also studying at the local university, but say they have no intention of ever leaving the co-op.

It's a very educational visit, not just in regards to coffee production but also seeing yet again how welcoming and generous people are here. On this trip I regularly find myself deep in thought as we drive away from a kind family's home, wondering why I never welcomed strangers into my life back in California and promising myself to be different in future.

But, here in central Guatemala the rain will not stop falling, so we head south to get back to the sun and the famous Lake Atitlan.

15

VOLCANIC ERUPTIONS AND BACK TO SCHOOL, AKA LIVING IN GUATEMALA

V ancito eases down a steep road, squeezing around dozens of tight switchback turns that each require a complete stop and multiple reversals to get around. Suddenly, we catch a glimpse of an enormous lake surrounded by towering volcanoes, with a scattering of little villages clinging to the hillsides. It's a startlingly picturesque sight.

Once we navigate the twisty road down to the rim of the lake, we squeeze through two villages to get out to a campsite halfway between the towns of San Marcos and Tsununa. It's the best camp we've had in months! Incredible views of the lake and volcanoes right from our bed, sunny and warm all day but cool at night, no mosquitoes (thanks to being at 5,000 feet), great swimming in the beautiful (but cold) lake, hiking trails leading in all directions, and total peace and quiet around us. John declares it's his favorite campsite of our whole trip so far. For me, it takes second place after the beach wildcamps of Baja. So we decide to settle down for a month.

As if the view over the lake backed by three enormous volcanoes isn't enough, we also have a live, erupting volcano in the distance to entertain us! I've sat at campsites watching every kind of nature in my outdoorsy life, but this is something completely new to me.

Volcan Fuego erupts most mornings and many evenings that we're there. I usually wake up at sunrise to the incredible view out my window and a clear blue sky, except for a big plume of smoke coming out of Fuego, which slowly dissipates over the course of the morning. And in the evenings, John and I sit outside in the cool air, totally mesmerized by the orange glow at the top of the volcano in the distance. We watch the orange smear of light growing and shrinking as lava spills out of the volcano and cools as it runs down the sides.

During our first week, on Jan 31st, we are treated to a particularly large eruption. We see the distant lava glow suddenly get much bigger and shoot upward, then slowly pour down the sides of the volcano for several minutes. The next day I see the news headline, *"Guatemala volcano eruption: Antigua in danger!"* The plume reaches 6,500 meters above sea level and travels 40 km, and the falling ash affects tens of thousands of people.

Although we love our beautiful campsite home, we are not particularly fond of the nearby town, San Marcos. It bothers me when tourists don't pay attention to local customs, try to learn the language, or respect the community they are visiting. Here I'll see a hippie foreigner walking around barefoot, her breasts almost hanging out of her skimpy shirt, trying to earn money from other tourists by selling necklaces on the side of the road. Then I glance around and see locals who are covered up from elbows to neck to calves, who wear shoes only if they can afford to buy them (and I see many barefoot workers carrying heavy loads over rough trails in the mountains), and who work hard to get their share of the tourist dollar. I notice the locals staring at the hippie visitors in disbelief – not bathing and not wearing shoes is a sign of abject poverty, not being cool. However, when I walk up into the hills full of small houses and no tourist facilities, it's a different world. The locals are so friendly, stopping to help me with directions or advice. It's amazing that two such different communities exist so closely together.

I plan to find a school where I can volunteer, hoping to repeat the great experience we had in El Remate, and John wants to take Spanish lessons, so when we hear about a small school that accepts foreign kids, we go visit to see if Lilly wants to attend.

Escuela Caracol is set up on the hillside, reachable only by hiking up a dirt trail, and is comprised of a series of small, open classrooms with waist-high walls. There are trees to climb, ropes to swing on, plants and little paths everywhere. The kids learn how to make tortillas on a traditional stove just like their parents do, they learn the local language Kaqchikel, they each have an assigned chore (Lilly has to sweep the floor), and they learn about the seasons at the lake. And there are only eight kids in each class, with two teachers – it couldn't be more different than Lilly's public school education back in California. Lilly loves it.

By contrast, in my search for a place to volunteer as an English teacher, we visit the local public school in the next town. There is a construction site spilling into the school grounds and we have to climb over a mound of dirt to get through the front door. As I wait outside the Director's office, kids keep coming to stare at me, but when I try to talk to them they just giggle. Finally a realization dawns on me and I ask tentatively, as though the question is too ridiculous to say out loud, "Hablan español?" (Do you speak Spanish?)

One says, "Un poco" (a little). I'm still not used to this idea that someone could live in a Spanish-speaking country but not speak Spanish. As I wait, two boys approach carrying a big, white, open bucket with some dark mush sloshing around inside, splashing onto the floor as they stagger past. I ask what it is and they tell me it's lunch for the kids today at school.

I end up visiting four different public schools in various towns around the lake and see that the facilities are similar in each. Concrete outdoor courtyard for PE, with classrooms in rows of concrete blocks, each packed with a grid of desks attached to chairs and lots of broken windows. The toilets have no seats, no toilet paper, and no soap to wash your hands. The most surprising difference for me is that the door to each classroom has a deadbolt, and the teachers often lock it during class! We decide to enroll Lilly in Caracol.

While Lilly settles into her new school, I figure out how to start teaching at the public *primaria* (primary school) just 10 minutes walk from Caracol. With the help of an American woman I met who's lived here for 17 years, I get connected with two of the teachers. They are both very enthusiastic about my taking over their English lessons because they don't speak English themselves. I hear the same story at all four public schools I visited, "The government mandates we give English lessons but doesn't provide a teacher who speaks any English."

My first day I teach two different classes. First, I join Mateo's second grade class where the kids are so excited that they keep running up to the front to touch me and hug me. The kids clearly adore Mateo, and he is really motivated for them to learn English. Next I walk into Freddy's sixth grade class, ready to start my lesson again, but the teacher first spouts off a long speech to the class about this great opportunity to be with a native English speaker and makes them all applaud for me! I am so embarrassed.

At the end of my first day, I'm walking out to pick up Lilly from school when a girl grabs me by the hand and drags me into a fourth grade classroom, disrupting a lesson in progress. The whole class starts applauding and the teacher gestures to me to start my lesson. I apologize, "Sorry I have to leave now to pick up my daughter."

There is much disappointed noise from the kids. "Come tomorrow!" the teacher demands. And thus ensues a debate because I already have three lessons a day and can't fit in another within Lilly's school hours. "It's not fair if you do five days with Freddy's class and no days with me, you should split," the teacher continues. I promise her I'll figure something out.

And this is how my first week continues as word spreads that there's an English teacher available. I get more and more requests, even though I tell anyone who'll listen that I'm not an English *teacher*, simply an English *speaker*. I end up committing to four classes – Mateo's second grade, a fourth grade, Freddy's sixth grade, and a second sixth grade whose teacher I won't name. Here's how my first day in that sixth grade goes...

As I approach the classroom, I find three teenage boys wrestling just outside the door. I hesitantly sidestep around them and look through the open door. The teacher who asked me to come is not there. Instead, there's a harassed-looking man sitting at a desk in the corner, attempting to hide from five kids who are leaning over the desk shouting at him. On the floor, between me and that desk, is a teenage boy in the fetal position with his hands up protectively and two other boys hitting him. There are a few girls sitting at their desks and one math equation on the whiteboard.

I stand still in the doorway for a moment, stunned. I think back to my own school experience in London and imagine how differently my life might have turned out if this had been my education. Eventually the math teacher notices me and jumps up looking very relieved. "They're all yours," he says, and jogs out of the room, stepping over the fight on the floor on his way out.

Teaching is exhausting. I come home every day with a sore throat from shouting so much. Even though most of the classes are not as bad as that sixth grade one, it is still a huge effort to control the kids. As soon as they see me waiting in the hallway outside their classroom, they start chanting, "Eeengleesh! Eeengleesh!" and the teacher has to stop whatever they are doing and let me in. Many of the kids are so excited to have an English speaker that they keep shouting out random phrases they know. I'll be trying to teach the kids how to count to ten, but have to raise my voice to make myself heard over the arbitrary cries coming from the back of the room, "Good morning good night my friend I love you!"

Although most of the kids are really keen to have an English lesson, there are a few disruptive boys at the back of every classroom who make it really difficult. Why is it never the girls? At one point one of the front-row-girls asks if I can make the boys leave the room so she can hear me better. It gives me a new appreciation for girls-only schools. It was so different when we taught in El Remate – those kids were voluntarily going to after-school English lessons and were excited to learn. I research online and brainstorm with John about ways to motivate kids who don't want to learn, or psychological tactics to deal with the misbehaving kids, but it is always a problem during my time here.

Generally, the teachers I work with are very committed and motivated, with the exception being that sixth grade teacher who leads the especially disruptive class I described earlier. They help with discipline if needed, or translate into the local language when the kids don't understand something I say in Spanish. I'm fascinated to learn that there are 23 different languages spoken in this country – in San Marcos, where I teach, the local language is Kaqchikel, but just 15 minutes away in San Juan they speak Tz'utujil. Many of the kids in my younger grades don't speak Spanish well yet.

By the second week, I start to recognize my kids all over town, but it doesn't feel as friendly as when we taught in El Remate. Perhaps it's because of the huge number of foreigners here – there's a definite divide between the white hippie tourists and the locals. But also I think it's because I'm teaching 80 kids rather than the dozen or so that I taught in El Remate, plus Lilly is not at the same school with me. All in all, it is a unique experience and I hope that I am helping these kids have a better chance to work in tourism here, but it is exhausting.

When we're not in school, we go for hikes to explore the hills above us or visit other towns around the lake. On these trips, and any time we're outside the tourist hub of San Marcos, we see people collecting and carrying *leña* (firewood). Men and women stack sticks of wood into a pile, then fashion a backpack out of rope around the pile, and hang the load from their heads (not their backs) using a wide strap across their forehead. I'm always surprised to see how much weight they carry from their heads, walking over uneven rocky trails in bare feet or thin flip-flops. The women almost always have a baby in a sling on their backs in addition to the leña backpack. It's a sobering but valuable reminder of how easy I have it. These women are so much tougher than I am.

I ask the father of one of Lilly's school friends about the constant search for leña. He explains that they collect wood every day to cook tortillas on their wood-burning stove. Propane/gas is expensive, so they trek into the woods, cut trees with their machete, and carry it back home every day. My privileged, first-world brain immediately wonders: why not collect enough wood for a week, so that you can get a better paying job the other six days and then eventually buy a gas stove? But they live in a daily cycle of collecting, cooking, and eating, and they are either uninterested or unable to change that.

One morning on a hike to a local waterfall, I notice two women carrying the typical stack of loose wood, and a young girl with them. She is perhaps 9 or 10 years old, and carries as much as the grown women. I try not to judge them in my mind, but I know that this girl could go to the free local public school and potentially learn enough to get a job that uses her brain in future... why doesn't her mother send her to school? Because she needs help to collect enough firewood to cook tortillas to feed them that afternoon. Just surviving day by day.

It makes me better appreciate what I have – we are living such a simple but happy life in the van. In future, when I'm back working a busy job again, I hope that these kinds of memories will help me appreciate the simple but privileged things in my life.

* * *

The beauty at our campsite and Lilly's love for her school keep us at Lake Atitlan far longer than we anticipated, but we're excited to continue exploring Central America. John and I debate if it is harder for Lilly to have temporary stability than no stability at all. I often wonder if our poor daughter will end up in therapy due to this crazy trip she's on, but we hope it's better for her than the stressful lives we used to lead where we hardly saw her. A parent's guilt and self-doubt never ends.

*Woman carrying leña. Note the strap on top of her head
holding all the weight, and the flip-flops on the rocky trail.*

View from my bed every morning in Atitlan

The picturesque city of Antigua

EL SALVADOR &
NICARAGUA

*We drove 240 miles over 1 week in El Salvador, then 100 miles across
Honduras in just 3 hours, then 750 miles over 3 weeks in Nicaragua.
All in March, 2018.*

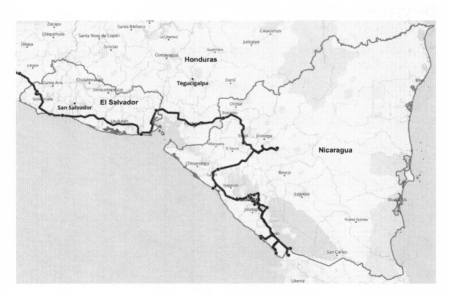

16

BRIEF JAUNT ACROSS EL SALVADOR

C *rack! I fall to the ground and roll around in the dirt on my back, clutching my hands tight to my head as if trying to hold the skull together. I hear John's voice calling urgently as if from a distance, "Where are you?" and then the sound of running feet coming closer. I peer through my tightly clasped fingers to see two men rushing toward me out of the darkness, each carrying a long, shiny gun. This is not how I envisioned our first night in El Salvador.*

We enter El Salvador with some trepidation. We try not to judge a country before we see it for ourselves, but it's hard to get over this one's reputation. In our five months of travel we've heard no stories of violence against tourists, but we hear four within 24 hours about El Salvador! On top of that, we have two El Salvadorean friends living in California who beg us not to enter their country due to the danger. And from a logistical standpoint, we are keen to get to Costa Rica before the rainy season arrives, so we plan to pass through El Salvador fairly quickly.

We are surprised to see lighter-skinned people here, often with blonde hair – we must have reached the end of the Mayan empire. The infrastructure seems far improved over what we've endured so far – the roads are in better condition and with better signs, and construction sites even have a uniformed man directing traffic – what a novel concept! We continue to see men collecting leña to fuel their stoves, but here they carry it on wheeled carts rather than on their backs like in Guatemala. And, in a final pleasant surprise, the currency is the US dollar! No need to exchange money and learn new coins and bills here.

To ease into this country, we camp our first night outside a hot springs complex with security guards present all night, rather than wild camping on the ocean in solitude. It's too hot for hot springs, but we spend a fun afternoon playing in eleven different temperature pools, all fed from natural springs in the mountains above, and our concerns start to fade when we meet a friendly El Salvadorean family who invites us to stay with them if we pass through San Salvador, the capital.

Getting ready for bed that night, I tell Lilly to come with me to the bathroom out by the hot springs. She and I step down from the van into the darkness outside, and I close the door behind us. I slip on my flip-flops and wait while Lilly slowly gets her sneakers on, having recently lost her third pair of flip-flops. Just as I'm thinking, *I ought to shake out her shoes before she puts her foot in them,* Lilly lets out a blood-curdling scream. My adrenalin spikes and my thoughts go into over-drive, *There's a scorpion in her shoe and she's been stung and should we drive back over the border to Guatemala for medical treatment or into the capital of El Salvador and is this one of the countries where scorpions are deadly or not-so-bad and why didn't I shake out her shoe first?!*

I drop to my knees and reach for her foot, not thinking about the fact that my head is now in perfect line with the opening arc of our van's door. As I'm lunging for her shoe, it feels like a horse karate kicks my head and I am whipped over backwards, landing hard on the dirt a short distance from the van.

Of course, John heard the scream, assumed Lilly was being attacked by bandits, and flung the van door open to leap out and save her. By this time, Lilly has already shaken out the ant or whatever it was in her shoe that had freaked her out, so John instead turns to look for the source of the low moaning sound coming from the dirt, "Mary?"

That's when the two security guards come sprinting toward us out of the darkness, carrying their shotguns. They heard Lilly shrieking and had the same reaction as John or any loving father would. Now they look confusedly between me and John, unsure what to do. John tries valiantly to use his few words of Spanish and some sign language to convince them he isn't trying to murder me, while I lie curled up in the fetal position in the dirt at his feet. I doubt they understand, but at least they don't shoot him.

The evening ends with a large pointed bump growing out of my scalp and a killer headache. As John is cleaning the torn knee cap that I sustained when I fell to my knees, I start shaking violently. It's hot and muggy outside, yet I'm freezing cold. John wraps me in sleeping bags and it takes ten minutes for the shaking to stop. I guess El Salvador *is* a dangerous country, but only because of our own stupidity!

At a campsite on the Pacific ocean the next day, watching a glorious sunset as we splash in the warm water, we start thinking about exploring the country further. The owner of the restaurant where we are camped has lived here his whole life, so I question him about the safety of traveling, "Do you think it's safe for us to go inland to visit the volcano?"

"Oh yes, definitely. It's much safer now than it used to be," he replies.

"That's great! So you haven't heard of any violence against tourists here?"

"No, hardly anything. Well... except on Wednesday at that restaurant over there," he points to the building three doors down, "some tourists were robbed at gunpoint."

"What?! Was it really late at night? Did the police come?"

"It was the middle of the day, and the employees couldn't really do anything so just stayed out of it. But the people weren't hurt." He states this matter-of-factly, as if telling us that we might get sunburned if we stay out on the beach too long.

That conversation, combined with the armed robbery we heard

about from a fellow overlander at the volcano we wanted to visit, seals our decision to travel quickly through this country.

* * *

Corn tortillas are a staple food throughout Mexico and Guatemala. Everywhere we went in those two countries, we'd see little homemade signs indicating a house selling tortillas for sale. Walking through the streets of any little town in Guatemala, you hear a familiar *slap slap slap* sound. Peering through the window, you see several women standing around a large round heated cooking surface, slapping little patties of corn dough into a tortilla shape between their hands, and alternately flipping and removing the tortillas. Customers call through the window how many they want, and then stand and wait while the ladies cook. These corn tortillas are served with breakfast, lunch, and dinner, no matter what you order.

Here in El Salvador, the omnipresent corn tortilla shifts to the *pupusa*. It's a thicker tortilla than we've been seeing in Guatemala and Mexico and they stuff it with cheese or chicken. We camp in the back-yard of a family who runs a pupusa food stand for a few nights, and eat enough pupusas to make up for spending so little time in this country.

Adela (the owner) lets me use the oven, which is something I miss dearly in the van, so I bake cookies and send Lilly over with a plate to share with Adela's family. Lilly returns with an empty plate and Adela by her side – she has come to ask if I'll teach her how to bake! She says she's always wanted to branch out into bread and pastries in her restaurant but isn't sure how.

So we spend the next day together in the kitchen, in a baking cultural exchange. I help her make bread and cookies, and then we all make pupusas together for her restaurant. Now Lilly has made tortillas in Mexico (invited into the kitchen of a restaurant) and Guatemala (her school at Lake Atitlan), and pupusas in El Salvador.

* * *

On this trip, I regularly read the local news for the country we are in, as well as for the country we're about to enter. I want to know the basics of each country we pass through – who's the President and what's the history, are there protests, elections, areas of violence we need to avoid?

So I've been reading about Honduras recently with increasing concern. They've just had an election but the results were not accepted by the general population and there are now protests and road blocks all over the country. Checking in with fellow overlanders, we hear stories of people stuck, unable to drive anywhere. Originally, we planned to go through northern Honduras to get a second crack at the incredible barrier reef that we enjoyed back in Belize, but due to election protests we skipped along through El Salvador instead, trying to avoid as much of Honduras as possible. But there's one unavoidable part of the country, unless your vehicle can swim.

So, on our last night in El Salvador, we sleep a stone's throw away from the border, make sure we have a full tank of gas, and prepare for our toughest travel day yet.

We wake up in El Salvador, drive five minutes, and cross the border into Honduras = 1.5 hours of mind-numbing bureaucracy.

Then we drive three hours across Honduras without stopping and cross the border into Nicaragua = 2.5 hours of brain-exploding bureaucracy.

Then we drive five minutes to an incredibly welcoming Nicaraguan family's house where we camp, I collapse exhausted from so much Spanish bureaucracy, and Lilly befriends a chicken named Jonathan. Seriously, she won't stop cuddling this chicken.

17

SIDE NOTE: CRAZY BORDER CROSSINGS

W hy does it take so long to cross a border with a vehicle? Firstly, every border is actually two completely independent processes – you need to leave the country you're in and then enter the next country – and both can be time-consuming with a vehicle to import and export. Secondly, it's a different set of burning bureaucratic hoops to jump through in every country, so it's always a guessing game. Here is generally how it goes for us:

STEP ONE: Leave Country

As we get close to the border, I dig out our passports, van title, and cash from our safe. We eat a snack and grab our hats and sunglasses ready to stand outside in the sun for hours. Lilly brings her iPad because, "It's gonna be some boring shit." Yes that is a direct quote from our sweet six-year-old daughter – gotta remember she overhears everything we say!

As we approach the border, the road typically turns to dirt and gets crowded with cars and people. Lots of men try to flag us down. We have to decipher which are legitimate border employees and which are random people trying to sell us things or change currency or get paid to "help" us cross. This is where the guessing game begins for John and me, trying to figure out where to stop and do the paperwork...

"Maybe that folding table under the tin roof is the immigration office?" I wonder out loud.

"Do you think that man waving at us with the hand-drawn cardboard sign is actually a border official?" John swerves to avoid him.

"I think we might have already crossed the border, let's go back and ask one of those truck drivers if they know where to go," I suggest.

Eventually we park somewhere and go on foot to look for someone official. Our experience in Nicaragua is the best example:

It appears that we have parked in the midst of a market or a festival, or perhaps a dancing contest? We walk between tables of merchants selling whistles, bottles of Coke, and carved wooden trinkets, toward the loudspeaker where a DJ is blasting music. As we cross the open courtyard from the parking lot (aka market) to immigration (aka the DJ) we are suddenly surrounded by a group of dancers twirling and stepping in time, wearing brightly colored matching costumes. We weave between them, feeling as though we've accidentally stepped onto a stage, and enter the building.

Inside, I approach a few different people, "Hello, we are leaving Nicaragua with our foreign vehicle, what do we do?" but everyone has a different suggestion. The general consensus seems to be, "Find a man in a blue shirt outside." So we go outside into the chaos.

There are hundreds of people milling about. The dancers are spinning. The music is so loud we can't hear each other or anybody else. I start approaching different men wearing blue but keep getting redirected. Finally, I feign zero Spanish abilities, and refuse to let go of one man-in-blue until he leads us over to the correct man-in-blue. This guy walks to our van to do an "inspection" (he doesn't even open the doors), then signs a piece of paper and points into the crowd, "Go find a man wearing a police uniform and ask for another inspection."

We're so grateful to the Nicaraguan government for organizing this really fun scavenger hunt for their border crossings. Especially in the middle of a blisteringly hot day with no shade overhead.

Eventually we find a policeman, show him the signed piece of paper from the previous man, and ask what happens next in this Game of Immigration. He tells us to write our names on the piece of paper and asks where the van is. I point through the throngs of people to the other side of the parking lot where one corner of our white van is barely visible. He glances that way and signs the paper. Second inspection complete!

We run the gauntlet through the dancing troupe for the third time, to cross the courtyard and re-enter the building. Inside, there are three different sections with no signs designating what each is for. I'm hearing game show music in my head as I arbitrarily choose to wait and find out what's behind door number three. But then the dancers finish their set and come inside, waltz up to the door we are waiting outside of, and disappear inside. They emerge a few minutes later in new costumes. This area appears to be the backstage changing room. We chose wrong!

"Shall we go try door number two?" John gently suggests.

John and I have accepted our respective strengths on this trip, and border crossings clearly fall into my job description. He makes a valiant effort to support and encourage, and prevent me from punching anyone.

I can't take it anymore, between the heat and noise and confusion, so go latch myself onto a man in uniform who takes pity on us. Maybe he's the director of immigration, maybe he's the janitor, I don't care, but he starts escorting us around the building, filling out this form, paying that fee, signing here, stamping there. Cancel the temporary import permit for the van, stamp out our three passports, go through customs.

One man behind a desk demands the fee that I know we paid when we entered the country. I explain this to him. No, no, you have to pay it again here. No, I already paid. We go back and forth a few times. I keep smiling and correcting him, until finally he stamps us out and waves us on. I guess if he tries that every time, he'll get some extra pocket money occasionally.

STEP TWO: Drive Through No-Man's-Land

Once you leave a country, you are now in no-man's-land. You're not officially in any country! And somehow we always seem to arrive here during lunch break when everything is closed. Several times we've left one country but then couldn't enter the next one because they were closed for lunch. We even camped overnight in no-man's-land once, in the Andes between Argentina and Chile. In Central America, the distance between two borders is usually just a mile or two. But, down in the rugged mountain area between Argentina and Chile, the distance can be 50+ miles because neither country wants their border post up at the high elevation of the true border.

When entering El Salvador from Guatemala, we drove over a bridge and got stopped by a man waving at us. We parked and approached, finding him sitting at a folding card table with an umbrella over his head for shade. He informed us that his boss had just gone to lunch. So then we all waited. For an hour. In the midday direct sun with no shade. The van basically turned into a sauna.

When the boss finally returned, he signed a paper and told us to go to a building down the hill to pay a fee at the bank. This is another oddity of these border crossings – there is usually a bank branch *at* the border and you have to go pay your fees at the bank, not at the immigration desk. Presumably this means there used to be a lot of corruption, and this is a way to take the cash out of the situation, putting it all in the hands of the bank.

An armed guard let me into an air-conditioned room where I waited to give money to the teller behind the desk. When I took out my phone he scolded me, saying phones are not permitted inside the bank. Never disobey a bored 18-year-old security guard with a gun as long as his arm. I put the phone away.

STEP THREE: Enter New Country

Entering a country is fairly similar to exiting. A confusing array of paperwork, desks, people, fees. Fill out this form, take it to that guy, pay someone else, get in another line. The difference is that you occasionally get searched, you often have to buy insurance, and you almost always get fumigated.

Fumigation is sometimes a bar lying on the ground that feebly sprays something up as we drive over. Sometimes we drive under a concrete arch with a thin nozzle on either side spraying some liquid onto the car. Every time, a man demands money from us for the privilege of having the van sprayed.

One time we were approached by a man wearing something resembling a hazmat suit. He carried a blow-torch-looking contraption in his hands, and was balancing an oversized backpack of chemicals on his back.

"Open your windows and get out of the van and go stand far away!" I could barely decipher his muffled cries through his full face-mask.

"What are you going to spray? That is our house! We sleep and eat inside." I protested.

"I need to fumigate the vehicle. Go stand over there away from the blast area," he insisted.

I continued to demand an explanation for what he was about to spray through our open windows, and finally when I mentioned Lilly's stuffed animal toys inside, he paused, lifted up his face mask, and asked in surprise, "You have a child in there? Ok, then stay inside and keep your windows closed." He replaced his face mask and sprayed the outside of the van as we sped through. Lilly saves the day again!

STEP FOUR: Relearn All Life Basics

Once you think you're in the country and start to accelerate to freedom, there is inevitably one more random person standing on the side of the highway, without even a sign, who flags you down demanding paperwork again. It's not until we're driving for a good 10 minutes that we feel like we can relax and celebrate. We smile and high-five each other. I can't believe we just drove into <insert country name here>!

In each new country, we start from scratch figuring out the basics:

Which bank will our ATM card work at, is there a black market or just a single exchange rate, which gas station can we trust to have decent fuel, is local insurance required and where do we buy it, what's the name for a big supermarket here, are there local laws that we need to comply with to avoid being pulled over by the police (eg. lights on at all times in Argentina, or special reflective stickers in Peru)... And, of course, we have to decipher the new names and brands of our favorite foods, "What on earth is a *palta*?" (Avocado is *aguacate* in all countries from Mexico to Ecuador, but further south it changes to *palta*.)

It feels like just as we are getting accustomed to all the rules and names in one country, it's time to move onto the next. But it's exhilarating and an endless process of discovery and learning, which is exactly why we are doing this trip.

18

NICARAGUA:
COMMUNE LIFE AND GIANT FISH

Two border crossings in one day left me completely shattered. Luckily, we arrived at a lovely family's home just a few miles past the border. Within minutes of parking on their land, Fausto brings us popcorn, then his brother shows up with some fruit, then a sister comes by with a bowl of freshly cooked beans. They bring over chairs and stay to chat, asking about our trip and our way of life back in the US. As I sit in the sunset light chatting with our new friends, I catch occasional glimpses of Lilly running with the kids, or chasing a pig/chicken/puppy across the hillside. She's certainly becoming an adaptable kid.

I realize we've traveled too fast when Fausto makes a comment to me, "They killed my father in the civil war in the 80s," and I have no response because I haven't read about the history here yet, this being our third country in as many days. But it's a similar story as in most of these Central American countries – civil war, government mistreating civilians, innocent families caught up in violence. Every one of these conversations on this trip reminds me how lucky I was to be born in England.

One fascinating aspect of vanlife is that we get brief glimpses into very different lifestyles. Perhaps I should have been an anthropologist

– I find it so interesting to chat with the different people we meet. On Fausto's property, I am intrigued by the commune-style living situation. The grandma had five kids, all of whom married and had their own kids, and now some of those kids are married and having their own kids. These four generations all live on the same parcel of land together. Each time a family member marries and starts contributing new kids, the family builds a house for them. One of the grandkids has recently had a baby, and so the men in the family are working together to build a new mud cabin. Of course the construction site for this new house is the preferred play area for the kids, so I keep finding Lilly chasing a pig or a chicken among machetes and rickety ladders.

It's such a different, but somewhat compelling, lifestyle. They often cook in one giant pot for everyone to share. There are always half a dozen kids running around playing together. Babies get handed off to many pairs of willing hands whenever a parent needs to work or just have some down time. So different from our fiercely independent living in the US. The grandma is always either rocking a baby on her lap in the hammock, or sitting in a chair being fed, surrounded by her family. What a wonderful retirement. No old ladies' homes here.

One afternoon I go looking for Lilly and find her with her favorite chicken, Jonathan, on the front porch of the house where the women typically do the communal cooking. The women take turns over the fire, feeding it leña (firewood) and stirring a huge pot with a wooden paddle. One of the daughters explains that they're boiling *maiz* kernels (corn) that they've grown, then they'll take them to a store down the road to be ground up into *masa* (flour) and then bring that home to make tortillas. Such a long process just for some tortillas! I join them briefly in the kitchen, but it's so hot and smokey in there that I wimp out pretty quickly. I wonder how their lungs are after spending most of their lives in that room.

Another common job for the women is to wash clothes by hand by whacking them repeatedly against a rock and then hanging them to dry on the barbed-wire fence that surrounds their land. When they're not cooking or washing, they're hanging out on the porch with their extended family sharing food and laughter.

It's interesting to see the teamwork of the family. Men building the houses and doing repairs, women doing the cooking and clothes washing, and everyone (including the kids) helping with planting and harvesting. They grow their own beans and corn, and raise their own chickens and pigs, which makes them fairly self-sufficient. Additionally, they all take turns leading canyon tours to get cash to buy the things they can't produce themselves.

In a way, it seems so perfectly simple and appealing. For a moment, I let my mind daydream about a life spent living in close quarters with a big happy family, away from the stress of high-tech jobs and busy schedules, rarely leaving my property, working the land every day to produce enough food to live, washing my brother-in-law's underwear by whacking them against a rock all day... ok, it's probably not for me.

* * *

It's a pleasure to discover that Nicaragua has the best roads of any country we've driven in so far. Paved, wide, and occasionally even a bike lane! And there aren't as many people using the roads as a walking path anymore, perhaps because more people here can afford to buy a vehicle.

The people continue to look more European, as we discovered in El Salvador, with longer faces and lighter skin and hair. We know that the Mayan empire reached down as far as Guatemala, and in Peru we learn that the Incan empire reached as far north as Ecuador – perhaps here we are in the dead zone between those two ancient civilizations.

We sleep at a waterfall that we use for a shower, at a coffee farm swarming with hummingbirds, in front of the bubbling steam field of the Telica volcano, and on the sand of many warm ocean beaches. And we enjoy visits from California friends who refresh our supply of homeschooling textbooks, and from my adventurous mother who flies by herself from London to stay in a rental house with us.

After two weeks of visits from friends and family, we are left feeling slightly lost. We've lived out of our van for six months now, driven almost 7,000 miles, and we notice that we're starting to lose our motivation to visit new places. In the first few months of the trip, we'd chase down every dirt road, every volcano, every waterfall – so full of excitement to explore. Whereas now we contemplate a 50 km detour to see an island or waterfall that everyone raves about, but prefer instead to find a campsite with a shower. What is wrong with us?

We decided to do this trip partly to get away from our stressful lives and have a wild adventure, but also with the goal of finding a new home, where we could live in a way that would make us happy in the long run. Maybe we're done with the adventuring, and it's time to focus on the where-to-live-next question? Costa Rica might be the perfect place.

But Nicaragua has one surprise left in store for us. We drive down a dirt track following the shores of Lake Nicaragua looking for a safe place to camp close to the border, so that we can deal with the inevitable bureaucracy first thing in the morning. A simple pull-out in the road, directly on the lakeshore, with no houses nearby looks like it will work for a night.

Within minutes of parking, a local family walks over to meet us and assures us we are welcome to stay there. They're expecting a dozen friends and family for the Semana Santa festival in two days, and are preparing the beach area to host them. So we help them clean up the sand and start building a shade structure for the weekend's picnic and festivities. The mother tells us to look out in the morning for the fishermen bringing in their catch, and puts her hand to her head to indicate the height of the fish – as tall as she is?! We assume we're misunderstanding something, until the next morning when we wake up to an unbelievable sight.

We're eating breakfast, looking out at the lake, when we see a fishing boat approach the shore near us and one man jump out. He pulls two enormous fish off his boat, and wades through the waist-deep water dragging one on each side of him, one hand hooked through each open mouth. Once he gets to the sand, he has to let one fish drop and focus on carrying just one at a time up the bank because they are so heavy. Another man on the shore lays out large plastic sheets on the sand, and the first man drags his fish up and lets it drop there, quickly returning to the other fish he left in the shallows before it can float away.

John, Lilly, and I walk over for a closer look, not quite able to believe what we're seeing. Each fish is longer than Lilly! We greet the fishermen and ask if we can help at all, but they have their systems dialed, one man dragging fish up to the shore as the other one works on removing the scales – with a shovel! They laugh as we take photos of Lilly lying next to the fish to show how big they are. Once we get internet reception a few days later, we research and decide they are probably saltwater tarpon. It would be terrifying to swim in the lake and spot one of these. But it made for a memorable last morning in Nicaragua.

Lilly checking out the giant fish

COSTA RICA

We drove 1,750 miles over 4 months in Costa Rica.
March to July, 2018.

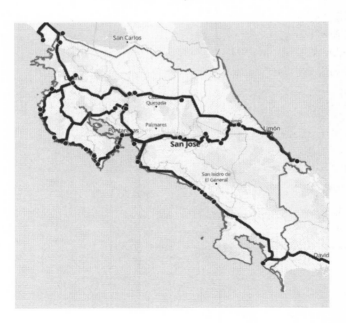

19

WE'VE REACHED THE PROMISED LAND

I can't believe we've driven to Costa Rica! We've been talking about this for five years. Crossing this border feels different than the others – this is a place we've already visited several times, and we've talked about moving here hundreds of times. After a bad day at work we'd research houses and schools and the cost of living in Costa Rica, and imagine how life would be if we just quit our jobs and moved here. It became our go-to refrain whenever we had had enough of the stress of Silicon Valley. And now we've driven here!

Barely half an hour after we cross the border, we are watching baby spider monkeys clinging to their mothers' backs scrambling across branches, and slow-moving sloths hanging camouflaged in a lush rainforest. Why does this country seem to be so much more full of wildlife than its neighbors?

Perhaps it's because the government and citizens work at it. Twenty-five percent of Costa Rica's landmass has been set aside as protected areas. We see many animal-crossing bridges over the roads. We learn that there is no hunting allowed, ever. It's illegal to keep any wild animal as a pet. Exceptions are made for injured animals who need a home, but then you'll be getting an annual check-in visit from the government. They take their wild animals really seriously here.

We continue to see the change in wealth, skin color and language that we have noticed ever since leaving Guatemala. Lots of the places where we camp are owned by foreign expats. Many of the Costa Ricans speak some English. Everything is more expensive. We see people out riding bicycles *for fun* – wearing lycra bike jerseys and riding expensive bikes. Previously we've seen people on bikes, but they were always junkers and being used to carry cargo or extra people. Similarly, for the first time on this trip we see people running *for exercise*, not because they need to get somewhere.

John and I laugh out loud at a sign, "Uneven road ahead" which is followed by a slightly uneven section of perfectly paved road – in Guatemala or Mexico that sign would not exist. In Mexico, we once drove around a curve in a mountain road to discover that the entire road had washed away down the hillside, leaving a barely passable section of dirt which we carefully inched our way around – no warning sign! Yet here in Costa Rica, they are warning us about a one-inch change in paved road. This country gave up their military so they can spend money instead on infrastructure and the environment. I can see why it's a favorite among expats.

Costa Rica is famous for its beaches and jungle wildlife, but also has a couple volcanoes worth visiting. We drive up to visit the 11,200 foot Irazu volcano late one afternoon, but find the entrance gates shut around 500 feet before the summit. Tardiness turns into opportunity when we drive down a little dirt side trail and find a perfect, deserted flat spot to camp for the night. No signs of life, just desolate landscape and the shadow of the volcano looming over us as the sun sets.

It's so cold that we cook inside the van – a very rare occurrence for us so far. It is incredibly still and silent. No bird chatter, not even a whisper of wind. That kind of silence that feels like there's a blanket over the air blocking out any sound. Also, it is pitch black outside – we can't even see the outline of the enormous volcano right beside us. The feeling of solitude is intense.

But then I glance out into the darkness and see the most unexpected thing.

Lights. Many lights.

There is a huge mass of lights flickering in a long row along the road as if a procession of angry townspeople is walking toward the van. Are they carrying pitchforks?!

When the lights are upon us, I hesitantly open the van door into the pitch darkness and find myself face to face with a dark figure that cheerfully greets me, "Hola, buenas!"

Like it's perfectly normal to appear at the door of an isolated camper van on top of an 11,000 foot volcano in the pitch darkness after the road closed to public traffic hours earlier?

Turns out the University of Costa Rica is doing an astronomy outing. Three school buses have parked down the road and about 100 people are marching along the path with flashlights to the deserted clearing to study the stars – exactly where we are camping.

This is just part of the wild camping experience – you never know who's going to walk up and become part of your evening. So we wrap up in coats and hats and gloves, and take our flashlights out to socialize at this most unexpected location for a party. One of the teachers hands us a constellation map and starts pointing out stars. Lilly runs from group to group saying *hola*. Every few minutes I hear her calling, "Mama? Papa?" and she runs over out of the dark to hug us and then disappears into the crowd again.

We retreat to the warmth of our little van later that evening, and just a few minutes later hear a tap at the window. A young woman pokes her head inside, "Do you have a toilet?" she asks, looking around our tiny space.

John misunderstands her, assuming she's asking for a tour of the van, which is what visitors always ask, and so responds, "Si" gesturing for her to enter.

"Great, can I use it?" she enthusiastically replies, starting to climb up into the van.

"Well," I interject, and point to the white bucket sitting on the floor next to me, "that's our only toilet." She decides to ask for toilet paper instead and retreats back outside. We can't stop laughing at the thought of this stranger peeing in our bucket surrounded by the three of us only two feet away!

* * *

The highlight of our time in Costa Rica is wild camping on the endless beaches. Nobody around for miles. Gorgeous sunsets across wide open sandy beaches. Warm water with friendly waves. It really is paradise.

Except for the crocodiles.

Imagine a picture postcard beach, endless soft sand to dig your toes into, bath-temperature ocean water full of inviting waves to play in, and... a sign that says, "Beware of crocodiles."

Is this some kind of cruel prank?

Inevitably, at each beach, Lilly starts sprinting for the water (can't read? or selective vision?), and we hold her back while trying to evaluate the situation. The few times that we find another person nearby, we quiz them and they invariably say it's completely safe.

"Then why are there all these crocodile signs?" I demand.

They just shrug, "Oh I suppose occasionally after the rainy season one or two crocs will swim out here, but they never approach people."

We've spent the prior six months in countries that wouldn't bother to put up a warning sign if there were a missing bridge on a highway over a river, so maybe we're being overly worried about these warning signs now? Gradually, after talking to more local families as we travel down the coast, we begin to trust them and start to enjoy the irresistible water.

I find a $10 boogie board and we have hours of fun. I put Lilly on my back and leap onto the boogie board at just the right moment to catch the whitewater. We bounce along together in the warm water, shrieking with laughter as the wind splashes us and we race toward the shore, sometimes only stopping once we're fully on the sand, other times crashing in a tumble of limbs and waves. Not a bad break between reading and math classes.

My favorite time of day at beach camps is always sunset. It's enchanting to be in water so warm that you can swim until dark, and then walk just a few steps up to your "house" for dinner when the wave drops you off on the sand. I'll never forget one evening bouncing along on my board on the warm waves, looking to my left to see the sun setting over the crest of the wave next to me and a flock of pelicans flying in formation through the orange light, then glancing forward to see our big white home welcoming me on the sand in front of my eyes.

We swim and boogie board, give Lilly's spelling lessons by writing in the sand, watch the unbelievable sunsets, then wash off the salt and sand using our solar showers and cook dinner. We always set up our stove and table and chairs directly on the sand next to the van, cooking and eating with the ocean just steps away. Sometimes at night, from our beds, we see heat lightning light up the whole beach – it looks like someone is turning on a giant light bulb every few minutes. Lilly snuggles between the two of us, exclaiming at the view and enjoying our front row seats.

These first three weeks in Costa Rica have been a highlight of our whole trip, but, as we discovered in Nicaragua, we are starting to tire of the constant movement of vanlife. Where will we sleep tonight? Do you think that hotel would let us use their shower? We have no clean clothes left again, and how do we drive through this town without hitting a kid/dog/chicken/person selling mangoes? It gets exhausting. On top of that, Lilly is starting to talk about missing her friends and our home. So, we traverse the country with our eyes open for a good place to potentially live.

After some searching, we find a good school that will allow a foreigner to drop in for a few months (Lilly's criteria), in a town with a good surf break (John's criteria) that has jungle and monkeys (Mary's criteria). So we jump into this new community, not knowing if we've discovered our new long-term home or we'll be full of excitement to continue the van trip after a few months of stability.

20

WATCHING MONKEYS FROM MY
SHOWER, AKA LIVING IN COSTA RICA

Our daily routine starts out just like back home in California, dragging sleepy Lilly out of bed and rushing to get her ready for school, but then we step outside into another world.

Walking down our driveway, we peer up at the monkeys living in the tree next to our house, who in turn eye us suspiciously and drop half-chewed mangoes at our feet. Turning left onto the dirt road, we dodge the bright purple pincers of halloween crabs scuttling by, and attempt to leap over the mud puddles that are growing larger as we get deeper into the rainy season. After dropping Lilly at the school bus stop, I walk along a dense jungle trail and pop out on the other side of town at the French bakery, where I line up behind surf tourists from the US and local Costa Ricans alike to buy a fresh baguette. Walking home, I pass elegant women's clothing stores and greet barefoot surfers walking to the beach with board in hand. What a diverse place! I am enchanted by the contrasts between jungle, beach, and town.

We have to commit through the end of the school year for Lilly to be accepted, so we rent a house for three months and move out of the van. Surprisingly, it feels quite exotic to stay in the same place day after day. I guess anything can become commonplace if you do it long enough.

It's such a novelty to sit at a table with space to stretch out my legs without kicking John. Or to be in separate rooms. Our new home has three bedrooms and yet Lilly usually ends up in bed with us. Are we building bad habits, getting her used to sleeping within a literal arm's-length from us in the van? Parent guilt tells me we are, but I know there will be an age when she doesn't want to be with us, so let's enjoy this while we can.

It's even more novel to be without Lilly for a few hours each day while she's at school. We go surfing most mornings, but also have to catch up on a lot of vanlife work. John is trying to fix the various small problems the van has picked up over the last 8,000 miles and order replacement parts that we might need in South America. I research second grade homeschooling, file our taxes, renew our insurances, calculate our spending to date to see how long we can travel, schedule dentist appointments for all of us, get Lilly's eyes tested – basically cramming a year's worth of life admin into three months.

This little beach town of Guiones is my first experience living in an expat community. I've always thought that an expat town meant a place full of 65-year-old retired Americans complaining about not having their favorite fiber cereal, but this town is the antithesis of that. Pretty much everyone we meet is 30 to 45 years old, with kids Lilly's age, and working interesting jobs.

Lilly has playdates non-stop. She's gone from being socially starved to needing alone time! John and I appreciate building friend-ships over several months instead of the brief encounters we've had with locals or other travelers so far. Typically on vacation, we seek out the most remote place to stay away from people. But after seven months in the van wilderness, we are loving being in the center of a lively little town.

I particularly enjoy meeting so many foreigners with unique life stories of how and why they got here. We've befriended flight atten-dants, hotel managers, online freelancers and restaurant owners. I loved hearing from a friend who left his high-tech career in California to start an organic farm here about the contrast between sitting in sales meetings with Apple or Google, versus this year trying to sell water-melons to hotels. It's fascinating learning about the varied careers that enable people to live here.

The other residents of this town that make it so unique are the monkeys. I am crazy about monkeys! I can watch them for hours. It's enchanting to see them effortlessly swinging from branch to branch using their ridiculously long arms that appear to dislocate with every swing, or hanging comfortably from their tail which is wound tightly around a branch above their heads. They always make me smile – it looks like they're having so much fun. I wish I could comfortably run through tree branches like they do.

Typically, whenever we see monkeys on a jungle hike, I'm the last person still looking up getting a sore neck while everyone else has continued down the trail. Lucky for me, here I don't need to go on a hike to see them, they are our ever-present neighbors.

Walking Lilly to the school bus stop in the morning, we usually see a howler monkey family commuting along the power lines, using them as a highway to get between trees. The males stride along, their glar-ingly white testicles swinging underneath them like two sagging water balloons. It seems like a poor evolutionary choice for an animal that is constantly leaping around in tree branches – how do they not get those things caught?!

No matter how late we are to the bus stop, Lilly and I stop and stare upward, holding our breath as we watch the balancing act. The big male always goes first, swaying precariously on the single thin power line until he safely reaches the other side. He howls impatiently and doesn't wait to watch as the mama and baby take their walk next. She is more top-heavy with a baby on her back so her tail waves furiously for balance as she sprints along. When I look closely, I see that the baby has its arms and legs wrapped around its mama's back, and its tail wound around the base of her tail – what a cute bundle of black fur! Occasionally, I'll see another male nearby and this inevitably provokes a lot of howling from both of them.

One morning while Lilly is at school, John calls me upstairs to join him because there's a monkey right outside our shower window, just three feet away. She's sitting delicately on impossibly small branches, tearing off pieces of leaf to put in her mouth for her afternoon tea. We watch her silently for a few minutes, feeling like we're in a National Geographic episode, until she turns her head and locks her eyes onto ours, startling herself and jumping back a little. She casually strolls away along the finger-width branches as if they were a wide sidewalk.

A few weeks before we move out of our rental house, a large family of monkeys moves in to live in the mango trees in our backyard. If you've lived next to a college fraternity, you may have experienced something similar – howling at all times of day and night, objects being thrown down at us every day (branches and mangoes), and piles of poop around the base of the trees. For Lilly's seventh birthday we had 10 loud kids at our house splashing in the pool, but this didn't dissuade the monkey frat boys. Several of them climbed down a branch that reached out right over the pool above us, as if intrigued to see what all the noise was about, and sat there eating leaves and tossing their leftovers into the kid chaos below.

I never thought it would happen, but I've had my monkey fill and I'm finally able to walk away from a monkey family on the trail before they walk away from me.

Of course the other thing that makes living here so attractive is the proximity to the ocean. It's so liberating to simply walk from your house, in your bathing suit, directly into the water, pausing only to kick off your flip-flops at the high tide line. Although this town is focused on tourism, the beach has somehow escaped development. There is not a single structure. Not one folding chair. No nagging vendors trying to sell you a massage. Just an open expanse of empty sand.

But at 5:45 p.m. every day, that open expanse fills up with people. The sunsets here are incredibly colorful and broad, and the entire town shows up daily to appreciate them. It's a social time – chatting on the sand with friends about school or work, and watching Lilly play in the waves with her friends. But my favorite moments are when the sun starts to touch the horizon and I go swim alone in the crashing waves, seeing the sky change colors all around me – what a wild and free feeling it is to be alone in the grand ocean as the sky darkens around me.

While Lilly is at school, John and I attempt to pick up surfing and boogie-boarding. I enjoy riding the smaller wave faces but the sport hasn't really grabbed me the way other sports have. John, however, has really fallen in love with surfing, and goes out once or twice every day. For both of us, it's wonderful to exercise daily for the first time since Lilly was born – our arms and legs and lungs are getting so strong from paddling and kicking and holding our breath. And, John has completed his surfer dude transformation as his hair has turned completely blonde from the sun!

But surfing can be scary... in John's first week, he went over the top of a big wave and his board snapped in half, leaving him with broken fiberglass shards to swim with. Over the ensuing months he managed to get whacked on the head by his board a couple times, get a bloody gash across his face, and cut his bicep in half. Please can we go back to safe rock climbing?

As for me, I had my closest-to-death experience I've ever had. I went to the "outside" (past the breakers) on a really big day and tried to catch the first set wave, but it closed out and I went over the falls. I tumbled for a long time until my air ran out and I involuntarily gulped water. I came up gasping for air and clutching my leash which had come off. I had just enough time to re-attach my leash before I had to dive under the next wave in the set. By the fourth set wave I had no air left but still had to dive under. It's a terrifying feeling to be entirely devoid of oxygen yet still force your body to dive down as deep as you can, then stay there while you feel and hear the chaos pummeling above you. When I finally staggered onto shore, I lay down without moving for over an hour.

I have spent most of my outdoor life in mountains or rivers, not in the ocean, so this visit is teaching me new respect for this powerful beast.

As much as we enjoy the people, the monkeys, and the ocean here, we can't avoid the realities of living in a jungle...

Some mysterious big winged insect flies into my face in the night and wakes me up with a start. There are dead bugs on the floor every morning, no matter how often I sweep. I walk into the kitchen and a black millipede crawls over my foot. I pick up the compost bin to empty it outside and a gecko jumps off. I lean my arms onto the counter to prepare breakfast and tiny spider babies run up my elbows. I open the lid of the honey and somehow, impossibly, there are ants inside – of a sealed bottle! I go outside and a mosquito bites me. I walk out to take Lilly to the school bus and accidentally walk through a spider web as I'm stepping aside to avoid a crab. IT IS TOO MUCH!

I guess you can't get the cute, furry jungle creatures without also getting the creepy-crawly kind.

One morning I'm walking out with Lilly to go to school and feel a painful bite on my foot. I glance down and see a solid black carpet of ants swarming the entire area. "Run, Lilly!" I shout. She sprints through the ant river with me and then we pause to look back.

It looks like a scene from a horror movie – the entire wall of our house is a black, seething mass of army ants making their way to the roof. I shout to John to come out, and he stands on the other side of the "river" looking in awe at the thousands upon thousands of ants.

I take Lilly to the bus and when I return home I find John standing outside waiting for me. "The ants have taken over," he warns. I take a running leap and manage to clear the ant river, then step hesitantly through the front door. John points up, so I glance up nervously. The entire ceiling is a moving black mass of ants heading for the second floor. John grabs my arm and we run out.

We tell everyone we meet about the ants (in a town of this size, you always run into friends when you go out) and the unanimous response is, "Just leave them alone for a few hours and they'll clean the dead bugs out of your house." They're right – we return later and there's no sign they were ever in the house.

Similarly, we've learned that you don't get the lush green jungle experience without an astonishing amount of rain. For most of our stay we experience a mild rainy season – a storm about once every two days for a couple hours. It lowers the temperature, cleans the dust off everything, and feels refreshing. But, there are times when it doesn't stop raining for 48 hours straight. It's impossible to get anything dry. Mold grows on our clothes and towels. The sky is always gray. The dirt roads that seem cute in the sunshine become a sticky mud bog. Not fun when you're walking to school in your flip-flops.

We occasionally found ourselves at the beach when a storm arrived, and we enjoyed the novel experience of swimming in the warm ocean under the rain. But, knowing that we didn't experience the real rainy season (which starts in September), I conclude that I would not want to live here year-round.

* * *

Costa Rica is the first country where we want to stay longer than the standard amount of time allowed by the government. Our US passports give us incredible privileges around the world, and I'm more grateful than ever for them, but we can't stay in Costa Rica longer than 90 days.

The only way to keep Vancito in the country beyond 90 days is to store it in a government warehouse or import it. We aren't quite ready to commit to living forever in Costa Rica, so we store it. It was wild to go from *living* in a vehicle, to having *no* vehicle at all. We bought bicycles and enjoyed the simplicity of riding or walking everywhere.

For our personal visas it's simpler – we just need to cross a border and return. So, we take a side trip to Nicaragua over a weekend in June. It's the same border we originally crossed to enter Costa Rica in March – remember the insane border crossing where it felt like we were in a Mardi Gras parade due to the crowds and music and dancing? Well, this time it's like entering no-man's-land during a civil war, because, well, Nicaragua is in the midst of a civil war.

What civil war? A brief history: On April 18th, three weeks after we left Nicaragua, the government there announced reforms to its pension system, prompting nationwide anti-government protests and a violent response from security forces and pro-government groups. In the ensuing months, hundreds of people were killed, and roads were blocked across the country making it impossible to travel. (End of history lesson.)

When we arrive at the border, it is absolutely deserted. What a contrast from when we were here just a couple months earlier!

The employees all look very bored, sitting behind their desks playing on their phones. We park on the Costa Rican side, exit the country, then walk about five minutes to get to the Nicaraguan entrance.

Immediately, there are guards with large guns everywhere, looking stern. We give our passports to the border patrol guard who asks, "How long do you plan to stay here in Nicaragua?"

I hesitate in my answer – generally countries don't like people doing "border runs" where you only enter/leave a country in order to get more time on your visa – but I decide in these circumstances I can be entirely honest. "Five minutes," I say quietly.

"Good idea," he agrees, and offers to process our re-entry without having to walk to the exit side of the building. It is spooky, and makes us appreciate our lucky timing having traveled through Nicaragua just before they broke out into civil unrest.

* * *

So have we found our forever home? It turns out that we are all feeling excited about living in the van again and getting down to South America. Plus, I haven't fallen in love with surfing like John has, and I need to have an outdoor activity in my life – there's very little climbing in Costa Rica. Living at the beach was a fun novelty, but I've discovered that I'm really a mountain woman at heart.

On top of that, I'm still conflicted with this ideal of wanting to live in a new culture with local people, not in an expat bubble that is far from the reality surrounding it. Our experiences in Guatemala taught me it may be harder to achieve than I think – it's tough to become close friends with someone who has almost nothing in common with you. Usually I make friends through a common activity or job but, as much as I hate to admit it, that's harder to do in places where people are more focused on survival than on an interesting career or having fun.

So our time in Guiones turns out to be more of a vacation than a cultural experience – it's a wonderful break, but leaves us excited to get back on the road.

Moving back into the van and traveling south, we enjoy the amazing creatures of Monteverde Cloud Forest, camp at one of the most beautiful canyon views we've ever seen, and zipline through the rainforest. But John is not enjoying himself. During our last week in Guiones, his neck started bothering him, possibly from an old injury re-aggravated by so much surfing. One morning, not long after moving back into the van, the pain gets so bad that he can barely breathe. So we drive straight to San Jose (the capital), and I call around trying to figure out how to see a doctor. It's intimidating to make phone calls in Spanish to large hospitals, with no clue as to how the health system works here, but we eventually figure it out. We stay one night in a hotel next to a hospital and John sees an orthopedic surgeon, a physical therapist, and an osteopath. The first two are no help, but the osteopath cracks him like a glow stick and runs electricity through his back. She's a miracle worker, and John feels ready to move back into the van that night.

The comical part of our brief big-city stay is my attempt to empty our portable toilet in the lobby of the hotel. Our toilet is basically a glorified bucket with a seat and a lid, which we need to empty every few days depending on how much we use it. So I carry this strange-looking dirty white box through the clean, tiled lobby, and then stand in line for the ladies bathroom while everyone stares at me. Once in the stall I try to pour it out quietly, self-conscious of the women seated either side of me, but it makes so much noise glugging and sloshing that I tip it totally upside down to get it over with faster. This just makes even more noise, and causes the lumpy liquid to splash out everywhere! So I spend the next few minutes attempting to wipe up my mess with some paper towels. This is the reality of vanlife that no one talks about!

In our last two weeks in Costa Rica, my favorite experiences are the endless wild beach camps: sunset swims culminating with solar showers at the van, cooking dinner on the sand and then snuggling into bed together listening to the waves crashing just a few feet away. Such simple, enjoyable living, and also a great way to camp for free in this, much more expensive, country.

I particularly enjoy the wild animal surprises at our camps. We hear the constant squawking of scarlet macaws overhead – their colors are so bright and contrasting that they look like something out of a toddler's coloring book. One morning I hear a familiar cry and am surprised to realize that I now recognize the toucan's call – I look up and immediately spot those impossibly huge beaks on a pair of toucans above. Another morning, we stand barefoot in the sand next to our van watching a sloth leisurely eating leaves in a tree. No wonder Lilly has trouble concentrating on her homeschooling lessons – it's like living in a zoo!

We always let Lilly sit on my lap in the front seat when we are trundling slowly down a dirt road, and these drives are some of my favorite memories of the whole trip. In Costa Rica, we explore countless dirt roads, always with our windows wide open to the warm air and jungle noises outside. Lilly loves reaching out to touch the endless green curtain of leaves around us, and we marvel at the sound of vines scratching on our walls and roof as we squeeze through a narrow track in the dense jungle. Whenever a low branch hits the windshield in front of us, we both instinctively duck and then laugh at our silly reaction. This full-immersion driving experience is a far cry from driving on a paved highway, and I love it.

When I look back on vanlife in Costa Rica, I will most remember the wild beach camps, the fascinating monkeys and sloths, and driving through lush jungle with Lilly snuggled on my lap. It wasn't the cultural experience we had in previous countries – we didn't learn about political protests like we did in Honduras and Nicaragua, or intense violent history like in Guatemala, or meet local families with very different lifestyles like in Mexico and Guatemala – but it was an incredible wilderness experience that will always hold a special place in my memory.

Lilly doing school in the van at yet another deserted wild beach camp

Our neighbors, the howler monkeys - notice baby on the back

PANAMA

We drove 385 miles over 2 weeks in Panama.
August, 2018.

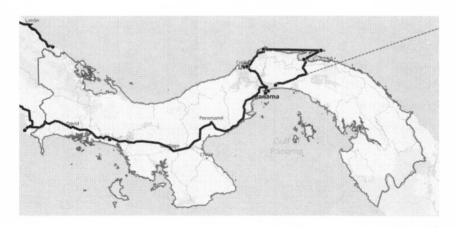

21

PAIN, PAPERWORK, AND PUKE

T he Panamerican Highway stretches 20,000 miles from Alaska down to the tip of Argentina, *except* for one little section of 60 miles between Panama and Colombia. This is the Darien Gap. Ruled by drug gangs and paramilitary guerilla bandits, covered in thick jungle criss-crossed with rivers and swamps, and full of poisonous creatures and infectious disease, it's not the first place you'd pick to go for a drive on a family holiday. There have been a few expeditions that tried to drive through it, but these were replete with sharpshooters, engineers, a construction team, and myriad other support systems.

Since I didn't fancy the logistics of parachuting car parts into the jungle, or the cost of a military escort to protect us from guerillas, or the effort required to build rafts at river crossings, we decided to take the easy road – a shipping container on a cargo ship for Vancito and three airplane seats for us.

So Panama never really had a chance to impress us. It was just a whirlwind of doctor visits for John's returning neck pain, and paper-work and bureaucracy to ship the van to Colombia. We spent almost our whole time there in big cities, meaning we were constantly packing and unpacking to stay in hotels (usually impossible to sleep in the van in big cities), and fighting awful traffic to get between the various offices for setting up Vancito's shipping container and doctors for treatment of John's neck. It made me appreciate vanlife so much more. We usually never plan anything in advance, and we always have all our belongings with us, so it takes some adjustment to carry backpacks and move in and out of different rooms every night.

During all this chaos, I had a zen moment at the Bridge of the Americas – what an appropriate name! I'm standing at the mouth of a man-made river, looking up through a gap that divides the North and South American continents. To my left is unbroken land all the way to Alaska. To my right is unbroken land all the way to Argentina. And in front of me is this sliver of man-made water breaking the two in half. Politically we are still in North America but geographically I consider this the entry to the South.

Finally comes the day to get Vancito into the shipping container. At the port, we meet our shipping partners. The shipping container is large enough for two vehicles, so most travelers try to find a shipping partner to split the cost ($2K becomes $1K each). We've read dozens of accounts from other overlanders who got matched with fellow travelers and became buddies, so we expect to find a family or a couple doing a similar trip to us. But, we meet two Mexican men in a flashy new Mercedes SUV. Tight jeans, bright collared shirts, spiky styled hair. No luggage.

We need to reassure ourselves that they are legit, since we're basically entering into an international shipping agreement together, so I try to casually question them.

"Where have you driven from?"

"Mexico."

"Wow, what an amazing adventure! What's the purpose of your trip?" I try to exude a nonchalant air as I question him.

"We just want to travel and see new countries," he tells me. Ok good, this is sounding plausible.

"And how long have you been driving?" I ask.

"Six days."

My jaw drops. I am speechless. These two men have driven in six days what's taken us almost a year, and yet they claim to be on a sight-seeing trip. They have no luggage. They're in a fancy car. They keep emphasizing their rush to get to Colombia, and that they will be returning immediately afterward.

Their car and our van will be searched by drug dogs. Together.

John and I do what research we can, but Google is not so helpful when you're searching for things like, "Will I go to a Colombian prison if my car shares a container with a drug smuggler?" Ultimately, we decide to take the risk, because surely we couldn't be held responsible for the contents of their vehicle.

We have one tense moment in Colombia when we watch the security guards fling open the doors of our van and the Mexicans' car, side by side, and a team of drug dogs goes through both vehicles. But, no alarms go off and we are not thrown to the ground in handcuffs. We never did figure out the true story behind those two guys, but I'm sure there was more to it than sight-seeing.

Since we are van-less for almost a week, we decide to do the thing that is hardest with a van – go to an island. The San Blas islands are off the Northern coast of Panama and I manage to find a boat charter that is available with only two days' notice.

Lilly is so excited about sleeping on a boat. She's wild about the movie character Moana and has been obsessed with ships since watching it. When we're camped on the beach, I'll often find her standing on the shore staring out into the ocean by herself, singing the Moana song ("I've been staring at the edge of the water") in a serious and melodramatic way. The night before our boat trip she says she can't go to sleep because, "I have to practice staying awake all night for when I voyage across the sea by myself."

For his part, John has often spoken dreamily about one day moving into a sailboat and traveling the world. Without a single day spent aboard a sailing vessel we have wondered if this is a pipe dream or if we could actually pull it off... we are about to get our first healthy dose of reality.

At first, the three of us stand up front on the deck of the boat, enjoying watching the enormous waves that approach and then crash improbably past us. There are a few that I'm sure will swamp us, so high do they tower above, but the little boat just rides up one side and then careens down the other. It's a fun roller coaster ride as the sun sets.

But soon it's too dark to see ahead of us any more, and the boat keeps rolling and pitching in unpredictable motions. John makes the fatal error of going below deck to help Lilly get to the toilet. When he returns, it's all over – he's puking over the side. Next is my turn. I go below deck to get John some seasickness medicine and, when I return, I join him puking over the side. Incredibly, Lilly feels not the slightest bit of nausea.

The intensity and duration of desperate retching from my body is awful, but even worse is my constant, helpless worry about Lilly. The three of us are sitting on an open-deck sailboat with low railings, it's pitch black outside, and we're in the open sea bouncing through big waves. It's impossible to move around without falling over, due to the violent jerking of the boat, but we can't keep an eye on Lilly. It's terrifying not being able to watch her, but John and I are both completely incapable of looking at anything but the waves, into which we are constantly puking.

I know that if Lilly falls overboard I'll jump in instantly after her, but I also know that won't end well. John and I take turns shouting into the darkness, "Come sit right next to me!" Then I feel the reassuring presence of her body next to mine, until I have to go hang my head over the side of the boat to throw up again. Eventually, she says she's tired and calmly walks downstairs and puts herself to bed. Amazing!

Then, John and I are only left to worry about each other. Unable to turn my head even a fraction to check on him, because of the increase in nausea that it causes, I occasionally shout, "Are you still there?" in between bouts of vomiting, and he does the same.

One curiously contrary moment during this horrible episode is the phosphorescence twinkling in the passing waves that I am desperately staring into. One small part of my brain is able to acknowledge and recognize it as beautiful, while the rest of me feels like I'm dying.

Eventually, through pure exhaustion, John lies down on the deck, wedging himself between the cabin and the wall of the boat, and I curl up behind his legs. We take turns napping and vomiting through the night. At some point, I manage to stagger downstairs and lie in bed, alternating napping and vomiting into a bucket. John follows suit and, in his state of confusion, lies down on the floor instead of our bed. At one point, I glance over to see him vomiting into our shared bucket and suddenly burst out laughing and can't stop. It is just such a ridiculous episode in our long and varied list of shared experiences.

When we anchor in the islands the next morning, everything instantly becomes calm. The sun shines, the boat rocks only slightly and in a predictable pattern, and our stomachs return to normal. It's one of those picture postcard scenes – brilliantly clear turquoise water surrounding the boat, with white sand palm tree islands only a short swim away from us. It's like we've sailed through hell and arrived in heaven.

I absolutely adore jumping off the boat railing into the ocean – the water feels like a refreshing hug when I land – so warm, clean, clear, and inviting. Plus, the visibility is amazing – we can sit on deck and clearly watch the fish swimming below us.

It's delightful to watch Lilly's confidence and strength in the ocean develop over the past year. At the beginning of this trip, in Baja, she bobbed around in the ocean in her lifejacket and would not jump off our kayak into the water. Now, she climbs up to the highest point of the boat railing and leaps into the deep ocean, far from land, no lifejacket, and comes up giggling wanting to do it again.

One evening, sitting on the deck after sunset eating dinner, I hear a huge splash behind me. I spin around to squint into the darkness and think I see a fin pass by. What?! Is that a shark? A few minutes later another enormous splash. I turn around to watch and wait. The boat owner turns on the external lights. At the next huge splash I see the shadow of a very long, dark shape passing by. The boat owners say it might be a barracuda, but I insist that the fin and body are far too big.

Finally, the large gray shape swims close enough to me that I can see the elegant smooth curve of a dolphin's back cresting the water. It jumps for another fish. Now we're all watching and ooh-ing and aahing. It's incredible how quickly it changes its speed from gently cruising past us, to unbelievable shot-from-a-cannon speed when it goes for a fish. I am crazy about dolphins, and if it were daylight I would probably jump in for a cuddle.

So what's the verdict? Does John still want to retire on a sailboat and sail around the world?

Hell, no! We never want to relive that night! Also, I think I'd get bored if we lived on a boat – there's really nothing to do but hang out on the boat or jump in the water. It's wonderful for a few days or weeks, but I don't think I'd want to do it for years. Van travel suits me well because you can cozy up inside together if you want, but you also have the option to step outside and hike up a mountain, walk around a city, surf in the ocean, swim in a river – the experiences are endless. But those three magical days among the islands are powerfully tempting, if we could one day solve our seasickness.

Lilly & Mary leaping off the boat in the San Blas islands

As we fly over the Darien Gap from North to South America, let's take a moment to ponder how far we've come:

This is day 330 of our trip, and we've driven 8,974 miles.

That's 190 miles a week, on average.

To put this in perspective, your typical San Francisco worker bee commuting to Silicon Valley drives more than we do in an average week!

Personally, when we lived in the Bay Area we rarely drove during the week (I rode my bike and John took the train) BUT we drove to Yosemite almost every weekend. Thus, we were driving more miles per week when we lived there, than we are now driving across a dozen countries. Hard to believe!

COLOMBIA

We drove 1,850 miles over 2 months in Colombia.
August to October, 2018.
We then spent 6 weeks visiting the US and UK, and returned to
Colombia for a few more days in early December before crossing into
Ecuador.

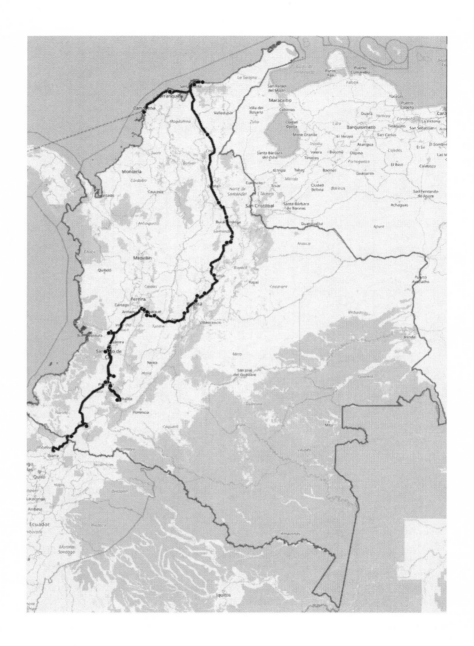

22

EXPLODING BATTERIES -
WELCOME TO SOUTH AMERICA

Asixty-minute flight delivers us safely over the Darien Gap, dropping us in the colonial city of Cartagena on the north coast of Colombia. We are dying to get back in our home on wheels to explore the enormous new continent at our fingertips. But, minor problem, where's the van?

We left poor Vancito sailing across the ocean without us, crammed inside a metal box stacked with hundreds of others like Legos on a huge cargo ship called the Vega Omega. Once it appeared to be in Cartagena, John commenced Mission Impossible: Locate and Retrieve Vancito from Shipping Container.

Day 1: Travel to the other side of town to find the shipping company's office to fill out forms. Then travel halfway back to find the customs office to fill out importation forms. Finally go to the port to, you guessed it, fill out more forms. John asks everyone, "Where's my van?" to no avail. No one has any idea which country Vancito might be in. At 6 p.m. the port office closes its doors and kicks John out.

Day 2: Return to the port at 8 a.m. and hang around the office *the entire day* trying to rescue Vancito. Finally, in the afternoon, John finds someone who tries to help.

"Ah, looks like the Vega Omega has continued onto the next city, Barranquilla. Do you want to go there?" the port agent cheerfully asks him.

"What?! Is my van there too or was it dropped off here first?" John asks.

"It could be there, or it might be here," the man says wisely.

"Well, can you find out?" John demands, forcing a smile.

After much back and forth between him and others at the port, the man finally returns to John with a conclusive statement, "It's 6 p.m. and we're closing." And they shut the doors and kick him out again.

Day 3: Return again at 8 a.m. Pester everyone all over again. No action all day again. But at 5:45 p.m. there's a sudden flurry of activity... and at 6:05 p.m. Vancito rides free!

But, not actually free.

The insurance office closed at 5 p.m. and we can't drive anywhere, legally, without insurance. Of course they don't let you buy insurance during the three days you wait around doing nothing, you have to wait until your van is out of the container... *sigh* ... gotta love bureaucracy. One more night for us in a hotel.

Day 4: Drive to the insurance office, fill out papers and hand over money, and we're finally free to explore South America! Nothing can stop us now. Unless the van almost blows up on the side of the road. But that wouldn't happen, would it?

We're barreling down the highway toward Barranquilla in northern Colombia, finally free from the bureaucracy of Cartagena's port. Behind me is a mess of loose backpacks and sleeping bags strewn about our van's living area – we were so excited to hit the road that we didn't move back into the van from the hotel properly, planning to do so at our first campsite.

It's unnerving to be driving so fast, at 65 mph on a paved road, after almost a year of bumping along small backroads. It's a two-lane highway, each side full of large trucks, and barely any shoulder on the sides, but this does not stop cars and motorcycles from passing us and each other constantly.

"It feels like I'm in a video game!" grimaces John, eyes focused intently on the busy road.

He carefully pulls into the left lane to pass a slower-moving truck, then I squeal, "Look out, there's a motorcycle passing *us*!" He corrects a little to the right to give this crazy motorcyclist more room, then notices there is another motorcycle passing us on *our* right, in between us and the truck that we are passing.

We are flanked on both sides by motorcycles, as we drive in the wrong lane of a busy highway trying to pass a truck. No one is touching their horn, just driving merrily along as if this were totally safe and normal.

Just then, "Beep! Beep! Beep!" An ominous alarm erupts from the back of our van, as if in protest to Colombian driving.

"What is that? Smoke detector? Carbon monoxide monitor?" I pepper John with questions.

"Do you smell that?" he responds, as an acrid, chemical smell wafts up from the back.

"Yes, and what's that other noise?" In between the alarm beeps, I am hearing a sound like pressurized air escaping from something. Pppssssssst.

John is looking desperately for anywhere to pull over. I open the windows for fresh air. The pressurized gas sound gets slowly and threateningly louder, building to a crescendo of terror in my imagination of what's about to happen. The chemical smell becomes overpowering.

John has no choice but to stop the van, simply pulling off the road as far as he can. We're half hanging into the bushes and half on the highway. I jump out with Lilly and send her into the bushes on the side of the road. John races into the back of the van, tracing the loud hissing sound back to the cabinet that houses our lithium house batteries. He throws off the lid to discover that one of the batteries is cracked and swollen with some kind of gas spraying out the side.

"Get the fire extinguisher!" he shouts to me. Upon hearing this confidence-inspiring cry, I direct Lilly to walk further into the bushes, as far from the van as she can get, and then I run back into the van to locate the fire extinguisher. John starts carefully removing the battery cables, while I force myself to stay calm enough to read the directions on the back of the fire extinguisher.

It's now impossible to breathe inside the van. John retreats outside and I open the back doors and all the windows. John tosses out all our belongings that are impeding his access to the battery – sleeping bags, backpacks, the kitchen table – all chucked out onto the highway in a panic.

He takes a gulp of air, as if he's diving underwater, and enters the van, holding his breath. He starts turning the bolt that is holding the battery cable to the terminal, but the terminal just spins. The entire battery is melting in his hands!

He jumps outside to take a few deep breaths, then returns to work. He gets the bolt loose but the result is more gas shooting out through the hole! When he finally manages to detach the battery, he looks at me for a second, "How do I pick up a melting plastic box that is spraying chemicals at me?" I grab two sacrificial dish towels and he's able to wrestle the battery out of the box and set it down on the side of the highway. We both back away from it, as if from a ticking bomb, and take some deep breaths while pondering our next move.

First priority is to get off the side of this highway where we could be hit by a truck at any second. But there is a melting, off-gassing battery now sitting on the side of the road. I'm ashamed to write these words but, we decide to leave it there. We simply can't think of any other safe solution. We've already got into the habit of picking up other people's trash on the beaches in Central America, but we now have a huge trash debt to repay in future. So, we throw all our belongings into the back of the van and escape from the scene.

Luckily, our second, identical battery is undamaged, so we have enough juice to power our fridge and lights, as long as we're more careful about usage. John spends most of his waking moments over the next month trying to figure out what went wrong, and, how on earth are we going to get a lithium battery shipped from North to South America?

But, we are finally free to drive south and start exploring this new continent.

23

FRIENDLY COLOMBIA

This was supposed to be a country to be afraid of, to rush through; somewhere to avoid interactions with strangers. But time and time again, strangers invite us in for coffee, bring us food, give Lilly toys, or insist that we sleep at their house for the night. The people we meet are surprisingly curious, generous, and welcoming – it's not what I was expecting from a country that has such negative press and history.

Almost every time we park, someone walks over to talk to us. When I look out my window in the morning, there's usually someone taking a photo of the van and smiling hello at us. We end up staying longer than planned at most camps because the caretakers make us feel so welcome. The north coast was chaotic, but driving through the center of this country turns out to be some of our best overlanding of the trip – not because of sights and landscapes, but because of the people.

We soon realize that we got comfortable and lazy during the past five months in wealthier countries like Costa Rica, and now it's time to adjust back.

At every speed bump or intersection there is someone trying to sell us something. Nobody speaks English. Doing our grocery shopping means searching at lots of tiny shops – one has milk, another has bread, and you find fruit on the side of the road – just like back in the small towns of Mexico or Guatemala. There's usually a Virgin Mary statue welcoming you at the entrance to every town, and there's always a central square with a big Catholic church. There's also much more waving and interest in who we are, like we last experienced in Mexico.

The food, however, is unfortunately not like in Mexico. It seems that every restaurant has the exact same, and only one, meal. The *comida corriente* (meal of the day) costs $2 to $3 and is always soup, fried chicken or pork, rice or french fries, and usually some onions they call salad. It's a cheap and tasty pile of calories, but we start to get sick of it after the first week. Once I asked at a hotel if they knew of any restaurant that served something other than *comida corriente*. She looked entirely confused, so I tried to expand on my question with examples, "Pizza, pasta, vegetables, stuff like that?" She simply looked at me like I was completely bonkers.

We learn about a new snack that we haven't yet seen – the *hormiga culona*. It basically translates as *big butt ant*, and it's honored in large posters on the walls of various buildings. Stopped at a park in San Gil for a picnic, I notice a lady perched on a plastic chair at a table with a big bowl in front of her. It's full of big butt ants, dead. She's separating them into two bags to sell as street snacks – butts go in one bag, heads in another – which is considered the more valuable, I wonder?

Another difference that is immediately apparent is the concentration of police on the roads, but we are confused about what they're doing. "Why are there two army guys, in full camouflage gear with rifles slung over their shoulders, standing on the side of the highway with their hands raised in a thumbs-up?" I ask in bewilderment.

"Is he trying to hitch-hike? Pull me over? Just saying hi?" John is equally confused.

We eventually learn that it's a show of force to prevent guerrillas from taking over the roads again. Local families explain to us that the roads were recently ruled by drug gangs and it was dangerous to drive anywhere. The government now positions armed men at intervals along the major roads, standing still with their hands in a thumbs-up sign to indicate that it's safe to travel. It's a good reminder of how recently this country pulled itself out of internal violence.

Colombia has the strongest police presence of any other country we traverse on this trip. In the North, we are stopped three times by cops in one day! They always reach into the driver's window to shake John's hand, look at his driver's license and/or passport, talk to us for a few minutes, then wave us on. Most of the time they are more curious than suspicious. We don't really fit any stereotyped profile for drug smugglers, so our interactions are usually friendly conversations.

One time they insisted on coming inside to search, which immediately made me recall all the horror stories we'd heard about police planting drugs in your vehicle and then "finding" them. I followed him inside, watching closely, but his zest for searching the van waned as Lilly started introducing him to each of her stuffed animals. Another time, one of the men actually got under the van with a mirror on a long pole to see if we were hiding anything under there.

"Why would we be smuggling drugs *into* Colombia?" is the joke John and I always make to each other after the momentary stress of each police interaction, but we never try the joke out on the cops.

There was only one time that we were asked for money by the police, and it was a situation where we were actually at fault. John passed a slow truck on a double yellow line, and the police pulled us over. The officer said we had to pay a fine and that it would be best to do it *en presencia*, which I guessed to mean pay him cash on the spot (aka bribe). I admitted our fault and apologized, but said that we'd only pay a fine at the police station, not *en presencia*, and eventually he waved us off.

Driving through central Colombia, we see hundreds of people walking on the sides of the highway. We've seen people using the highway as a walking path throughout this trip, but this is different – these are entire families carrying luggage. It's the first time we're exposed to the plight of the Venezuelans.

While camped on the edge of Chicamocha Canyon, enjoying breath-taking views from our van, we meet our first Venezuelan family. Raul tells us that he was the manager of a large store in Venezuela, but

as the situation deteriorated in his country he had to leave everything
behind. When it got to the point that he could no longer buy enough
food to survive, he started walking. He had to leave his car because he
could not find enough gas to drive it out of the country, so he walked
over a thousand miles until he found employment here in Colombia.
Now, he wakes up at 5 a.m. each day to collect eggs and feed pigs on
this farm that has taken him in – what a life change!

Raul gives us a tour of the farm, where Lilly delights in helping
him feed the pigs, and then invites us into his modest home for coffee
and a chat. He proudly takes out his Venezuelan passport to show us,
and tells us that they used to receive tourists from all over the world.
He describes the beauty of his country, and emphasizes that he'll return
as soon as it is safe again. In the meantime, he's already found a job for
his sister, who just arrived with her husband and baby, and he's sending
money to his parents back in Venezuela. I'm shocked when he explains
that it currently costs about one month's salary to buy a dozen eggs, so
his parents can't survive without his help.

Leaving Chicamocha Canyon a few days later, we've enjoyed
waking up to birdsong every morning, watching the intense sunset over
the canyon view from our van, and trying various foods and coffee
delivered by Raul's sister next door. But what we'll most remember is
our personal introduction to the situation in Venezuela. This will stick
with us for the next year as we travel in parallel paths with the
Venezuelans through this continent.

We meander generally south, heading toward the capital city of
Bogota where we hope to find a battery to replace the one that
exploded. We stay on the goat farm of a Colombian/English couple and
make our own goat cheese. We visit the charming colonial towns of
Barichara and Villa de Leyva, see the biggest preserved Kronosaurus
fossil in the world, and go rock climbing for the first time since
Yosemite.

And almost every time we park our home on wheels, we are
approached by curious and friendly local people...

Walking back from swimming in a river, a woman calls out from
her house as we pass. We end up sitting inside her home, in our wet

bathing suits, drinking coffee with her and her husband until the sun sets and we run back to the van.

Camping on a hilltop behind a family's house for a night, they invite us in for juice and give us bags of guayaba, raspberry, and mango from their fruit garden. The teenage daughter paints Lilly's toenails, and we can't leave the next day without an entire bag full of hand-me-down toys and a new pair of shoes.

Visiting the breath-taking Zipaquira underground salt cathedral, the Colombian tourists seem more interested in our van than in the cathedral. We have non-stop visitors knocking on the door, even though we try to tuck out of sight in the far corner of the parking lot. The most unique visit was by a young man who turned out to be in a punk band – when he saw John's guitar, he hopped into the van and sat down and started playing and singing for us!

Stopping at a mechanic's shop outside of Bogota to ask for help procuring a new lithium battery, the mechanic leads us through the gates of his large property and invites us to camp in front of his house. His mum invites us into her kitchen for coffee and tells us to use her shower and stay as long as we want. We don't make any progress with the battery, but we enjoy the visit with this generous family.

Colombian curiosity and kindness is endless and everywhere.

Leaving the mechanic family's compound just outside Bogota, we head south and west to the *Eje Cafetera* (coffee region) and Valle de Cocora, home of the giant wax palm trees. The road is full of slow-moving trucks on a very curvy road. It's painfully slow, not to mention scary, with cars and motorcycles continually making dangerous passes on blind corners. Examining the map, I find a possible alternative on off-road tracks that would avoid the busy highway, so we turn right into the unknown.

It turns out to be three of our best driving days. Slow, safe driving with virtually no other vehicles or people around. Incredible canyon views almost the entire drive. Lilly sits on my lap in the front seat with the windows down as we trundle along on the dirt listening to music and pointing out things down the hillside.

We camp in a little pullout overlooking the valley, with great views and total peace and quiet, the only disturbance being some kids riding horses to school the next morning! I really love wild camping – it's like backpacking into the wilderness, except with the creature comforts of home and no backpack to carry. What an amazing combination.

Even out here we aren't able to escape Colombian friendliness. A 100-year-old man (ok, I'm estimating) walks by with two horses in the morning, and stops to chat. He's walking from a village that took us an hour to drive from yesterday, to another town we don't expect to reach until tomorrow! All this just to sell some of his produce for cash. (Cue reminder of how lazy and privileged we are.) We do the usual Q&A and van tour that has become routine in Colombia, then say adios and gracias to his "Que Dios les bendiga" (may God bless you) as he walks down the hill.

That afternoon, we see him slowly returning up the hill toward us, on his way back home. (Yes, we still haven't moved – homeschooling eats up our every morning.) As his horses continue on ahead, he walks over to our van, approaching Lilly. In his outstretched hand is a small orange, "Toma, nena." (Here, little girl.) It's such a small act of kindness, but leaves me agog, knowing how far he's walked and how little he likely has to give. The people I meet on this trip are constantly reminding me to become a more generous person.

On the second day of our dirt road detour, we summit an 11,000 foot pass while surrounded by... palm trees? Now that's unexpected! They are called wax palms and they thrive up here. That night we sleep in a little pine tree grove away from the road. It feels like we're back in Yosemite – the carpet of pine needles at our feet, the last rays of sun lighting up the tree tops with alpenglow, the smell in the air – every little detail feels so familiar.

On the third day, we reluctantly return to civilization and paved roads, but happily park at an overlander campground with hot showers and internet. Lilly makes friends with a French girl, and it's fascinating for me to listen to the pair of them playing together speaking only broken Spanish. (French girl speaks no English, Lilly speaks no French, so Spanish becomes the common language.)

We still haven't figured out what might be wrong with the electronics, so we head to the big city of Cali to look for new batteries, nervously checking the battery temperature every hour as we drive.

Vanlife is not conducive to city visits – it's hard to drive such a big vehicle in crowded streets, impossible to park anywhere while we do our errands, and campgrounds rarely exist. Luckily, we again find a friendly mechanic who lets us camp in his shop. We get the tires rotated, check the brake pads, and he sends one of his employees motoing around town to find new air filters for us. We finally give up on the impossible quest to find a replacement lithium battery – they just don't exist down here – and decide to go buy a lead one instead.

Looking for a place to park so we can buy the battery, we stop in front of an office building and I poke my head through their open window to ask if we can block their doorway. Of course this results in a conversation and van tour and, when we return to the van 30 minutes later, they insist on giving us a t-shirt, hat, coffee mug, and flashlight, all branded with their logo. (Most of which we distribute to people we meet in the subsequent week.) But we get the new battery!

On our way out of Cali, we find a large supermarket and delight in buying hard-to-find foods like good bread and cheese. I take Lilly to the bathroom and, while I'm waiting for her, a message arrives in the cell phone John and I share.

"Hi John, it's Eduardo, here's our address, we look forward to hosting you."

What? John is organizing a secret meeting with some guy called Eduardo?

Colombian hospitality strikes again.

In the five minutes I was gone in the bathroom, someone approached John in the supermarket aisle and insisted that we go stay at his house. (You have to remember that we look very different from your average Colombian, so we visually stand out even when we're not in our giant, foreign-plated van.) We were leaving town that day so we declined, but a week later when we returned to Cali to extend our visas, we did take him up on his offer.

As we approach the winter holiday season, several friends are discussing visiting us but struggling to fit it into their schedules and deal with expensive flights. We realize that *we* are the ones who have no time constraints, so maybe it makes more sense for us to visit everyone in one big trip, at a less expensive time of the year?

How much would that cost? Where could we store the van? Would our Colombian visa let us leave without the van?

And the bigger question: doing this would rule out the possibility of getting to Patagonia in time for this summer season (Jan/Feb 2019) – are we willing to commit to this trip taking an extra year?

Back in Mexico, we quickly realized how much we enjoyed this new lifestyle, so I created a budget and started carefully tracking our spending. Now, we conclude that we can cover over half our expenses using the income from our rental house back in California. So, if we can find ways to make up the difference while traveling, we won't be touching our savings and could do this indefinitely. We agree that a trip back to the US will include researching options for freelancing jobs, so we jump into the logistics of how to make the trip happen.

The best flights we can find are from Popayan, in southern Colombia, so we drive there a few days early to secure safe van storage and enjoy the hot springs in the area. We also find a propane station willing to fill our cooking tank that we haven't filled since Guatemala.

As the friendly owner, Diego, is filling our tank, John and I are discussing our one remaining problem – where to store the van during our trip – when we both notice an odd smell.

"Check the battery!" John shouts. I run inside and don't even need to open the battery compartment to feel that it's boiling hot. John leaps into action just like back in Barranquilla with battery #1 melt-down, while I throw open the doors to pull Lilly outside. Luckily we catch this battery much earlier and it's out on the ground before the gas starts spraying. But, it is in thermal runaway and will burst if not immediately cooled.

Now what?

We're standing inside a propane filling station, looking at our about-to-explode battery sitting innocently surrounded by a dozen human-sized cylinders of highly flammable gas, while a patient queue of customers await their turn to fill their personal tanks.

Cue Colombian hospitality.

Instead of asking us to get out and take our dangerous battery with us, Diego invites us inside for coffee. Because that's just what Colombians do when they see someone who needs help.

One of Diego's employees strolls over in his grease-covered trousers and begins spraying water on our steaming battery like he is watering his tomatoes. Eventually he realizes the futility of that endeavor, and instead fills a wheelbarrow with water and manhandles the battery into it. As an afterthought, he throws an old piece of cardboard over the top.

"What's the cardboard for?" I ask, curiously.

"In case it explodes, it will soften the impact of any flying parts," he explains. I retreat hastily.

Inside the small employee area, Diego pulls out extra chairs while his elderly father sets out three plates of sweet bread on a small table, gesturing for us to sit down. This is usually when I start feeling uncomfortable about the generosity of strangers, but right now I'm frazzled by the battery tension, and grateful for the momentary peace. We chat with them about our trip and the battery situation, while sipping coffee and watching Lilly eat most of the sweet bread.

"This coffee is the best I've tasted here, which brand is it?" remarks John, who really loves coffee and is looking for one to bring home to our friends next week.

Diego pulls out a bag with a simple sticker label on the front, "My family grows and processes it on our farm down the road."

Our jaws drop. They grow and roast their own coffee! Just as John is about to ask more, Diego's dad interjects, "You must camp on our coffee farm tonight. You're welcome to stay as long as you like. In fact, you can leave your van there during your trip home to see your families. I'll have our security guard watch over it for the month."

Why does it seem like everyone in this country wants to help so much? Are they taught this in school? Is all of South America like this? Do they only act like this to foreigners?

Over the past year, John and I have spent hours debating and analyzing poverty, education, building materials, country borders, and languages. But now we find ourselves discussing – what could make an entire nation of people more kind than another?

We do tour Diego's coffee farm later that week, fascinated to see all the machinery for processing coffee on a much smaller scale than we saw back in Guatemala. But we decide not to store the van there because there's no roof and it's the beginning of the rainy season. We do, however, buy ten bags of his coffee to bring to friends in the US and UK.

Ever since battery meltdown #1, John has spent every waking moment researching, experimenting, and calling experts in the US trying to figure out what is wrong with the failsafe system he designed. Finally, after meltdown #2 he discovers the issue. The solid state, military aircraft grade switch John found to protect the batteries from over-charging failed. The manufacturer confesses they made a bad batch but haven't recalled them yet. Of all the luck! They agree to ship an urgent replacement to us so that we can retrieve it while we're in the US, and we pack up the faulty switch to ship to them once we arrive. We spend an afternoon thoroughly cleaning Vancito for his hibernation, then leave him in a roofed parking area and take a taxi to the airport.

24

DOUBLE CULTURE SHOCK

After 13 months of living in our tiny home with no schedule, few visitors, and a very slow pace of travel, we fly half-way around the globe in one day to drop into a busy household in central London. Lilly takes the jet lag in stride and delights in playing with her cousins every day. My sister and brother-in-law welcome us with open arms and we merge into the chaotic family routine. School pickup, homework nagging, nanny coordination, late-night work meetings, sick kids – it's just like our old lives in California.

What's the most surprising thing about our return to civilization? My appreciation for hot showers! It seems so trivial, but it is such a luxury that I have missed. You don't *need* hot water to wash yourself, so in most of the rural areas we travel through, it's cold. Washing your body is a chore – you steel yourself for impact, rush under the icy water with short deep exhales of shocked breath, quickly step aside to soap thoroughly then mentally prepare for impact #2 to rinse off. The warm shower is a completely different experience – a place to relax, think, sing – an unnecessary luxury that many do not have.

And the stores, oh my! The first day in London, John and I start walking to the grocery store but never make it because we stop at the gas station store and it feels so big that we can't imagine needing to go anywhere else. It becomes the joke of the household: "Mary and John's favorite grocery store is the gas station."

Lilly's hardest adjustment seems to be toilet paper – she can never remember to put it in the toilet bowl, she's become so accustomed to putting it in the trash can. My poor sister and brother-in-law keep discovering piles of poop paper spiraling out of their bathroom trash cans. "Are we going to get cholera?" they joke.

Returning to our home in California is surreal. Everything seems exactly the same as when we left – our neighborhood, our friends' houses, our offices where we used to work. How can so much have happened to us in the last 13 months, and yet this place feels like we left just yesterday?

One thing that feels very different is driving. I'm amazed by how wide and organized the roads are. Clear lane markings, almost no motorbikes, obvious road signs (in English), no one trying to pass you on both sides at once. I feel like I could drive while sleeping.

Ironically, after 13 months on the road traveling through 10 different countries with no sickness, Lilly comes down with an ear infection and we have to visit her old pediatrician in California for an antibiotic prescription. Driving slowly through countries is a very different hit on the immune system than flying thousands of miles in one day.

Being back home talking to my friends with their normal lives and stable friendships and progressing careers, makes my mind go back to worrying about things I've been mostly ignoring this past year.

When will we start building our careers and savings again instead of gallivanting around the world? Should we get Lilly officially tested for dyslexia and put her in some special tutoring? Is it irresponsible to be living so far from good emergency medical care? Will Lilly be mentally scarred for life because of the instability of her home and lack of friends?

John helps me to rationalize. This is the perfect age to do a trip with Lilly. She does miss her friends but she is so happy to be with us day in and day out – I doubt she'll want to live in a van with her parents when she's a teenager. And, she's getting daily private tutoring with a reading syllabus specifically designed for kids struggling to read. Back at our public school she was in a class with 24 kids, falling further behind every day. She cried so many mornings when I dropped her off at school, and she'd come home telling us that she thought she was stupid because everyone else could read but she couldn't. Now she gets to learn at her own pace and is starting to fall in love with reading. So maybe we're removing as much mental scarring as we're adding?

This visit also makes me realize the depth of friendships that I've been missing on the road. Traveling through Latin America we're constantly meeting kind and generous people who welcome us in as if we are family, but we have no history with them and we are unlikely to ever see them again. This visit back to the US reminds me how much I value good friends.

* * *

Three flights and 24 hours of travel later, we are overjoyed to be reunited with Vancito and drive into the unknown again. We had spent 13 months driving in Latin America and yet, after leaving for only six weeks, it is quite the culture shock to return. We'd become accustomed to the sights and sounds, but now we're surprised once again, pointing things out to each other every few minutes...

I see ladies tending to open-air smoking campfires, roasting something unidentifiable for sale, right on the side of the road amidst the diesel fumes and dust...

People hanging onto the side of a truck as it drives up the road because there's no space to ride inside...

Laundry hanging out to dry beside every house we pass...

Men walking down the side of the road with a machete strapped on their hip, on their way home from work...

People standing in the middle of the street at every speed bump or pothole, trying to sell us mysterious plastic bags of things that we assume are food but don't recognize.

But at everything I point to, John replies, "I can't look, I'm trying not to hit someone!" The road is only two lanes wide but there appears to be an unspoken agreement among drivers to use it as three lanes. There are motorcycles constantly swarming around us passing on both sides – John refers to them as "the mosquitoes." Surprise potholes around bends in the road. Stray dogs and kids running everywhere.

And, the houses! That's perhaps the most striking difference after our time back in the US/UK. Four posts of wood or bamboo or sometimes concrete, with corrugated steel lying across the top forming a roof. Always a *pila* outside (big container for catching rainwater for washing dishes and bodies) and the ubiquitous laundry strung up everywhere trying to dry in the unreliable rainy season.

Twenty-four hours ago we were in Silicon Valley sleeping in large houses with guest bedrooms, and driving in borrowed cars down roads that you could navigate with your eyes closed. The difference is overwhelming. It's a cultural chasm. But humans adjust easily, especially when living in a bubble of comfort in a big white van.

* * *

I am bracing myself for the emotional trauma of the Colombia/Ecuador border crossing. Thousands of Venezuelan refugees are walking through Colombia to get to Ecuador or Peru, and many of them get stuck at the border, living in makeshift roadside encampments while they wait for the immigration office to decide their fate.

Since entering Colombia, we've seen obvious groups of Venezuelan refugees on the side of the road, always walking south – away from Venezuela. I torture myself by reading about their plight online and feel guilty that we don't help them somehow.

I read one interview with a woman who walked with her 10-year-old daughter from Venezuela to Peru. Yes, you read that right – they walked through four countries! The mother talked about trying to carry her exhausted, crying daughter on endless long walking days, while being passed by countless trucks that did not stop to pick her up. I know the roads she's talking about because I've driven them. Narrow, winding, often no shoulder, on a cliff, up a steep mountain. Plus, it's now raining most afternoons. Maybe I was one of those trucks that did not stop?

John and I debate it every time we pass people walking on the side of the road, but ultimately decide not to invite a group of desperate young men into the back of our van with Lilly. I try to reduce my guilt by saying that if we see women with children alone we will pick them up. But we only ever see large groups of mostly men.

Arriving at the border, with my heart in my throat, we park amidst chaos. There are crowds of people everywhere. Crying kids, tired older relatives, parents trying to hold their family together – all hoping to get across the border. It's like we've walked into a scene that you'd see on the news on TV – a refugee crisis in some far-flung country. Except we're standing in the middle of it. It's overwhelming and distressing.

The people are carrying as much of their worldly belongings as possible, in a haphazard array of plastic bags and disintegrating back-packs. I see a mother sitting in the dirt nursing her baby, with her free hand resting on a child who is napping on a piece of cardboard next to her. It's clear that this crowd of homeless people have been here for days, but buses keep arriving and disgorging more.

There's a large Red Cross tent with a long snaking line of people waiting in front. I want to do something, anything, so I march up to the front with a fistful of money. I have no idea what I'm hoping to accomplish, and the tears in my eyes are making my vision blurry. I can't find anyone who looks like they're in charge, so I go around the back, but have no luck there either. What am I expecting, a donation box nailed onto a post here in this dirt parking lot?

I decide I will give money directly to a family instead. I walk around feeling like a complete idiot, trying to make eye contact with someone, as if I'll be able to magically tell that they are desperate enough to accept money from a stranger. Each time I start to approach someone, they look away, and I feel too awkward to walk up asking if they need help. Finally, I give up and walk sheepishly back to the van where John and Lilly are waiting patiently for me.

We gather our paperwork and start looking for the immigration office, picking our way through groups of families sprawled out on the dirt road. We're not surprised to see an enormous line of families in front of the immigration desk, waiting to plead their case to the border guard. The line snakes back and forth with hundreds of people.

We're going to be here for hours.

But as we approach, US passports in hand, a security guard sees our white faces and motions us over to a separate line. It only takes about 20 minutes and then we are through, moving on to do the van paperwork and then driving into Ecuador while the Venezuelans stay in line. I can't help but agonize over the obvious question, "What makes me any different?"

Please take a moment to appreciate your citizenship right now.

Dirt road detour through the wax palm trees in central Colombia

ECUADOR

We drove 3,160 miles over 5.5 months in Ecuador.
December, 2018 to May, 2019 (including 3 weeks on Galapagos
islands).

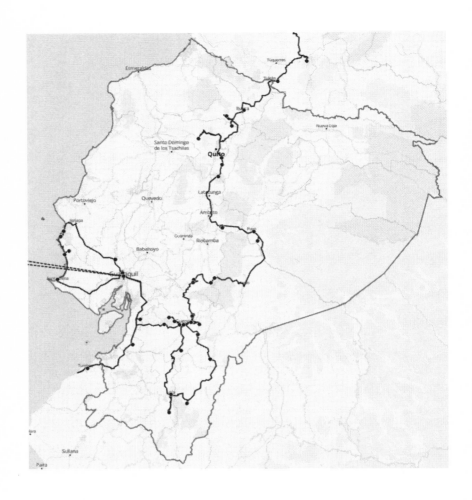

25

AMAZING ECUADOR

F rom snow-capped volcanoes to the Amazon rainforest to surf beach towns – Ecuador has it all. We initially debate whether to drive down the western coast (beaches), or through the center (volcanoes), or hug the eastern side (Amazon jungle), but we ultimately decide we're ready for a change from Central American beaches and jungle. So, we drive down the center of the country, criss-crossing the Ecuadorian Andes, past dozens of volcanoes, the tallest of which reaches over 20,000 feet. We are loving being back in the mountains.

But first, we have to deal with some van and human health logistics.

John installs the replacement switch that we brought back from the US, and we buy a pair of new lead batteries to finally put our battery troubles behind us. Unfortunately, we couldn't bring new lithium batteries with us – for some reason the airlines don't let you fly with a potentially exploding box – but the lead batteries work out just fine.

On a trip of this length, you have to deal with healthcare at some point. I was tempted to put off non-essential things like a mammogram until after the trip, but then I heard from a friend about her stage four breast cancer diagnosis. So I spend a morning googling "mammogram

Ecuador" and making tricky phone calls in Spanish to hospital recep-
tionists, then John drives me to the clinic. I'm taken in immediately to
the big machine for the scans, and then directly to the doctor's office
where she talks me through the images that are already pulled up on
her screen. She then does an ultrasound to get better pictures, which
she says is standard here, and gives me print-outs of all the results to
take with me. Finally I return to the front desk where I pay... wait for
it... $75.

Ironic timing because the next day we get a $220 bill from the
pediatrician in California from when Lilly had her ear infection there.
We'd spent five minutes with her and no tests were administered. That
$220 did not even include the cost of the antibiotics. The US health
system is really not an option without insurance.

Then finally we're back on the road, heading south. Driving is so
relaxing compared to our experiences in Colombia. The roads are in
great condition, with signs and on-ramps, and there aren't "mosquitoes" (motorcycles) swarming all around us constantly – it's all so
orderly! Also, the currency is USD, and the emergency number is 911
– little things that make traveling here feel slightly easier.

Our first stop for gas leaves us somewhat confused. Our 25-gallon
tank was almost empty and yet the man is asking us for only $17.
Something must be lost in translation. But no, we realize that diesel
here costs less than $1 per gallon! We later discover that it's heavily
diluted with water, which explains both the price tag and the later
issues we have with our fuel system.

I'm tired of being in a city dealing with logistics, so we aim for a
wild camp on a lake, Laguna Mojanda. We bump slowly along a dirt
road, so Lilly climbs onto my lap in the front seat. The road progressively gets worse as we get closer to the lake. We keep arriving at large
flooded sections that Vancito plows right through, until eventually we
find ourselves driving right up to the lake itself. I guess we'll camp
here then! Not surprisingly, we don't see another soul.

It's cold and cloudy, over 12,000 feet elevation, but there is beautiful sunset light streaking through the clouds as we hike along the lake
edge that evening. We have an absolutely silent night of peaceful sleep.

In the morning, we sit at the water's edge bundled up in coats and drinking coffee/hot chocolate, while Lilly jumps through imaginary portals between the muggle world and her magical world, loving being in the wilderness again.

I catch a glimpse of an airplane above and point it out to John, just as the thought forms in my mind, *That's not an airplane!* We sit in silent astonishment enjoying our first sighting of giant Andean condors. These enormous birds reach up to 10 feet in wingspan! It's easy to imagine we are watching a pterodactyl flying overhead.

I roll out my yoga mat in the sandy dirt next to the lake, and do my usual morning back exercises that keep my back pain from an old injury at bay. I then lie flat with my eyes closed, listening to the water lapping and feeling the sun on my face and the cold high mountain air blowing across my body. Today is the first day that I feel like we are really, truly in South America – this is what I'd expected from this continent.

We detour into the jungle and cloud forest of Mindo for a few days, a town that reminds me of Monteverde, one of my favorite places in Costa Rica. We walk through a huge enclosed area full of butterflies in all stages of life that prompts Lilly to write her first book – the four stages of the butterfly. We drink tea at an outdoor cafe and watch the whirring wings of hundreds of hummingbirds dipping their long beaks into the colorful flowers surrounding us. We hike past waterfalls in the lush, green jungle. Every time I hear a rustling in the trees above me, I look up expecting to see my monkey friends, but it's just the wind.

On one wet jungle trail we stop short of walking straight into a big spider web stretched across the path about chest-height – perfect viewing for Lilly. We happen to arrive just in time for the 10 a.m. show. The spider crawls over to an insect caught in her web, frantically wriggling. We watch in morbid fascination as the spider pulls thread from her body to wrap around the bug, and then uses her legs to carefully spin the poor bug around and around, rolling it up into an unrecognizable bundle of silvery thread. The wriggling gradually subsides to stillness. We duck under the web and continue our hike. When we hike back that same way an hour later, there is nothing left of the bug.

We pass through this country's namesake, the Equator, and pay $5 to get a photo of us straddling the Northern and Southern Hemispheres. There is some debate as to the precise location of the Equator, and many enterprising locals try to convince you to stand on *their* painted line in the ground.

Also at the Equator monument is a small pen of cute fluffy guinea pigs. We ate *cuy* (guinea pig) once in Colombia, trying to be open-minded about eating local delicacies, but I don't think Lilly has matched the food to the creature yet. She's delighted to see these little fuzz balls in their open pen, and squats down next to them, petting their furry orange bodies and playing with them until we finally drag her away. Then, she steps outside to see their siblings skewered from head to tail on a metal stake roasting over a fire. "I'm never eating cuy again, Mama!" she declares.

We skirt around Quito (the capital city) and then veer off the main road, aiming for Cotopaxi volcano. It's the second highest volcano in Ecuador, at 19,000 feet, and we camp right at the base. We're teased by glimpses of the snow-covered symmetrical cone summit towering before us, but the clouds never part sufficiently for the full spectacular view. Similarly, as we pass the highest volcano in the country, Chimborazo, a few days later, the clouds also block the peak. But what we miss in view, we make up for in wildlife sightings...

Bumping down the dirt road to get to the volcano, we spy our first llamas of the trip. They look so odd with their thick lips and long necks, and walk right up to our window as we trundle slowly by. I am delighted to see this quintessentially South American creature looking at me eye-to-eye right outside my window.

While cooking dinner at our campsite, we again see several of the impressively large condors circling above us with their tell-tale white collar. The size of these birds is just unbelievable. No wonder Ecuador has chosen the condor as its national bird, and put it front and center on their flag.

After a cold but beautifully silent night, we are woken up in the morning by owls hooting outside the van. John ventures out into the cold, foggy air and finds a pair of large bushy great horned owls in a tree. I join him and we stand marveling at the proximity of these wild-looking creatures. One has its eyes closed as if asleep, and the other is staring right at us suspiciously, head cocked slightly to one side. As we are doing school with Lilly in the van later that morning, the hooting sound becomes much louder and we see our owl friends have moved to a tree right next to us, letting us watch them from the comfort of our warm seats inside.

After passing the biggest volcanoes in the middle of Ecuador, we decide to turn left (east) toward the Amazon. I've heard about a monkey preserve that accepts volunteers, so of course I'm navigating John right to it. The road plummets in elevation and the temperature climbs. It starts to feel tropical, with thick, lush jungle surrounding us. There are waterfalls pouring down the sides of the roads everywhere we drive, and for the first time in months we are sleeping with our windows open and digging out our swimsuits to bathe in rivers. My favorite alarm clock has returned – the dawn chorus of so many different bird tunes enveloping our van. But still no monkeys. Let's go find some.

26

MUGGED BY A SQUIRREL MONKEY

We find *Paseo de Los Monos* at the end of a dirt road, and park outside a neighboring family's house for $1 per night. The three of us venture down the muddy trail and I tentatively approach the first person I see.

"Um, we are looking for someone to talk to about maybe applying to volunteer?" I ask hesitantly.

The person, who turns out to be the owner, replies without a moment's thought, "Great, we need to count out 346 bananas and feed the appropriate number to each animal," she points me to a wooden shed that I discover is full of enormous banana bundles.

"And someone needs to go to town to buy more chicken for our Christmas dinner tomorrow," she throws her car keys to John.

"Don't forget to wear the special gloves when you grab the banana bundles because there are poisonous spiders inside them," she shouts to me as I turn toward the banana shed.

"And can someone pull that tortoise away from the other one he's trying to hump?" Lilly climbs over a fence and starts a futile game of pulling tortoises off each other.

"And the collared peccaries need this bucket of food." She sets down a bucket which I dutifully pick up, and pauses for breath.

I take my chance to ask how to find the collared peccaries, not admitting that I have no idea *what* a collared peccary is, and she explains, "Walk down that trail on the right until you hear a parrot saying *hola* then turn left until you smell pigs and you'll be there."

I am in love! This is my kind of volunteering.

A Swiss-Ecuadorian couple is running this place, and they fall appropriately into their cultures' stereotypes. Lisette, the Ecuadorian, kisses and hugs us and invites us to Christmas dinner with the family the next day. Yvan, the Swiss, demurely greets us between drags on his cigarette and invites us to do whatever jobs we can find.

It's amazing what they have done with only one hectare (2.5 acres). They have a variety of cages – smaller enclosures for keeping babies, a medical area for sick animals, and enormous, expansive enclosures where the monkeys can run and climb freely. They've built a system of wire tunnels about ten feet off the ground that the monkeys use to travel around the entire property. These tunnels go over the walking trails, past the river, near most of the other animals' cages, even *through* the humans' living room in the main house. This allows the monkeys to get used to being near other creatures if they are comfortable doing so, and provides them the option to be near humans if they prefer (since many used to be pets). Whenever I enter the house, there is always one particular capuchin monkey sitting by the front door in one of the tunnels, reaching out his arm for a handshake, even though his tunnel extends all over the reserve. Lisette explains that he was a pet, kept in a small cage for a long time, and they doubt he'll ever be released back into the wild.

When cooking in their kitchen, it feels like *we* are the ones in a cage – the entire kitchen is enclosed in wire because otherwise the monkeys will run in to steal food. When we sit at the dining room table to eat, there is almost always a monkey or coati outside peering in at us to see what's going on. Other volunteers tell us that the night before we arrived, the kinkajou strolled through the tunnel over the dining room and pooped onto the table while everyone was trying to eat!

We learn about lanudo monkeys (chorongos, aka woolly monkeys) who look like a stuffed animal toy (Lilly's favorite), spider monkeys (my favorites, more on them later), squirrel monkeys who roam freely on the trails stealing food, capuchins who like to throw things at passersby, and chichis which are about the size of a hamster. There are also tortoises, peccaries (which I discover look like a gray bristly pig), coatis (which we saw frequently at our home in Costa Rica), loros (parrots), snakes, spiders, kinkajous, and a margay (nocturnal wild cat).

Most of the creatures were brought here because they were kept illegally as pets in someone's home, or were found injured or orphaned. Ultimately, for the few that are able to survive in the wild, Paseo works with the Ecuadorian environmental agency to release them to a safe place in the jungle.

CRASH! Our morning wake-up call comes from one of the capuchin monkeys who has a sheet of tin in his enclosure and bangs on it each morning as if demanding, "Hey where's my breakfast?"

We have breakfast sitting at our little table outside the van, from where we can see monkeys climbing the taller trees nearby. Then we walk down to the reserve, greeting all our favorite monkeys on the path down – most of them immediately bound up to greet us at the fence and shake our hands.

The work varies depending on what needs arise each day, although the feeding and cage-cleaning job is never-ending. John builds a roof onto an enclosure, I repair the little structure for newborn creatures, and Lilly actually does work for the first time in her life cleaning the baby coati cage. I was sure she'd whine and quit after five minutes but she sticks it out until we're completely done. She also helps clean up food leftovers from each cage after morning feeding, but mostly runs around all day playing with the various creatures. In the afternoon, once we complete whatever job we set ourselves that day, I walk down to the river for my daily bath. What a luxury being able to wash myself every day, even if just in a river.

My favorite time is at the end of the day, when the tourist groups have left and the sun is starting to set and most of the volunteers are in the house. Lilly and I walk the series of trails around the preserve to say good night to all the creatures. The parrots start chattering away. They squawk *Hola* and *A comer* (time to eat), though for some reason they are mostly quiet during the day. The margay (tiger cat) comes out of hiding and the kinkajou also wakes up and starts racing around its enclosure. We always stop at our favorite spider monkey and lanudo monkey spot to hang out with our buddies. Lilly feeds the lanudos some leaves plucked from the nearest bush and shakes hands with them, while I watch and laugh at Lisa, the goofy spider monkey.

The first time I "met" Lisa, she walked right up to me then turned around and sat with her back toward me. She looked the other way, pretending to ignore me, while she snuck her long, strong tail out of the cage to check me out. Her tail wrapped around my arm, then went into my pocket, then up to my face – all the while she was pretending to look at something on the other side of her enclosure. So curious and hilarious!

When I talk to her, she looks over her shoulder at me and furrows her eyebrows as if saying, "Who are you talking to? Oh, me?!" and makes this surprised "O" shape with her mouth. Her facial expressions are so human! Periodically, she'll get up and saunter away upright on two legs, which just makes the similarity with humans uncanny. With all these monkeys, after so many handshakes, I've noticed that their hands are very reminiscent of ours – soft inside, rougher outside, with fingernails just like we have. Spending close-up time with these amazing creatures makes me realize just how similar we are.

For our second Christmas on this trip, we join the family and other volunteers for a big Christmas Eve dinner in the main house.

I decide to bake two large banana breads to share with everyone, so stop at the animal feeding kitchen to pick up some bananas. I carefully put on the anti-poisonous-spider gloves and pluck five bananas off the giant stalk. Then I walk down the trail to the main house, juggling the bananas as well as several zucchinis and carrots for dinner.

Suddenly something lands on my shoulder. Squirrel monkey alert! He wriggles his hands (paws?) through my pile of food until he gets hold of a banana and a tug-of-war commences. For a creature weighing only 2 lbs, he has a surprisingly strong grip on my banana, plus I'm trying to carry too much stuff so can't really battle him. He ultimately wins and I scold him but can't stop laughing as I continue down the trail to the house. I guess I'll be making four-banana bread instead of five!

I would be happy to stay at the monkey reserve much longer, and Lilly is in heaven with so many creatures to play with, but there isn't a good accommodation setup for us, plus there is some silly politics going on between the other volunteers, so we decide to move on. But it forever remains one of my favorite weeks of the trip.

27

THE CONTRASTS OF ECUADOR

W e swim in a waterfall surrounded by dense, green, lush jungle in the tropical Amazon lowlands, then drive through highlands with scraggly grass and an occasional flower at 13,000 feet elevation, and end up in a large, modern city celebrating New Year's Eve in the partying streets – all in the space of seven days and a couple hundred miles. And we haven't even been to the coastal beach area yet! This country is impressively diverse, particularly given its small size – it's only about as big as the state of Colorado, or slightly larger than the UK.

We first travel south from the monkey rescue center, hugging the western edge of the Amazon. People are taller. Faces are different, almost Asian or Hawaiian looking. There are signs for tours to see native tribes, or get your face painted like an Amazon warrior, or try out blow darts. Compared to the mountainous center of Ecuador, we see lots more people walking on the side of the road. Maybe it's a cultural thing, or maybe it's as simple as the climate being warmer down here.

We camp in the parking lot for a waterfall, and the following morning enjoy a peaceful jungle hike to the deserted pool framed by trees. The falls are perfect for a shower, and I marvel at the lush jungle view around me as I stand in chest-deep water shampooing my hair. But that afternoon, we ascend almost 10,000 feet in one day and the scenery and people change dramatically.

We marvel at huge, open valley landscapes with dramatic green carpets of hills, backed by rocky peaks further in the distance. The vegetation is short, shrubby grass with the occasional flower struggling up in the thin air. The people are all wearing colorful clothing, which makes for a beautiful and striking contrast against the green hills. It's almost like a uniform – every woman has a brightly-colored (usually orange, red or pink) poofy skirt over some kind of white petticoats, a similarly-colored blouse and shawl, very long black hair usually in two braids, and a black hat and boots. And, everyone is tending animals – usually cows, horses, goats or pigs.

What a change from just a few hours ago when we were in dense green jungle inhabited by scantily clad tribal-looking people peddling blow darts!

We pass Laguna Atillo and see that the main road marked on our map now goes way up north and then doubles back on itself south again. Surely we can avoid that by cutting across the blank section on the map for a better adventure? So we turn left on a random dirt road that heads in approximately the right direction...

Within 30 minutes I am out of the van, sloshing about in ankle-deep mud in my flip-flops, attempting to direct John who is desperately trying to keep the van moving before it sinks. He manages to get onto some fairly firm dirt and guns it ahead out of the mud, where we accept defeat on this particular stretch of road. We see other dirt tracks that head in the general direction we want to go, but it's starting to get dark so we change focus to looking for a safe place to tuck out of sight for the night.

I see a spot of color down the hill, and realize it's a brightly-dressed man walking some horses near a collection of huts. We manage to get close enough to chat with him and ask if we can spend the night on his property. He immediately offers us a room in his house to sleep in, which we politely decline since we have our own house on wheels. Would you invite some passing foreigners whom you'd just met to sleep at your house? Each time this happens to us, I remind myself to bring this mindset of generosity and openness home with me after the trip. Our host, Humberto, sells us trout from his farm for $1 and we cook ourselves a fresh fish dinner before going to sleep on yet another foreign but welcoming stranger's property.

The next day, Humberto points to a dirt road that he says will connect across our blank section of map, so we head west once again, this time with more success. The scenery is breath-taking. I'm hanging out the window gazing across the wide, open hillsides breathing it all in, as John slowly guides Vancito along the muddy dirt road. Once again, we're so glad to have taken a dirt road detour, plus it's always fun to see the little blue dot representing our location on Google Maps simply floating in space with no roads or landmarks near it.

A local guy flags us down and we give him a ride. As we drive through the mountains together, we trade questions and answers – as intrigued about his life as he is about ours. This is one of the most remote areas we've visited, and I'm curious about how he and others here make a living. He explains they focus mostly on their animals for wool and meat, and ride a bus to the nearest town for supplies they can't produce themselves. We make it to Laguna Ozogoche where we drop off our new friend, and eventually we return to the paved road (phew!) We descend in elevation and head south toward the big city of Cuenca, just in time for New Year's Eve celebrations.

As we approach civilization, we start seeing kids in the streets with home-made mannequins asking for money. Once in the city itself, we see these mannequins everywhere – shop windows, outside of restaurants, stuck on top of cars driving by. The markets all have mannequins for sale, along with masks and wigs and make-up. It's like a strange combination of Halloween in the US and Guy Fawkes in the UK. What is going on?

The family whose yard we camp in explains the New Year's tradition here in Ecuador: Everyone makes or buys something to represent the bad from the past year. The great majority of these tend to be imitations of an unpopular political leader, hence all the mannequins we are seeing. At midnight on New Year's Eve, everyone burns these figures to represent the forgetting of the bad events of the past. On January 1st, they write down their goals for the next year, put them in an envelope and don't open the envelope again until the following December 31st.

Lilly surprises me with a home-made cardboard representation of a car battery for her bad thing. She hadn't seemed too concerned during our near-explosion on the side of the highway in Colombia, but maybe it affected her more than I realized. It did feel good to burn it in the street that night, like a way to erase an unpleasant memory.

New Year's Eve itself, (or "Old Year" as it's known here), is very different from other New Year's festivities I've experienced. There is no giant street party with music and dancing, instead the celebrations are small and fractured around the city. There are hundreds of small fires with a family crowding around each one, but no big organized central bonfire. There are fireworks shooting off in every direction, but I don't see any city-organized displays.

It's relatively tame, as city parties go, but it's also strangely surreal, with a post-apocalyptic feel. Standing on a street corner in the dark, you see small fires burning all around, you hear and smell rockets blasting off from every direction without warning, and there are small groups of people wandering around aimlessly. Zombie apocalypse?

The funniest part of the evening is watching the men dancing for money. Imagine a hairy man in a pink dress with a blond wig on his head. He stands in the center of the street, blocking traffic, and doesn't allow approaching cars to pass by until the driver gives him some money. He sometimes throws himself on the hood, sometimes dances, or sometimes misses the car entirely through his drunk, blurry vision. Car after car stops to hand him a coin. Everyone is in good spirits, most people give him money, and I am very glad we're not attempting to drive anywhere.

28

FOUR EARTHQUAKES AND A LOT OF HOMEWORK, AKA LIVING IN ECUADOR

We always thought that we'd stop in Costa Rica and in Ecuador during this trip, to find out if they are contenders for our forever-home. I adore the jungle and wildlife of Costa Rica, but there's no rock climbing and the rainy season is just too much. So I'm hoping we may find in Ecuador the perfect mix of climbing, good school, and community.

We find a house for rent on top of a hill with gorgeous sunset views. Cojitambo, a great little rock climbing area, is 15 minutes north, Lilly's school is just down the road, plus there's the modern city of Cuenca full of amenities 20 minutes west. But the best part is that we're renting from a loving family who lives next door, and they fully adopt us into their clan. They check on us daily, invite us everywhere, bring us food and share meals, and generally make us feel like we have a supportive family unit around us.

John and I both focus on ways to earn enough money to continue this van lifestyle that we've fallen in love with. I start freelancing for a friend's company which I can then continue to work for part-time when we're back in the van, and John builds a business with friends back in California, even flying back to the US twice during our stay to get it to a point that he can manage it from the road. Our goal is to figure out how to travel for the long-term without eating into our savings.

John finds an excellent osteopath who treats him every week throughout our stay for his lingering neck pain that started back in Costa Rica. He also gets x-rays and MRIs and sees an orthopedic surgeon, trying to figure out what could be causing his pain. He improves during our stay, but we're realizing we may have to deal with this more seriously in future.

We enroll Lilly in the Asian American School, but don't let the name mislead you – Lilly is the only non-Ecuadorian in the school. When we visit, she is welcomed into the second grade classroom while John and I meet with the Director. It just happens to be English class at that moment, so Lilly gets to experience being the star pupil. I see the teacher hold up a picture of a duck and ask the class what it's called in English. No one knows the answer, but visiting Lilly eagerly raises her hand and shouts, "Duck!" with a big grin on her face.

I don't think the other classes are going to be so easy, my dear!

We spend the next entire day traipsing around the nearby city of Cuenca with a three-page printed list in our hands to buy the various notepads, text books, special pencils, and uniform that she needs. I give Lilly a crash course in Spanish letters over the weekend ("i" sounds like "ee," "j" sounds like "huh") and let her go on the first day of school. I think I'm more nervous than she is.

This is Lilly's first experience in a serious academic setting since we left California. In Guatemala and Costa Rica she was only in kindergarten due to the age cut-offs they had there, so it was only play-time. Here, she has homework every night, presentations to give, and exams after the first month. She is exhausted during the first couple of weeks, but quickly gets into the swing of things.

Every afternoon I sit down to help her with her homework. Social studies asks her to identify which type of house belongs on the *paramo* vs the *playa* vs the Amazon – I don't know! Or science demands a presentation on how the stomach works, and I'm looking up words like *digestion* and *intestines* in Spanish. At first, John gets off scott free, but over time his Spanish reading improves and he's helping with math word problems.

No one at the school speaks English, and so Lilly's Spanish improves dramatically for the first time on the trip. In her first week, she tells me that she raised her hand in English class to correct the teacher's English, and I'm not sure whether to scold or praise her? Of course there are some confusing moments. She lost her sweater at school and tells me she had to go to "the secret room" to check the lost and found. I'm confused, but eventually she tells me the name in Spanish – the *secretaria* (secretary) which she translated as 'secret room' – she's doing her best trying to guess the meaning of unfamiliar words.

EARTHQUAKE #1 – Magnitude 5.7 on Jan 26th. John & I at home, Lilly at school.

I've felt them several times in my life in California but they're usually over before you even realize what's going on. This was the first time it lasted long enough for us to actually walk outside. The whole house was shaking on its foundation – I'll admit it was a little freaky! The parents started frantically messaging each other asking if the kids were ok, then the school sent a photo of all the kids safely evacuated outside on the lawn.

Lilly said the alarm went off suddenly and they all filed outside but she had no idea why. She was excited telling us about it when we picked her up that afternoon, but mostly because they had been in *Lengua* (Spanish Language Arts – her hardest class) and got to play outside instead. She joked about how silly they all looked because they were told to walk outside with one hand on their head and the other straight out in front of them like a zombie.

While Lilly is at school, John and I alternate working days and rock climbing days. I am in heaven to be able to climb regularly again. The feeling of searching out holds and ascending a seemingly blank rock face, the views and contentment when I'm sitting at the top of a hard lead belaying John up to join me, and nudging my body back toward the stronger version of itself that used to be my normal – I have missed it so much since Lilly was born.

To get to most of the climbs, we have to walk past a quarry and we usually hear the distant "ping ping" of hammers on rock while we are climbing. The guys working the quarry have one of the toughest jobs I've witnessed. Each man picks an area and sits there all day under the hot sun with a hammer turning gigantic boulders into perfect little building blocks – all by hand! Next time you're feeling like you hate your job, remember these guys.

We find an easy route for Lilly and it becomes her project. She gets up only about 15 feet the first time then cries with fear and comes down. Next time, we take our Ecuadorian family with us, and with the help of their cheering she gets halfway up but then gets too scared and comes down. The next time she says, "I'm going to do it," and she does! She's not a natural when it comes to being up high off the ground, but she is really trying hard to overcome that fear, and I'm proud of her determination.

EARTHQUAKE #2 – Magnitude 7.5 on Feb 22nd. All of us asleep in the van.

This was by far the longest earthquake I've ever felt – it just kept going and going. Many buildings were destroyed, and there were several injuries, but miraculously none were serious. The epicenter was right by our monkey preserve up in Puyo. I checked with our friends there and they said it felt like their entire house had turned into a swinging hammock!

We were on a mini van trip to renew our visa and were fast asleep in the van on a hillside above a river. I woke up from the van shaking so hard, and John woke up thinking someone was driving the van on a bumpy dirt road, but Lilly didn't even roll over. John and I conferred briefly and decided it would be safest to stay inside the van – that's what the suspension is for, after all!

* * *

Most of the families we befriend live with or next to their extended family, and they seem to do everything together. The family we live with is grandma, grandpa, adult daughter Belen with her two kids, and adult son Manuel with his two kids. When we took the granddaughter climbing, the entire family came along to cheer for her from the base of the climb. They all go together to every bike race the grandson has. When Belen drove John to the airport, her teenage kids came along in the car with us! It's beautiful seeing such close, supportive families who truly enjoy spending all their time together. I hope we can somehow retain this aspect of Latin American culture as Lilly grows up.

Logistically, this closeness with the grandparents makes it so much easier for working parents to handle child care. When the school emails, "Surprise! We'll be closed in two days," (which they did three times during our three months there), the other parents don't seem bothered even though typically both parents work, because they have grandparents on hand to help watch the kids.

The downside for us is that it's slightly harder to make friends here because everyone's priority is their family. For example, I ask most of Lilly's friends if they'd like to join us for a hike one weekend, but all of them have standing commitments with their extended families. Back in California hardly anyone I know has family nearby, so friends become the priority.

Greetings are also much more important here than in the US. People always walk up and kiss/hug/shake hands with everyone they come across. Our host family, whom we see every day, always makes a point of walking across the lawn to greet each of us individually and ask how we slept, even as we're running late to the school bus stop. I learn to build in an extra few minutes to my morning walk to the bus just for this.

We have to remember to walk up to each and every person in a room, even those we do not know, and formally greet them one-by-one rather than just waving and smiling broadly hello, which I would do back home. Lilly's social studies textbook has a whole unit on the importance of greeting people and saying goodbye to people. When we go to the dentist for a teeth cleaning, she kisses each of us on the cheek in greeting, even though we've never met.

Even in a text message, I find myself getting straight to the point, "Hi, what time does the bus come today?" but the response is always, "Dearest mother of Lilly, I hope this message finds you well and you're having a good day, the bus should come at 2:15 p.m. today." It takes a while to adjust, but now I always stop myself when I start typing a message, and first make sure to say some friendly greeting at the beginning.

They are also so much more affectionate. It was only about two weeks before the grandpa of the family started calling me *mi'ja* (my daughter), and it was only days before they started referring to Lilly as "my precious" or "my life" or "my love." Years later, they still end text messages to us with, "We love you."

On the other end of the spectrum, we are always surprised to hear the nicknames conferred among friends. Time and again, in different groups of friends, we overhear the same set of *not* politically correct nicknames. The heaviest friend in a group is lovingly referred to as *Gordo* or *Gordita* (fatty), or for a really special friend, *Chanchito/a* (little piggy). Whoever has slightly darker skin than the others is *Negro/a* (black). I am always called *Flaca* (skinny). These nicknames are used in absolute affection, but still surprise my politically correct US ears.

EARTHQUAKE #3 – Magnitude 6.1 on March 23. I am home alone, John in the US, Lilly at school.

By now I know the routine – the parents all text each other until someone gets through to the school and confirms the kids are all ok. Then they send photos of the kids all outside, evacuated. Then when

Lilly comes home I ask her about it and she responds, "What earthquake?" Yup, three times now she didn't notice.

* * *

It's funny how quickly we get back into a routine. John and I work most of the time that Lilly is at school, we help with homework in the evenings, Lilly has playdates after school, and on the weekend we do laundry and go for hikes in the local national park. We've completely turned back into normal people with a routine.

We are also meeting more like-minded people during this stay. Typically, traveling in the van, we sleep on farms or in the wilderness and mostly meet people living very simple lives working the land. Now, living near a modern city and building a community of friends with the parents we meet through Lilly's private school, it's like our lives back in California. The parents we meet all work intellectual jobs, live in nice homes, plan vacations during school breaks, worry about their kids' education and talk about their work-life balance – it's just like talking to my friends back home, except in another language.

One weekend, our neighbor family invites us to go watch their son compete in BMX (bike racing) nationals in a nearby town, so 13 of us all pile into their van and spend the day sitting on a hillside watching the races and cheering. It's enchanting to watch parents encouraging their kids, checking their bikes, fastening their helmets; to see their pride when their kid wins or just completes the course.

I see a tiny girl, probably six years old, with a pink helmet, pedaling furiously around the course. When she gets to the finish line, her dad sprints down to greet her with a huge grin on his face, they high five and he wraps her in a bear hug. For some reason it brings tears to my eyes (I've gone totally soft since Lilly was born), but it also brings home the fact that people are the same everywhere. I think about this girl's upbringing – she has parents who love her, who have enough money to buy her a bike and uniform, and who are devoted enough to spend their weekends taking her to a race – is her upbringing really any different than a kid in Silicon Valley's?

EARTHQUAKE #4 – Magnitude 6.2 on March 31st. All of us at home asleep.

For all the teasing I gave Lilly for not noticing the last three earthquakes... I didn't notice this one! It was fairly big, but at 2 a.m. so we were fast asleep in the house. I guess I'm adjusting to life here?

* * *

Three months of stability has been great in many ways. I've kicked off remote online freelancing, John has started a new business, and Lilly had a great school experience, but we're all looking forward to returning to vanlife. The city of Cuenca feels too busy for us to stay long-term, and the little suburb where we live is tiny, with no community. Plus, some California friends have coordinated with us to fly to the Galapagos a few weeks before our Ecuador visa will expire, so we are excited to go join them there.

It's amazing how quickly we settled into a routine while here – staring at computer screens most of the day, rushing Lilly to get her homework done before bedtime, waking up tired to an early alarm clock. It makes me miss the quality time we have together when we're in our tiny van home together 24 hours a day, and I feel excited to return to it. It can't last forever, from a financial perspective, or once Lilly gets a little older and her need for stable friends is stronger, but I'm loving it as long as it does.

29

GALAPAGOS

bout 1,000 km west off the coast of Ecuador, sitting right on the equator, are 127 islands comprising the famous Galapagos. The typical way of visiting these islands is a cruise on a live-aboard boat. My memory of puking over the side of the boat in Panama is far too recent to be ignored, so I'm hesitant to step foot on any more floating vessels. On top of that, I learn that prices for Galapagos tours are around $3,000 per person per week! We'd spend half our year's budget on a two-week tour! So instead, we fly out to the islands, stay in last-minute hotels or rentals, and just wing it exploring independently for three weeks. We spend a week on each of the three largest islands, and are joined for part of our stay by friends from Costa Rica and California.

From the first moment, it's clear this is a different kind of holiday destination. Before boarding the plane, our bags go through an extra check for fruit or soil that could bring unwanted species to the islands; and when we arrive, sniffer dogs check the bags again before we can touch them. We pay a Galapagos island tax and they give us a booklet explaining the rules of the islands. Example: stay two meters away from the animals – this proves to be impossible within minutes of arrival as I have to step over sleeping sea lions blocking the path at the boat dock!

We transit briefly through Santa Cruz island upon arrival, and I'm surprised to find a busy little town of restaurants, tour offices, and trinket shops. It's quite a change from our last several months in South America, now seeing so many white faces in matching zip-off cargo pants and designer sunglasses. There are 25,000 people who live on the islands, so of course there are schools and houses and cars, but the tourists outnumber the locals here about 10 to 1!

Our first day on Isabela island, before our friends arrive, we rent three bicycles and set off on a 12 km ride along the beach. We've underestimated the sandy track, under the hot, cloudless sky, wearing just flip-flops and bathing suits, and we soon wish we'd brought more than one bottle of water. It is magical to pedal alongside the wide open white sand beach, but Lilly starts complaining of hunger at the 6 km point. Oops – we are getting complacent after living in the van for so long, always having everything we need with us. Luckily there are gorgeous beaches sprinkled along the way where we stop and swim in clear turquoise water with gentle waves.

On the short walk to the first beach stop, I have to grab Lilly as she almost walks into a pile of marine iguanas sunning themselves in the sand. We stop to study the prehistoric looking reptiles for several minutes, and they aren't in the least bit concerned by our presence.

At another spot, we walk through a mangrove tunnel and emerge at a river of cold water. Usually mangroves mean crocodiles, but not here, right? We sink our overheated bodies into the cold river and suddenly a big dark shape comes swimming toward us and I almost pee my bathing suit in terror! But then a cute whiskered sea lion face pops up to check us out and swims around for a few minutes before disappearing again into the mangroves.

Back on our bikes, Lilly is lagging behind as we ride up a slight hill. "Is that a speed bump?" John asks, pointing in front of him and slowing down.

"I think it's just a big mound of dirt we can go around," I respond.

Realization dawns on both of us at the same time, and we let Lilly go ahead to get the first close-up look.

"A turtle! A giant turtle!" she shrieks, dropping her bike to go investigate her discovery.

There's nothing like coming round the bend and hitting the brakes because you're about to ride over a giant tortoise! We sit down on the hot road, next to our bikes, watching in fascination as this creature bites right into the huge spikes on the cactus plant, and slowly chews it up. From that moment on, whenever we see a chewed-up cactus plant on any hike in the Galapagos, our minds return to this memory. The tortoise seems not to care at all that we are there.

(Linguistic side note: in Spanish there is only one word – *tortuga* – for both "tortoise" and "turtle." So we have picked up the bad habit of always translating it as "turtle" or just using the Spanish word.)

All three of the main islands have a giant tortoise breeding center. On Isabela it's a short walk through a flamingo-populated lagoon. As we walk around reading about the history of these creatures and watching them laboriously wander around their enclosures, I notice a group of teenage boys clustered together giggling and taking videos. No big surprise what they're staring at – it's not every day you see giant tortoises mating! There's an amusing HUMMMPPPHHH sound emanating from the upper tortoise every time he makes a slow-motion thrust. That is, about once a minute or so. Why rush when you're a protected species?

We learn that these tortoises got very close to extinction because of invasive species on the islands (rats, goats, and dogs) and because pirates in the 18th century used them for food on their long voyages. Apparently these creatures can go up to a year without eating or drinking! So it was an easy way to store meat for a long time without refrigeration. The pirates would carry the tortoises down into the hold of the boat, stack them upside down in a pile, and eat them when they ran out of meat later in the trip. It got to the point where there were only 2 males and 12 females left. Scientists carried these 14 to a safe place and protected them over the years, and now there are thousands of them. We got to meet Diego, the tortoise who helped bring the species back from the brink of extinction by fathering over 800 tortoises since the 1970s!

For our first paid tour, we pile into three kayaks with our friends from Costa Rica and paddle out from the sea lion-covered beach. We see cute little penguins hanging out on the lava rocks and watch them zoom by us in the water. They are much smaller than I expected, and incredibly fast.

One of my favorite moments is when we first jump into the water and immediately see a huge turtle swim by. The rest of the group continues on, but I stay by myself with this turtle. It's surreal to be swimming in his territory so close to him. I watch the colorful fish clustering around his head, I look at his unique mouth and stare into his eye. What does he think about me – clumsy, awkward swimmer who can't hold my breath very long hanging out in his neighborhood?

Eventually I swim over to the rest of the group. John and I dive down to check out a big school of fish, and as I'm coming up for air, a large, dark shape whizzes by me. My heart stops for a second, then I see it's a sea lion! It seems to show off spinning and turning effortlessly through the water, while we watch in delight.

As it disappears into the distance, a smaller dark shape zooms by me. Penguin! It's so fast at first that it's just a black and white blur, but then it loops around and comes back, in no hurry, and I get a close up view of this foreign creature. What a unique experience to swim with penguins in warm water.

It's the best ten minutes of snorkeling in my life.

Next up, we spend a week on Santa Cruz island, where small sharks constantly patrol the water around the boat docks, and sea lions have taken over most of the benches. It's entertaining to watch a tourist roll their wheeled suitcase along the dock and stop at a sleeping sea lion blocking the path, not quite sure how to proceed, then lift up the suitcase to step delicately over the sea lion and continue. Walking past the fish market in the morning, I always see one sea lion eagerly standing next to the fishermen selling their fish, like a dog waiting for its owner to throw him some leftovers from the dinner table.

We rent a kayak and cram the three of us into it (this is becoming harder as Lilly gets bigger) and paddle out from Playa de los Alemanes. Almost immediately we see a turtle head popping up to breathe. Then another. Then a pair of them. Then one swims right under our kayak. Lilly delights in counting turtles as we head out into the bay.

We see a crowd of birds up ahead, circling in unison while taking it in turns to dive bomb into the ocean. From afar, they look like arrows being shot into the water. As we approach, one arrow-bird shoots down near us, and when he pops up right next to our kayak I see the distinctive crazy eyes and blue feet of the blue-footed boobies. We paddle through as they dive bomb the water around us, seemingly not caring that we're traveling through their dinner table.

Next I see a strange fin that is not moving. We get closer and the fin disappears underwater. Suddenly I hear a loud exhalation right next to me and there's a black whiskered face looking at me, six inches from my kayak paddle. Creatures here really have no fear of humans.

Arriving back at our pier, we jump out, barely glancing down at the usual baby sharks that always swarm the dock, but Lilly tells us to look – there is a huge school of about 30 rays calmly floating by underneath us!

We paid $40 to rent a kayak for a couple hours and we saw turtles, sea lions, blue-footed boobies, sharks, and rays – the Galapagos is famous for live-aboard boat cruises, but we are discovering that solo travel can be a great alternative.

For our third and final stop, we take the public ferry boat to San Cristobal, the easternmost island in the archipelago. While Isabela seemed to be the island of iguanas, and Santa Cruz the island of baby sharks, San Cristobal is definitely the island of sea lions. There are hundreds upon hundreds of them, and they are everywhere. I never realized the multitude of weird sounds they make – barking, burping, roaring. It is hilarious listening to them having a conversation back and forth. After dark, when they start falling asleep all over the town, it's like seeing passed-out drunk frat boys. You're walking along and there next to a trash can, lying in a puddle of pee, is a sea lion totally passed out on its back with one flipper draped over an empty whiskey bottle. (Ok, maybe I invented the whiskey part.)

We do a paid tour to a nearby island (Isla Lobos) and go for a walk along a lava trail, jumping between jagged black rocks. I'm walking behind the guide when he suddenly steps to the right and points to the ground to his left. I follow him and look back and there's a blue-footed booby sitting on her nest, mere inches from my feet, watching us suspiciously with those crazy eyes. These birds are famous for the comical mating dance they perform which involves waggling their blue feet at each other. The result is a nest full of eggs, but also hundreds of t-shirts for sale in town that say, "I love boobies." The guide tells us that every booby lays three eggs, but only ends up with one surviving chick. Why's that? Whichever chick is born first gets stronger first, and pecks at its younger siblings until it eventually tosses them out of the nest to be eaten by other creatures. Nature is so harsh!

We also get a much closer look at the frigatebirds that we've been seeing overhead these past two weeks. Several males are perched together in a tree, puffing up a massive red sac under their necks in an attempt to attract the females. As if these comical red balloons weren't enough, they also make a loud and constant gobble gobble sound to draw the ladies' attention. The females fly around above the tree, peering down at the various males and occasionally approaching to get a closer look. A male will wait in his tree for several days or even weeks until a female lands beside him, indicating he's been chosen. When the males are not sitting around gobbling for the ladies, their red balloon sac hangs loosely like old neck flab as they fly along – not the most attractive sight.

While we're watching all of these scenes play out before us, we notice a mother frigatebird fly down to a nest where a baby is calling frantically. The large, black mama bird makes a couple of jerky motions with her head, like she's about to vomit, then opens her mouth wide. Next, the baby bird sticks its head deep into her throat! Is the mother eating the baby? As the baby pulls back for a second, I catch sight of a fish being regurgitated from the mother's throat, and then the baby lunges its head again into its mother's throat and pulls the fish out to eat. Nature is fascinating!

Also on San Cristobal, we somehow manage to convince a dive boat to let John and me share a pair of dives, so that one of us can watch Lilly while the other dives. It's my first time diving since before Lilly was born. What a wonderful feeling to sink down into the water calmly breathing and equalizing my ears as fish swim into view around me.

We immediately come upon an enormous school of fish which is so huge that it's disorienting. It completely surrounds me and entirely blocks out any light. I feel hypnotized as my eyes track the thousands of fish swarming around me, and I'm only jolted back to reality when I check my depth gauge and realize I'm sinking rapidly.

After swimming out of the fish school, I see the other divers looking up, so I turn on my back to see what's there. A dozen hammerhead sharks are silhouetted by the sunlight shining down on them from above, and I lay motionless on my back watching the eerie shapes pass over me.

Meanwhile, John and Lilly snorkeled together through Kicker Rock, which John said was his best adventure ever with her. They linked arms and he kept her close by his side as they swam through the cavernous gap between the cliff walls, surrounded by schools of fish.

Our last day in the Galapagos is one of my favorites. We rent a kayak for a paddle around the point, seeing the usual cast of characters (boobies, turtles, etc) and jump out to snorkel in a calm bay. We are soon joined by the most inquisitive and playful sea lion yet. He swims toward us and spirals around and behind us, as if showing off his superior swimming abilities. Then he disappears and we swim away, only to see him again on the other side of the bay. He dances around us in the water, charging toward us then carving away gracefully at the last moment, blowing bubbles at us. I find myself laughing out loud through my snorkel!

Back on shore later, Lilly is playing in the small waves in the knee-deep water when a juvenile sea lion swims up to join her – what can you do about the two meter distance rule if the animal approaches *you*?

They ride the waves back and forth together, with the sea lion dancing around Lilly as if really trying to play with her. I watch closely, half concerned and half amused at their play date. The sea lion is about the same size as Lilly, but certainly stronger and a far better swimmer. Then I hear a loud barking sound and see a much larger sea lion approaching rapidly. This mama swims right up to Lilly then barks at the juvenile sea lion like, "Hey it's time to come home for dinner, didn't you hear me calling you?" and they both disappear. It's so entertaining and unique to be with these wild creatures in their own habitat.

Deep Thoughts about Happiness: Coming back to the same hotel three weeks later and moving back into the van feels somewhat surreal. We looked forward to this trip for months and now we are back and everything feels the same, as if we'd never left. If we were returning to our normal busy lives and this were our once-a-year holiday, it would be depressing. But we have made our normal everyday life *be* the thing that we look forward to, so I don't feel sad that this trip is over.

It reminds me of something I read in a happiness book once – it's much more effective to make small changes that increase your daily happiness than to plan one big thing that will give you temporary high levels of happiness. If you can make a change in your daily commute to work, or the place you eat lunch every day, or the amount of time you spend with your kids before school in the morning – something that improves your everyday living – that will have a much larger impact on your overall happiness than working long hours to save up money to go on a two week holiday to the Galapagos. (End of happiness lecture.)

Some of our woolly monkey friends at the Puyo monkey preserve

When you live in a van, you shower wherever you can!

Lush green jungle

Lilly's playdate with a sea lion in the Galapagos

John & Lilly snorkeling through Kicker rock in the Galapagos

PERU

We drove 3,550 miles over 5.5 months in Peru.
May to October, 2019

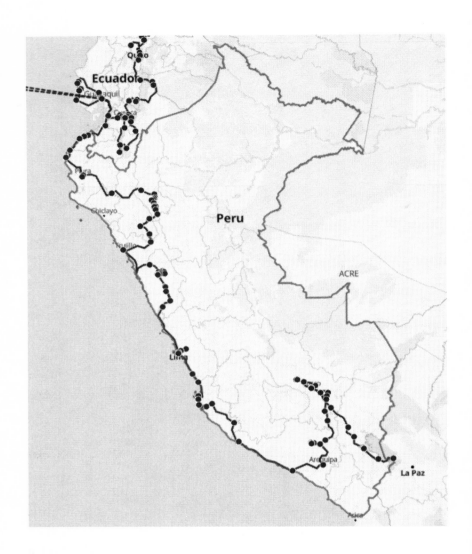

30

BROKEN DOWN AND
STUCK AT THE BORDER

C LUNK! CLUNK! CLUNK!
We are parked in no-man's-land between Peru and Ecuador when the van starts making violent crashing bangs from the engine bay. It sounds like there's an angry gremlin hiding inside our engine swinging a hammer around.

This is not good...

John, Lilly and I have been stamped *out* of Ecuador, but not *into* Peru yet.

The van is still stamped *into* Ecuador, and we can't stamp it out without driving 4 km to the customs office. But, it sounds like the engine will explode whenever we turn it on.

There are only three days left on our Ecuador visa and there's a $390 per day fine if the van overstays.

We stand outside under the blazing sun, staring into the engine, sweat dripping down our backs, and realize that it's Saturday so no mechanic will be open. And thus begins the worst two weeks of our trip. I guess our luck had to run out at some point.

John starts poking around in the engine while I research mechanics and look for the closest place to camp. It is miserably hot with the blazing sun directly overhead and nowhere to hide – why did this have to happen right at the border in no-man's-land? We are feeling sorry for ourselves when I glance up and see a Venezuelan family stagger past carrying all their worldly belongings in haphazard plastic bags and broken rolling suitcases, trying to get away from an unlivable country. It's a good perspective check for us. We are safe, healthy, and have useful passports. First priority, get all *four* of us legally into the same country!

John gingerly turns the engine back on – we are pretty sure no country would accept a foreign vehicle being towed across their border – and the angry gremlin recommences his banging. We limp the few kilometers to the Ecuador Customs office to check Vancito out, and then to the Peruvian offices to check all of us in. It's the usual bureaucratic dance to get all passports and the van permit completed, but the confusion and hassle feel trivial compared to the unknown problem awaiting in our home's engine. With no other options available, we drive the van to the first beach camp we find, grimacing at the painful crashing noise constantly emanating from within and wondering if it's causing permanent damage to our home.

We spend two nights camped on the beach near the border, at an ironically beautiful campsite directly on the sand which we don't appreciate, while John tries to figure out what's going on. After various tests and hours of online research using our weak cell phone signal, he concludes that we need a scanner to do a "buzz test" to see if the injectors are buggered.

We take a public bus into the nearby town of Puyango to visit mechanics and see if anyone has this scanner, but it's impossible to get a straight answer out of anyone. We have no choice but to pick the best of the poor options, and we call a *grua* (tow truck) to tow us there. It takes one hour to go 14 miles, but we make it to Alex the mechanic's shop. They are of course all out to lunch.

Day One in our New Home

At 2 p.m. Alex returns from lunch and listens to the engine. He states with confidence, "It's definitely a mechanical problem, not electrical.

We don't need the scanner, we'll disassemble the engine to see which part is broken." John explains to me that this means they think the actual engine block is damaged, which would be impossible to rebuild here.

My heart falls into my stomach.

Then my brain goes a million miles an hour asking John questions to which he doesn't know the answer, "What if we could get it to Lima, could they repair the engine there?"

"I don't know."

"Would it have to get all the way to the US to get repaired?"

"I don't know."

"How expensive is it to rebuild a motor? It is even worth it?"

"I don't know."

"Is this the end of our trip?" I finally ask, with tears in my eyes.

"No!" he states definitively.

I turn my mind to worst case scenario planning – could we ship the van from Peru to the US if this is unfixable? And to logistics management – where can we stay in this dusty border town while we are dealing with this?

Meanwhile, mechanics start swarming over and under and inside the van, and John tries to oversee the tearing apart of his baby. The language barrier is significant. Most of the words are things I don't know even in English so our conversation is a repetitive version of something like this:

John, "Ask him if he thinks it could be the camshaft."

Mary, "Um... what's a camshaft?"

John, "It's like a rod with lobes on it that spins around and pushes the valves open in sync."

Mary, in Spanish, to the mechanic, "Could it be that thing that's like a long stick with bits coming off that goes around and around and makes the valves work?"

Mechanic looks bewildered

Not much progress is made on disassembling the engine that afternoon. At 6 p.m., closing time, we sadly pack up a couple of backpacks and say goodnight to Vancito. Alex doesn't want us sleeping in the van in his shop, plus the temperature here would make that unbearable.

We dodge rusting cars and piles of dirt to walk along the side of the road – there's no sidewalk here – to the local hotel. This dusty town of Puyango has two hotels and, shockingly, one Airbnb rental but they didn't answer my email.

Our $13 room has just enough space for two mattresses pushed together, with no shelf or table to set anything. With our backpacks taking up the precious little floor area, there is only space to step into the room and then lie down on the beds. In the tiny bathroom is a cold water trickle of a shower. When I sit on the toilet, my knees are bumping into the sink. Air conditioning doesn't seem to exist anywhere in this town. But look on the bright side – we have wifi, which John uses until late in the night trying to figure out what could be happening to this, allegedly indestructible, engine of ours.

Day Two

We return at 8 a.m. on the dot and John has renewed energy to plead his case that the problem may be electrical, not mechanical. Alex and team want to remove the engine and open it up to see what's wrong inside, at which point we'd need to find somewhere that could machine new parts to rebuild the engine. This shop definitely can't do that, plus Alex has already told us that he can't get replacement parts for anything that's broken in there. Taking apart the engine here kinda feels like signing up for open heart surgery in a small rural medical clinic.

John insists we do the scanner diagnostic before they touch the van again, so finally Alex sheepishly hands us a box and walks away. Inside lie the scanner tool and an instruction manual, looking new and unused. Now we understand why he didn't want to do the scan – he has no idea how! So we spend the day googling how to use this device and solving myriad stupid technology issues...

It can only run on Windows, how do we do that on a Mac?

The scanner only works via WiFi but its software only sees Blue-tooth-connected devices.

It's asking for an activation code, anyone know how to find that? (Alex suddenly disappears.)

I've bought two other scanner apps but they're not compatible with this scanner device.

It's a frustrating day. Especially because we could buy the tool we need for $5 on Amazon and receive it the next day, if we were in the US. Eventually we give up on the scanner and attempt manual tests instead to figure out if there's an electrical problem.

"Hold this wire, and touch it to this terminal," commands John. "Your hands are dry, right?" So I contort my body to fit on the floor between the two front seats of the van, and reach my arm into the engine compartment. I'm clutching a wire and pushing it against the terminal that John indicated, while he is trying to fiddle another wire through a small opening to the other terminal to test the resistance, when a hand reaches up through the opening in the floor below us asking for our flashlight. I pass the mystery hand a light and John barely has time to mutter out loud, "I wonder if I should check what they're doing down there," when we hear an almighty horrible crunch. John curses, jumps out of the van and wriggles underneath to join the three mechanics all desperately searching for what they broke. We never find anything. This does not fill me with confidence.

We ultimately conclude that the buzz test cannot be done with this scanner, and we can't learn anything definitive from the manual tests. But, we do convince Alex that we think it's more likely to be an electrical problem and to STOP taking apart the engine! Alex has his guys put back everything they took out on day one, and promises to find a better scanner the next day.

I am so impressed by John chasing after three different mechanics, each possibly helping or damaging the van, while corralling the boss to get information about what tools he has, in Spanish, while conversing with Ford mechanics in an online forum that he's joined, in English, and remaining calm and positive throughout the whole experience.

And part of my distracted brain is pleased to notice our teamwork, without blame or bickering, in this stressful situation.

* * *

The restaurants in this tiny town are just the front room of someone's house with a few plastic chairs and tables set out, and two or three options for a meal. On our first night, we are eating at one of these little dining areas, when the woman at the next table turns around to stare, then asks, "Disculpe, usted es Mary?" (Are you Mary?)

John and I look at each other in amazement. We're in a tiny border town in Peru, at a hole-in-the-wall restaurant, and a stranger is recognizing me?!

Turns out she's the owner of the Airbnb I emailed. She says she guessed who we are because there are no other foreigners in this town – no surprise there! We get to chatting and she insists we come to her house the next day for dinner with her family. Kindness of strangers strikes again!

So after another hard day at the office (mechanic's shop), we go home (dump hotel) to shower and change, and then walk to Dalila's house for dinner. She cooks us a feast of shellfish, stew, and plantains, and I bring over my baking supplies to make banana bread for dessert. She says it's the first time she's ever used her oven! We adults stay up late chatting about work and life and family, while all the kids watch TV. What an unexpected ray of sunshine in an otherwise very depressing 48 hours.

Day Three

A mysterious man in an orange jumpsuit appears and sits in the driver's seat, messing with the van. He refuses to communicate with us, but we soon hear the sounds of the buzz test that we've been trying to do the past two days. Four of our eight injectors are not "buzzing" which either means all four have died at the same time (unlikely) or the computer that powers them is broken (more likely). Finally, we have information!

Side note: John would like to point out, like a proud father, that his van successfully drove 50 miles on only four cylinders. End of side note.

We need an oscilloscope to test the IDM computer, but no one in this town has one. Alex says he knows someone in Lima who has one and organizes for this guy to fly up to us. They also recommend bringing four replacement injectors so we can try them out to see if that solves the problem.

We make the decision to trust this remote guy because Alex says he knows him, and because we don't have much other choice. The guy, Celestino, insists we deposit the full cost, S/2,200 (about $650), into his bank account. This involves multiple trips to banks in the next town and wastes another day.

Day Four

Once the cash is deposited, Celestino calls to request that we pay for the flights. An argument ensues about what the S/2200 included. Alex hands me his phone to deal with Celestino directly. He first demands the full cost of the flights, then says we can pay half, but ultimately I say we'll pay no more until the guy arrives. He books his technician on a flight out that evening. We lose another day.

By now, we have settled into a depressing routine. We wake up in the crap hotel and put back on the dirty, sweaty, grease-stained clothes from the day before – because why bother putting on clean clothes when they'll instantly get dirty and we have no way to do laundry anyway? Then we pack up and check out of the hotel, just in case this is the day we fix the van and drive away. You gotta think positive!

We look for somewhere to get breakfast that isn't fried fish. We know one place that can make us eggs and so we go every day, but they never get our order right. I'm impressed that they can come up with so many variations on the same theme without hitting the one we actually order.

We walk up the hill in the hot morning sun with our backpacks on, dodging huge piles of dirt, bags of trash, plastic littered everywhere, random ankle-breaker holes in the ground, skinny street dogs, the occasional open sewer, and ladies selling gas in plastic bottles because there's no gas station here. We also need to constantly jump out of the way of traffic passing us within inches because there's no sidewalk.

We arrive at Alex's shop and greet all the employees, who know us well. Lilly sits in her chair in a corner and plugs her headphones into her iPad, while John and I talk to Alex to discuss the plan for the day. I try to do some school with Lilly, but I jump up every time I see John communicating with anyone so I can help translate. We are both so worried that the van could be unfixable and this stress weighs heavily on us the whole time we're at Alex's shop. Lilly, however, always looks on the bright side, "At least I get to watch my iPad all the time now!" she says with a mischievous smile.

After another failed day of trying to fix our home, we pack up the backpacks again and trudge back through the dirt to the same hotel, "Would you like your usual room #9, señora?" for a shower and sleep, before starting all over again the next day.

This is one of the most depressing towns I've ever stayed in. I try to appreciate the life experience of being here, but it's hard to muster up the philosophical appreciation. It's eye-opening to think about people who live here their whole lives.

Day Five

The tech doesn't arrive until 2 p.m. Then he spends two hours trying to get his computer to connect to our van. He calls his boss and figures out that he needs a password to download the right information and the boss won't give it over the phone. I call Celestino to demand the password but he won't answer the phone. Ultimately, we decide we can at least try out the injectors, even if we can't diagnose the problem.

We open the injectors. They are used and stained, with old gaskets. What have we paid for? Celestino won't respond to phone calls. We want to refuse them but Alex says we should at least try them because if they work then we'll know that the injectors were the problem. John figures out how to install them because the tech has never done it on a vehicle like ours.

Around 8 p.m. the new injectors are in, we turn on the engine, and oil sprays out wildly everywhere from the turbo. The old gaskets on these used injectors are letting the oil leak out and potentially we have now just broken our turbo, in addition to whatever problem we already had.

This is probably the lowest point of our trip.

Everyone else has gone home. We sit down on some folding chairs in the dark workshop with Alex, his wife, and the visiting tech, and have a long discussion about what to do. Alex feels bad for having recommended Celestino. He's pushing for us to have the van towed 30 hours to Lima to make them do the work. John and I are so distrustful of this guy that we say absolutely not. Plus, we are fairly sure that we need a new IDM computer, which this guy does not have in Lima, so it wouldn't help us anyway.

John announces that he's going to fly to the US to bring back a new IDM computer and eight new injectors. I bring out a bottle of whiskey and we all toast to the decision.

John and the tech get to work removing the faulty injectors. Since John's going to buy a new IDM computer anyway, Alex breaks open our existing one to find... water inside! It took a week but we finally know what the real problem is. It could have been so simple if we'd had the right diagnostic tools initially.

(We later learn that Celestino fires the tech and the tech's boss. And, after much arguing from me, he reluctantly reimburses us one-third of the money we paid him. What a crook.)

At 11 p.m. we stagger out exhausted. We walk down the trash-covered, sidewalk-less street, dodging limping dogs and three-wheeled taxis. We go to our usual dump of a hotel and they have no room for us. What?! This zero-traffic-light town has other visitors besides us?

We go to the only other hotel in town and check-in. It's even cheaper than our usual place – all this time we've been paying $1 more than we needed to! Ha! We walk upstairs and fall into bed. Lilly notices there are only two pillows, so I send her back downstairs to ask the reception desk guy for another pillow. She returns with him, and the ensuing conversation is hilarious.

Hotel employee, "Your room only has two pillows."

Mary, "Correct, can we have another one please?"

"No. The Venezuelans took your pillow."

"Ok... so someone took a pillow, don't you have any others we could have?"

"No."

"What about from the other room you offered us when we checked in?"

"Ah, yes. Room five." A wistful look passes across his eyes as he reminisces about room five. "That's a better room. It has three pillows. You should have taken that room, I told you that room was better."

"Um, no you didn't, but anyway can we have a pillow from that room now we're here?"

"No, you're here now, can't move, too late."

"We don't need to move rooms, can't we stay in this room and take a pillow from that room?"

He looks flabbergasted at this wild idea, "No, we can't move the pillows!"

"But, we paid for a room for three people...?"

The guy disappears for a few minutes and returns with the sacred pillow from room five. I've totally lost my noodles at this point. I have to hide in the bathroom while the man is giving John the pillow because I'm laughing so hard he'll think I'm insane.

We all shower and I get into bed, but then I hear Lilly cry out from the bathroom.

"What's wrong?" I ask, knowing that she's exhausted and has stared at her iPad for the better part of a week, so isn't in a great state of mind.

"I cut my leg sitting on the cracked toilet seat!" she cries. Oh wow. Could it get any worse? (The cut did get slightly infected over the next two days, but we didn't have to amputate anything, and the hotel was forever known as the CrackedSeat hotel.)

Day Six

The next morning, Lilly and I are brushing our teeth when we hear a loud, rhythmic moaning coming through the thin wall from the room next door. Clearly sounds of shagging. I am wondering if I should say anything to Lilly when she stops brushing, cocks her head sideways and reports, "It sounds like that lady also cut herself on the toilet seat." Her expression is serious and concerned. I am laughing so hard I choke on my toothpaste.

* * *

Since we can no longer do anything at the mechanic's, we leave Vancito behind and I find us a rental house on the beach about an hour away. It has a small pool, sunset views, and even a nine-year-old girl living on the premises. What a change from the CrackedSeat hotel!

I spend our first day there in a whirlwind of research. Unfortunately, foreign car parts are not allowed into Peru, so I contact customs and shipping experts locally to see what we can do. Everyone tells me the parts will be confiscated if we try to mail them to ourselves here. But I do find some accounts of people who've flown in with car parts in their luggage and made it through customs.

So we choose between almost-definite-failure and unknown odds, concluding that John will fly to the US and attempt a smuggling mission. It will all come down to whether he can get through customs without being searched on arrival.

It's a hectic journey for John. Four flights, one night in Lima, one night in Miami, one night back in Lima, only sleeping a few hours each night. But he manages to get the IDM computer, eight new injectors (because ours were damaged in all the chaos), a scanner (in case of future issues), and some tools that Alex requested for his shop.

While waiting for his luggage to arrive at the carousel in Lima airport, John studies his escape path through customs, as if plotting his escape through a guarded jail. There are two customs agents watching everyone pass, and most people are allowed through without being searched. John's hopes are raised. Once he gets his luggage, he waits until one of the guards – I mean agents – appears distracted, then tries to saunter casually, but quickly, through the narrow hallway.

"Stop!" calls a young man in a uniform, suspiciously eyeing John's bulging backpack and two cardboard boxes.

And so begins John's toughest Spanish test yet.

The two customs agents grill him on what he is carrying and its value. They both state, with absolute certainty, that he cannot bring car parts into Peru. John argues. The men don't give an inch. It's against the rules. You cannot do it.

It's impossible to convey the importance of these obscure car parts to someone unfamiliar with our plight, but John keeps repeating the Spanish sentences he's memorized, "My family is stuck here unless I can get these parts to our van." The customs guy becomes slightly more friendly, but explains that no one can bring in more than $500 worth of car parts, and this is obviously more than that.

"I'm not leaving this airport without these parts," is John's final word on the matter.

So he is escorted to another room in the airport to meet the big boss. There he sees another customs agent, presumably the boss from the look of her fancier uniform, arguing with a man about his luggage. She glances over as John walks in, clearly annoyed that he's distracting her from her current goal, "What is all this stuff worth?" she barks, pointing to John's boxes.

"About $450," replies John. Obviously.

And she waves him out the door.

While John is enduring his mission, I'm back at the rental house with Lilly. Did I mention it has a pool?

I'm sitting outside reading while Lilly and the Venezuelan caretaker's daughter play in the pool together. The other girl's parents are nowhere in sight. As the sun slides behind the horizon in the distance, the other girl's dad walks up to chat with me.

"Wow, I can't believe my daughter is in the deep end of the pool." he remarks.

"Why is that surprising?" I ask him.

"Because she can't swim."

I can't conceal my surprise and criticism. She's been playing in the deep end of the pool on an inflatable toy with no parent in sight for 30 minutes, but she can't swim?!

The dad walks over to the pool to congratulate his daughter. Just then, she falls off her inflatable into the deep end. By now, it's dark enough out that I can't clearly see what's happening. I start to get up but stop, because her dad is standing right there, so the girl must be fine, right? Then I see Lilly swim over and dive under the other girl, so I jump up to investigate.

Just then, there's a blur of action as someone else comes sprinting from the other end of the property and leaps into the pool with all her clothes on. She grabs the girl and pulls her out. The girl is crying hysterically, taking great heaving breaths of air, and I see Lilly swimming away safely.

I am totally confused, but I later learn that the dad cannot swim either! The owner of the property knew this, so raced over when she saw what was happening. The dad stood at the edge of the pool watching his daughter struggle, but was frozen in fear. What an awful feeling that must have been. Lilly saw what was happening and told me that she swam down under the girl and tried to push her up from below. I praise her intentions but caution her about the danger of such action, and I pay much closer attention to the pool the next day.

* * *

Back to Alex's shop.

Back to the CrackedSeat hotel.

Back to our "favorite" breakfast restaurant.

We walk up the dusty road to find that Vancito has been pushed out into the street to make way for other customers while we were gone.

So, John replaces eight injectors and one computer on a dirt road outside the mechanic's shop in the full sun by himself. Well, I stand behind him holding an umbrella to help reduce the heat, but that doesn't count for much. Even Alex is impressed, "Un muy buen mecánico," he comments, as John turns down his offer of a job in Puyango.

The buzz test now sounds perfect but the engine is burning oil, causing smoke to pour out as we drive. We hope it's just the remaining oil puddle from the crappy injectors that we briefly installed, but it's possible that they damaged the turbo, which would mean a whole new problem to solve.

So, we spend yet another night in the clean, scenic, delightful town of Puyango. We have a joyful reunion with the reception desk lady at the CrackedSeat hotel, and give our breakfast restaurant one more chance to get "three fried eggs" right (she doesn't). This time, there is a quinceanera party going on across the road from our hotel, and the music is so loud that our walls are reverberating all night. We turn on sound machine apps on both our phones and push the fan as close to us as possible, but it's still impossible to sleep. It seems a fitting end to our ordeal in Puyango.

The next morning, after about two hours of sleep, John drives around until the oil has all burned off. Our new scanner is still reporting two concerning codes, but our online Ford mechanic support team says it's probably nothing, and John points out that Alex wouldn't be able to help anyway, so we decide it's time to get the hell out of Puyango.

We drive slowly and nervously down the coast, stopping at a few beach camps on the way. We're overjoyed to be living in our home again, and even more overjoyed that the van runs smoothly every time we turn it on. In fact, John reports that it sounds better than before. Who knows how long Vancito has been running on a computer full of water?

But we have a new level of respect for the importance of the van functioning. John decides he wants to solve two potential problems that have been nagging at him for the past year, just in case. We don't want to find ourselves in a pile of poo(yango) ever again.

So in the first big city, Piura, we find a large, professional mechanic where we make two big upgrades. Vancito gets a new diesel tank (old one may have been leaking paint chips) and air intake system (old one was letting dust in). John, of course, does most of the work himself, parked in the mechanic's shop for shade and equipment and occasional advice.

Ever wondered what it's like living in a mechanic's shop for a week?

We wake up in eerie silence, surrounded by shells of vehicles with their insides eviscerated and lying all over the floor. I weave my body between car doors and hop over various extricated car parts to make my way to the toilet. We cook breakfast on our stove that is wedged between our van and the neighboring broken-down car with its hood open and engine missing. I wash our dishes in the communal sink while someone is banging on a piece of metal a few feet away from me. But this feels like a five-star holiday compared to Puyango! We're sleeping in our own home, and the mechanic's shop is larger and cleaner and has a bathroom, but the main difference is that we're here by choice, doing preventative maintenance that we can control. I confidently look forward to our departure, rather than worry endlessly about our future.

And, in a pattern that is becoming normal whenever we have problems, John meets a guy who drives him all around town helping to find a particular part he needs and then insists we join his family for dinner. We gratefully accept and enjoy a fried chicken dinner with him and his wife and kids one evening after a day in the mechanic's shop.

Finally, after a month stuck with mechanics near the border, we are ready to explore this new country.

31

RUINS AND REMOTE PUEBLOS OF NORTHERN PERU

P eru. You immediately think of the famous Machu Picchu ruins and the Incan empire. But you never hear about the dozens of remote pre-Incan ruins up in the far north of the country. They are sprinkled all over the cliff faces and hilltops, usually down long dirt roads with no hotel or restaurant nearby, and loosely governed by whatever local community lives the closest or cares the most. It turns out to be a perfect area for vanlife exploration – we drive down many dodgy dirt roads and see very few other tourists, but always find ourselves surrounded by curious and welcoming people.

Our first night in this region, we drive later than usual because we're so excited to be back in the van after a month of van troubles in Puyango. It's starting to get dark, so we pull off the highway into a village and I ask some elderly ladies by the side of the road if we can park there for the night. They direct us to the main plaza, where we see a church that looks like it hasn't been opened in years, and a couple of houses. When we park and emerge from the van, we're immediately surrounded by boys who pepper us with questions.

"Where did you come from?"

"How do you say my name in English?"

"What's 7 times 9?"

They are so curious! We invite them inside for van tours and answer their questions. I crouch down to lay out a map of Peru on a park bench and am instantly crushed by a pile of kids crowding over me to see what I have. I show them where their village is and how we drove here, and I point out the size and grandeur of their country compared to little Ecuador.

Two adults walk over to see what the commotion is about and shake my hand. I ask them if we'd be bothering anyone if we spend the night in our van here, and they emphasize how safe their village is and how welcome we are – two phrases that we become accustomed to hearing over the next two weeks.

Previously on this trip, we only wild camped when far from any civilization, but after this experience we commonly park our house on the main plaza of whichever village is closest to the ruins. I always walk around first and ask a few people if it's ok, and then we settle in to watch the daily life of these highland villagers. These camping experiences turn out to be just as educational and thought-provoking as the ruins we've come to see.

Traveling further south we veer off the main road into the town of Mud. I mean, LaMud. Pronounced "la mood." Either way, it tries to live up to its name by providing us with our second consecutive day of rain, turning the all-dirt roads to mood, I mean mud.

We want to visit the remote ruins of Pueblo de los Muertos nearby and, after some confused driving in circles and even more confusing pointing from locals, we finally start up the correct dirt track. But about 30 minutes later we find ourselves almost sliding off the side of a steep, muddy, gooey trail in the pouring rain.

And then the unthinkable happens… John says it's too dangerous to continue, and turns around! *Who are you and what have you done with my husband?* I think, but do not utter aloud, knowing full well that he'll be the one digging us out of the mud if we get stuck.

So we pat ourselves on the back for being so sensible and cautious, and head out to the more popular ruins of Karajia instead. I locate the ruins on my phone map and hit "navigate," then sit back to enjoy the scenery for the 30 minute drive.

Two hours later I am starting to feel a little nervous about my lax navigational efforts. Upon closer examination, there are two tracks to Karajia. We are on the north one which we discover is not really fit for vehicular traffic, at least not in this rain that's turning the narrow dirt path to mud. We haven't seen a single other vehicle, and we've been in 4WD the whole way. I admit to John that we were probably supposed to go the other way. He valiantly shrugs it off and says we're committed now, so we continue slowly ahead.

We come around a corner and I gasp aloud at how deep the mud is ahead. "I don't think…" I begin, but John is already charging into it.

The van slows down and teeters around violently in and out of the depths of black goo, like a bicycle hitting sand, but keeps plowing forward. Suddenly there is a sickening crunch sound from underneath us and we feel some large object dragging beneath the van, tearing and bumping in the mud.

"Stop! You're going to break something!" I shout.

"If I stop now, we'll be stuck in this mud forever," comes the grim response.

So John continues dragging the unknown part of our van through the mud underneath us until we make it out to the other side. We both jump out and look underneath, terrified at what we might find.

Luckily, it's only the storage box that holds our climbing gear.

The good news: it did not damage anything else during its violent and protracted departure from the undercarriage of the van.

The bad news: it is still very much attached to the frame of the van, rendering us effectively attached to the mud beneath it. John spends an hour lying in the mud with a hacksaw before we are able to drive away. I don't comment on the irony of his turning back on the other dirt road only to end up here.

It is now approaching sunset. Our home is full of muddy items – the gear that had been in the storage box, our shoes, and John's body from the waist down – as we continue toward the town of Karajia only a few miles away, hoping to find a place to camp.

I zoom in on the map to discover that the final 500 meters look like a child's violent scribbling. I check the elevation at the beginning and end of the zig-zag to conclude that we are headed for some insanely steep switch-backs. We come around a bend in the road and spy the final ascent.

It looks about 45 degrees. It's rocky and muddy. I can barely walk up it. It involves three hairpin bends that will require multi-point turns to get the van around. I declare firmly, "We are not driving up that, let's sleep right here and turn around tomorrow."

John walks all the way to the top of the climb – really it would be far too generous to call this thing a road – and returns ten minutes later grinning, "I think we can make it."

I know my husband well, so I give him the ultimate test, "So, do you want Lilly in the van with you, or outside with me?"

When he says it doesn't matter, I know he must really think it's safe. Personally, I feel sick at the idea of sitting in our gigantic van teetering up that steep trail. So I get out and run ahead, while John chugs slowly up the hill without incident. It's a huge relief to pull into the tiny village and park along the edge of the main square.

As usual, we talk to the locals who emphasize how safe their town is and welcome us to sleep there. They also invite us into the one-room building that serves as the town's only restaurant. I feel like I'm in a Western movie when the three of us walk through the doors and everyone inside turns to stare. However, instead of reaching for their guns, the locals shuffle around to make space for us on the few chairs set up inside, and a woman offers us beers. It is freezing cold here at almost 10,000 feet elevation, and everyone is distracted watching a football game on a small TV, so we opt for hot teas back at our van instead.

It's such a relaxing walk to the ruins of Karajia the next morning, after the heart-pounding drive to get here. From the trail, we can see five complete sarcophagi, but from online photos we see that there used to be seven. We are told that they are gradually falling down from earthquakes or simply old age. From the plethora of human bones we see lying beside the trail, it's clear that there isn't much maintenance.

Each sarcophagus holds one mummified person, tied tightly with ropes to hold him in the fetal position. The ancient people believed that the dead would go on to a new life and should arrive in the fetal position inside a new mother's womb. The mummies themselves are all gone, either looted or moved to the Leymabamba museum, which we visit later.

We drive back on the *other* road from Karajia to LaMud – which is an easy 30 mins instead of the terrifying three hours we did the day before – and find a little tourist office in town. We ask the lone employee, Roxana, how to get to the Pueblo de los Muertos ruins that we tried to visit a couple days earlier. She says only about 100 people per year visit them, so she's not familiar with the road conditions, but guesses it will be better tomorrow after a day of no rain.

We decide to give it another try, so Roxana gives us a key that will let us through the final gates into the ruins themselves. She gives us her cell phone number and says to text her when we get back to return the key. I like this laid-back village security!

The drive is much better than a few days ago and we make it to the top of the dirt road without issue. Then we walk along a beautiful trail on the edge of an enormous canyon, enjoying views of Gocta Falls in the distance, and spying smaller versions of the Karajia sarcophagi in the cliff across from us. Eventually the trail switchbacks down steeply and crosses over a pass into the next canyon.

The trail gets progressively narrower, with the hillside rising to our right and a steep drop-off to our left. We walk carefully, with Lilly in between us, until we reach a dead end. There's a cliff-face in front of us with no way around it. To the right is a vertical wall extending up, and to the left is a cliff face dropping down.

But... there's a small door in the middle of this blank rock face. We look at each other in disbelief. John reaches into his pocket for the key that we got from the tourist office lady, and he fiddles it into the gate lock. It opens! It's a bit of an Alice in Wonderland moment – stepping through a portal into a blank cliff face using a magic key entrusted to us by the queen of hearts, I mean, LaMud.

This would be a good time to remind you that John and I are rock climbers. We've each spent hundreds of hours clinging to cliff faces, or hanging out on narrow ledges, almost always with a rope attached to us. Being up on the narrow ledge of Pueblo de los Muertos is like being a couple of pitches up on a climb and stopping for a lunch break at a natural ledge, except, no rope!

I am absolutely gobsmacked that they let random tourists like us just wander around up here. It is a cliff face with at least 100 feet of vertical drop below. The path is at times less than *one foot* wide. It's crumbling dirt with stones piled underneath for strength, and it was built ~1000 years ago. The builders clearly did an excellent job, but I'm pretty sure it wouldn't pass building code. Not even in Peru. Probably not in the last century.

We escort Lilly to one of the little rooms which are about eight feet wide, then take turns with her while the other one of us explores a little further. I love being up there because it feels like being up on a climb, sitting at a comfortable belay ledge watching the view, except with little caves and windows to explore. The human bones lying around make the experience just a little more unique.

We return to LaMud that afternoon without incident, and return the magic key.

Despite the name, LaMud is a lovely little spot. One evening, we walk past a lady cooking something mysterious in the street. I ask what it is, but don't recognize the name. I try to ask basic questions like, "Is it sweet or salty?" but she just keeps repeating the name of it.

I'm about to give up when an old man on a nearby bench shouts, "Here, try mine." I look over and he's ripped off a piece of his and is holding it out to me between his fingers. You sometimes have to throw away thoughts of germs on a trip like this. I thank him and put it in my mouth. Oh, it's like a sweet doughnut! I tell the lady I'll buy some. She reaches her bare hand into a mushy red substance and digs out a little. She shapes it into a circle like a skinny doughnut and drops it in the pan of oil, then repeats this process five times. I get my plate of six and go sit on the bench next to the friendly man and hand him one.

We sit and chat about this town and our travels. He calls his wife over. School kids appear because the afternoon session just let out. He shouts across the plaza to one of them, "Come meet my new friends!" His daughter walks over, an embarrassed teenager, and her dad tries to make her practice English with us. An ancient man with no teeth comes out of a nearby store to join his friend whom we're sitting with. I ask him how big the town is and he says about 500 people, and that he knows "everyone." They all know about the big white van that appeared in the field on the edge of their town a couple of nights ago, and emphasize that we are welcome to camp there. It's a beautiful late afternoon with the sun starting to set, and I appreciate the experience of hanging out chatting to these varied characters – all because I accepted some mystery food from a stranger.

We head south from the LaMud area to go to the most famous ruins around here – Kuelap – known as The Machu Picchu of the North. It is incredibly organized and busy compared to the middle-of-nowhere we just came from. This is not, "Here's the key and just bring it back tomorrow." There are guards stationed everywhere shouting rules:

No eating!

You must walk the loop in a clockwise direction!

The last bus leaves at 3:30 so you have to keep moving!

The ruins are interesting, but we prefer our experiences at the lesser-known ones. Kuelap will hold a stronger place in my memory for the little celebration we had for Lilly's eighth birthday than for its namesake ruins.

At this point, we've seen enough ruins that we know how they look from afar, and we start noticing them all over the place. John will be driving along and suddenly stop dead in the road. (It's so deserted here that there's no need to pull over.) He'll grab the binoculars from under his seat and, sure enough, we spot walls and windows and doorways hundreds of feet up on a cliff face in front of us. They are simply abandoned up there. No one is maintaining the structures or trying to study them. It is mesmerizing staring up at these impossibly high buildings, still clinging to the cliff face after thousands of years, imagining the lives of the people back then.

We continue south from Kuelap and detour to visit one more little village reminiscent of LaMud, this one called Revash. These ruins are similar to Pueblo de los Muertos except they don't hand out the gate key to any old tourists, so we only see it from far below. But our time in the village itself proves to be far more interesting than the ruins.

In the afternoon sunset light, walking back up the hill toward the van, we see a little sign "Restaurant" tacked up on a mud-brick wall of a house. We poke our heads inside. It's a simple house with dirt floors but the main room has two tables set out each with four chairs. I ask the man if they have any food. "Come back in half an hour and my wife will make you something," he replies.

Back up in the main plaza we are the entertainment for the whole town as we attempt to find a level spot to park our van for sleeping. John circumnavigates the square while I follow behind on foot, eyeing the sloping ground. Each time he stops the van, a friendly face pokes out of the house in front of him, welcoming him to camp there.

Once parked, we return to the "restaurant" and the family starts cooking for us. While we wait, I peek into the kitchen and see an open fire powered by leña, and reflect again on how easy our propane stove is compared to how most people cook here.

Of course the family has several kids and Lilly quickly approaches the one nearest her age, "Quieres jugar?" (Do you want to play?) This refrain, repeated so many times on our trip, always makes me think of the first time back in Mexico when Lilly was the shy girl being asked to play. This time, the other girl is initially shy, but is soon grinning and following Lilly around. Within a few minutes, curiosity overcomes the rest of the family, and Lilly soon has a group of four kids chasing her around the house. She has become so much more confident with new kids in the past year.

Plates of *trucha* (trout) and chicken appear, heaped with rice and french fries. Usually in these high mountain towns we are served hot tea with dinner, whereas in the lowlands we always get whatever fruit juice is found locally. Tonight, however, steaming mugs of brown liquid are served. The señora explains that it's *cafe* (coffee) plus *cebada* (barley) plus a word I don't recognize that she says is like beans. They grind all these up and add hot water and presumably some sweetener. It's mysterious but pretty good.

The five kids run around the house/restaurant playing while John and I chat to the adults. (Of course there are no other guests here.) The grandmother tells us that her ancestors have lived here for generations. She shows us the walls that are made from wooden posts filled in with mud and straw, and the stone floor in the dining room that has a natural drain out to the road for easy washing. She explains that this little town has a small primary school, where her four grandkids go, but next year the oldest will have to walk an hour to the nearest secondary school. The community tries to encourage kids to stay by helping them build their own house when they turn 18, but she says most of them prefer to move to Lima.

It's hard to tear Lilly away from her new friends, but eventually we say thank you and goodbye, pay S/24 (about $7) and traipse up the dirt trail in complete darkness, thinking we'll be climbing into the van for the night.

As we approach the main square, we see people congregating and a man waving us over to join them. I recognize him as the father of the grandkids Lilly was playing with in the restaurant. They are having a *dansa*, practicing for a parade in the nearby larger town of Leymabamba. We are directed into the open area next to the tourist office (where we had earlier been advised to camp for the night because "no one would be using it" – I'm so relieved we didn't!), to find most of the town milling around waiting for the dansa to start.

An older gentleman immediately welcomes us and introduces himself. Someone runs off and reappears carrying a bench, telling us to make ourselves comfortable, even though everyone else is standing. I put Lilly on my lap and gesture to the older man to join us on the bench. A group of about 15 boys shuffles into position, with bells hanging off their ankles and wrists, and they start stomping in time to a single drum beat.

The older man tells me that this is a traditional dance passed down over many generations, and that he did this very same dance when he was a boy. He was born here and has lived here his whole life. The town has 290 people and everyone knows everyone. I ask about his kids and grandkids, but he reports sadly that they've mostly moved away to larger cities. It's the same story for small towns the world over, I think.

It's a somewhat surreal experience. Here we are in this tiny village high in the mountains far from any tourist hub. It's nighttime, there are no electric lights around us, and we are in a dirt floor building watching a dozen young boys stomping their feet, surrounded by friendly people who've all lived here for many generations. It feels like we've dropped in from the sky and we shouldn't really be here, but the locals make us feel welcome.

The next morning, it's intriguing to wake up to the sounds of villagers walking by, calling hello to each other as they pass. I look out my window to see a little girl by herself, maybe six years old, walking quickly and determinedly across the square with her backpack on, clearly in a rush to get to school – how do kids get so much more independent and responsible here?

The house next door to us starts playing some music. A small group of men gather on a bench to weave something. John goes to investigate – they are making the ankle bracelets full of bells that the boys were using in their dance last night.

An older lady approaches the van, curious about us. She's wearing the traditional attire of colorful poofy skirts, black heeled shoes, and thick tights. She asks me where we come from, how does the camper van work, can she see inside, where are we going. We chat outside in the sunlit square while John sips his coffee and Lilly snores in her cozy bed.

These are the experiences that make me so appreciative of van travel. We can wake up surrounded by day-to-day life of regular people, in a tiny town high in the Andes. The experiences are much more diverse and authentic when you can appear in the middle of a remote village and stay the night, without need for hotels or public transportation. Of course it helps that we speak the language and that our daughter breaks the ice by befriending local kids, but mostly it comes down to stumbling upon villages full of friendly people.

We stop in our first town in a while, Leymabamba with 3,500 people, to have a look at the mummies that were removed from the sarcophagi. It is somewhat creepy to see the skeletons lined up in rows on shelves in the museum, like canned food on a supermarket display.

I'm a little worried that Lilly will have nightmares, peering into the eyeless sockets of these skeletons with sparse hair still sprouting from their skulls. The hands are pressed either side of the face as part of the fetal positioning, and the mouths are agape, making it look like the classic horror movie shrieking face, except, in a skeleton! But Lilly says matter-of-factly, "They're just skeletons, they're not bad," so we let her inspect them. And, she's right. While she can't read Harry Potter #2 without having nightmares, she can look at real skeletons in various states of decay and have no issue sleeping that night.

We ask a few locals where we can camp for the night, and we're instructed to set up our house on the edge of a football field. Lilly immediately makes friends with a seven-year-old girl, and within 10 minutes has a small crowd of kids around her. I wonder what it will be like to be a normal kid in a crowd, rather than an interesting foreigner, when we eventually return to the US?

The next morning, Lilly disappears into the kids' house to play for a while, so I follow to check on her and introduce myself to the parents. It's eye-opening to walk around this little house looking for Lilly, imagining what it would be like to live here:

I open the front door and step inside to see that the floors are dirt just the same as outside. How would I keep anything clean if this were my house?

The walls are made of mud, but I notice kids' drawings stuck up there, just like we do on our fridge at home.

I peer through a doorway to see a separate room with two beds pushed together, covered in a pile of clothes. There is no sign of closets or dressers, so the beds function as the clothes storage.

Through the next doorway is an outdoor area that must be the kitchen. There is some leña piled closely together with a pot balanced on top – any time you want to cook, you have to start a fire. The toilet is an outhouse hole in the ground, and the laundry is a cold-water faucet outside with a nearby line to hang everything for drying.

It's always a reality check when I see inside a regular house in these rural areas.

Eventually I find Lilly playing with the *cuy* (guinea pigs) in a straw-filled pen behind the house. Most places we go, we see a little area dedicated to raising cuy near or inside the house. The owners throw them food and let them breed, and simply grab one for dinner now and then. Perhaps the local kids just don't see them as cute or fun to play with, like Lilly does?

The road to get back down into civilization in Cajamarca is unbelievable. It's the narrowest possible sliver of path you could cut out of a steep mountainside and still fit a car on it. As John white-knuckles around one particularly narrow section he says, "It feels like I'm 1,000 feet up on a rock climb, except I'm driving a van!" I've been on trails like this many times before, but always on foot.

John honks the horn at every bend in the road to warn oncoming traffic – there are actually signs telling you to do this! Luckily we only come across a handful of other cars the entire drive. Each time we do, there is a stare-down between drivers – who should reverse back to find a wide enough spot for passing? If you want the experience of hiking through high mountains, but without having to do any exercise, then this road is for you.

The frequent elevation changes are also impressive. We drive over a 12,000 foot pass, stopping to take in the view while shivering in the cold and gasping in the thin air. Then only a couple of hours later, we stop for lunch in a town and have to strip down to shorts and t-shirts and flip-flops. We swat mosquitoes while sweating in plastic chairs in a restaurant, and buy local mangoes from the overflowing tables out in the street. I thought Ecuador was geographically diverse, but Peru takes the cake!

We briefly touch in with civilization, for the first time in weeks, in the city of Cajamarca. It's famous for being where the Spanish captured the Inca King Atahualpa and demanded a ransom of gold for his release. The Incas provided the ransom but the Spanish killed the King anyway. And now they all speak Spanish instead of Quechua. Our modern-day battle here isn't with the Spanish, but with Customs and Immigration to get an extension on our visas. We fight valiantly through many flaming hoops of bureaucracy and win another 90 days.

This remote area of northern Peru has been a wonderful return to vanlife after our miserable month in Puyango. It turned out to be a great mix of adventure driving, remote camping, and cultural learning – more so from interactions with the people living in these remote villages than from the 1000-year-old ruins themselves. But we have seen enough ruins to last us until Machu Picchu – let's head into the mountains...

32

INTO THIN AIR

T he Cordillera Blanca, or White Mountain range, is a 200 km chunk of the Andes that contains an impressive network of hiking trails snaking between and over its many peaks. The combination of volcanic rock for fun climbing, high alpine lakes for jaw-dropping views, and the endless panorama of white mountain tops in every direction make this area one of my favorites of our entire trip to date.

The road to get here from the coast is an adventure in itself. Remember how I thought that road from Leymabamba to Cajamarca was so exciting? Ha! A walk in the park! This road is one lane and goes through countless long, dark tunnels cut through the rocky mountains.

Yes, one lane.

Long and dark.

No shoulder or traffic lights or anything to prevent head-on collisions in the middle of the tunnel.

How does that work, you ask? Some luck, some bravery, some peeing your pants.

I nicely solved the problem by sitting literally on the edge of my seat, with my nose pressed up against the windshield so that I would have an extra split second of time to warn John if I saw a car coming. That should do the trick, eh? There might have been some wet underpants too.

The other technique that we employed was to honk the horn like crazy around every bend and when entering every tunnel. We've noticed in this country that honking your horn is almost meaningless – drivers just randomly honk all the time, as if to say hello – but we hoped it might give an extra second of warning for an oncoming truck barreling toward us from the other direction in a one-lane tunnel.

By the end of the Cañon del Pato road, John was merrily tooting away on the horn every couple of minutes without hesitation – he's practically Peruvian now!

Having survived the road to get into the Cordillera Blanca, we stay a month hiking, climbing, and gaping at the scenery. After my bad experience at elevation on the volcano in Mexico, we decide to start with a test before doing any long hikes, so drive up to camp at Laguna Paron (4,200 m / 13,800 ft).

This is one of the more popular lakes in this area, getting a lot of day visitors but few who stay overnight. It's cold, high, and doesn't have much in the way of facilities, but we find a great spot for van camping. It's cloudy and we get some rain showers, but we luck out for a few hours of the impressive view. Everyone around here claims that it's the mountain from the Paramount Pictures logo.

We see a few local women tending campfires along the edge of the parking area, so we approach to see what they are selling. They are all wearing the voluminous, colorful skirts and surprisingly tall, formal top hats that we see on women everywhere in these mountains. It makes me pause and mentally examine my own attire as I walk toward them. I'm wearing:

- Black pants and sneakers – would only be worn by men around here. These women are all wearing skirts and stockings and black, low-heeled shoes.
- Puffy down jacket zipped up to my neck – renders me

entirely shapeless, compared to their fitted V-neck cardigans showing their curvy chests.

- Tight fitting black wool hat – this is so practical for this harsh environment, but the women all have airy top hats on, with glittering dangly earrings hanging from their ears.

I must look as strange to them as they look to me.

The women are boiling water in large tin pots balanced on rocks strategically positioned around firewood to form a stovetop. We buy some corn with fresh cheese from them and sit nearby to eat, giving us an unfortunate front row seat for the next event: The biggest pot of water is now boiling, so the lady goes to fetch a mesh bag that I hadn't noticed, tucked away behind the rocks. She carries the bag back to the pot of boiling water and we notice that it's squeaking and wriggling. She reaches in and pulls out a cute, furry *cuy* (guinea pig). We all look on in dread, unable to turn away, as if rubbernecking at a car crash.

I exhale a big sigh of relief when I realize she is *not* about to toss the living creature into the pot of boiling water, but then inhale again sharply as she starts casually sawing at its neck with a blunt knife. When it stops wriggling, she puts it on the plate and reaches into the bag to grab another one. Cut, drop, grab another, repeat. Once the entire bag is empty of wriggling cuteness, and the plate is full of motionless bloody bodies, she starts tearing off the fur from each body. At this point we decide to walk away.

It's thought-provoking to see her treating these animals the same way I treat an apple or a hunk of cheese. She's clearly been doing this her entire life and it's completely natural. It makes me wonder why I consider it wrong to kill this particular creature, but ok to kill a chicken? Who decides which animals are for eating, and which are for cuddling as pets?

Local folks will often ask us if we eat cuy. I always explain that, for us, cuy are pets like dogs or horses so we don't eat them. I ask if they ever eat dogs or horses? The response is violent head shaking and surprise along the lines of, "Of course we wouldn't do such a thing, what do you think we are, savages?"

I guess we all have our double standards, including me – I eat chicken one day (causing its death), and then feed a stray dog the next day (prolonging its life)... doesn't really make sense.

Since none of us has any issues with the elevation at Laguna Paron, we're excited to get off the roads and further into the mountains. We sign up for the Santa Cruz trek which is 50 km over four days – much more than Lilly has ever walked before! We join forces with a wonderful family who has kids about the same age as Lilly, and the three kids walk almost the entire way, making us parents exceedingly proud. Lilly (just turned 8) and Aviva (9) chatter nonstop as they walk, imagining dragons and fairies at every bend in the trail. Each day when we arrive at camp, the adults relax with hot tea but the two girls disappear down to the riverbank or into a tunnel of bushes and immediately start building fairy houses or a bakery or a store. I am so impressed at their imaginations and energy levels.

The scenery is stunning, the company is wonderful, and the style in which we do this trip is totally new to us: donkeys carrying all the bags and a cook preparing the meals and washing the dishes! It is amazing to wake up in the morning with a coca tea delivered to our tent, sit down to a hot breakfast that we don't have to carry or cook or clean up, then saunter up the trail with a small daypack holding only snacks and water. Wow, it will be hard to return to normal backpacking after this luxurious trip.

This hike marks the highest I have ever been. No, we didn't consume any mind-altering substances – we walked over a 15,600 foot pass! I've climbed the highest peaks in the continental US but they top out around 14,500 feet (Whitney, Shasta, and Rainier) so it is exciting to propel myself into a new stratosphere of the Earth, and I am so impressed at my little daughter walking up there with nary a complaint.

Less exciting, but more entertaining, is the HAF. A climbing buddy had warned us about High Altitude Flatulence when I told him how high we'd be sleeping, and I laughed at another of his silly jokes. But then in the middle of the night, lying in my sleeping bag wondering if I could brave the bone-chilling cold outside to go pee, I hear Lilly moan, roll over, and let out the loudest and longest fart I've ever heard from such a small body. Moments later John joins in on the loud sleep-farting, and, I have to admit, I am also contributing to this symphony. What is it about elevation? Perhaps the lower pressure outside our bodies causes the gas inside to escape more easily? Whatever the reason, HAF is real!

We so enjoy the four-day Santa Cruz trek that we are very tempted to do the ten-day Huayhuash trek next – after all, who knows if we'll ever be in this part of the world again with this free time and physical fitness? We talk to a dozen tour operators looking for another family to join us, but no luck. As we ponder whether to just go on the hike by ourselves, we stop at the nearby climbing area of Hatun Machay and remember… we are rock climbers, not hikers!

We arrive in the late afternoon and find a burned-down building, a partially destroyed toilet block, and a sea of tents pitched in a sloping field. Apparently, the guy who built the refugio house had a falling-out with the local community and got kicked out.

"If I can't have it, no one can!" we can imagine he shouted, as he doused the refugio in gasoline and tossed a match over his shoulder, driving away in an angry cloud of dust.

Now there's a new caretaker, Alsi, who doesn't have the anger issues of his predecessor. He's trying to rebuild the refugio but so far only has a cold water tap and a bucket-flush toilet. I am surprised to hear him call the faucet the *pila* – a word we haven't heard since Guatemala. He does have a very cute tiny puppy, so Lilly is in heaven. And John and I are so happy to be back on the rock – I love the feeling of waking up with sore muscles, eager for the next day's climbing.

Lilly's fear of heights that she fought to overcome in Ecuador has returned, but she is still determined to climb. Unfortunately, about 80 feet up her second climb she is gripped by terror and comes down crying, so we spend some cozy hours sitting together at the base of the rocks in the sun doing school and reading. Another afternoon, we go for a longer hike around the back of the formations and discover a rickety ladder that leads up to a cave full of ancient paintings of hands and animals – it's an unexpected Indiana Jones moment and makes for a fun history lesson.

We've been at high elevations for several weeks now – here at Hatun Machay we are living at 14,000 feet – and it's interesting to notice the little differences of life up here. We sleep much more than usual, about 11 hours a night. However, I never sleep very well because it's so incredibly cold that I can't move a muscle without cold air sneaking into my sleeping bag. Our seven-liter water bottle is often frozen solid in the mornings. Our olive oil starts to coagulate, turning solid. We start heating water to wash dishes and our hands – first time we've done that on the entire trip. It takes forever to hard boil an egg, so we don't even attempt to cook pasta. We go through a roll of tissues every day because our noses are constantly dripping. The cold, dry air leaves our lips cracked, our faces dry and the backs of our hands crispy. It makes me wonder what it must be like to climb the really big peaks in the Himalayas – I don't ever need to find out, this is high enough for me!

Despite the cold and elevation, I am overjoyed to be climbing every day, so we stay at Hatun Machay as long as possible. We eat our emergency stash of canned food that we've had for months, trying to eke out one more meal so we can stay one more day. But canned food and wet wipes only go so far – eventually we run out of food and can't stand how dirty we are. John's muscles are cramping, I want to wash my hair, and we're all craving fresh fruit – it's time to drive back to the town of Huaraz.

Huaraz is "only" 10,000 feet, so it feels warm and easy to breathe. Last time we were here, just a week ago, I would go out in the evening wearing a sweater and coat and hat, but our first evening back here after Hatun Machay I go out in just flip-flops and a long sleeve t-shirt! I'm surprised at how quickly my body adjusted to the cold.

Huaraz is my favorite town of the trip so far – I see majestic white mountains in the distance any time I walk anywhere, it's full of mountaineers and climbers (my kinda people) and there are great rock climbing areas and hikes surrounding it. It's also a great size at 120,000 people – big enough to have interesting restaurants and stores, but small enough that you can easily walk around.

It's not quite big enough to have a huge grocery store, but I come to love the different style of shopping for food. Here's a typical grocery shop for me in Huaraz:

I start walking to the market with my empty backpack. On the way, I see a lady sitting on the sidewalk, enveloped in her huge, colorful skirts, with a large woven basket in front of her. "How many bread rolls for one *sol*?" I ask. She pulls back the white sheet covering the mountain of bread that she baked that morning and hands me five rolls, which I stuff into my backpack.

Continuing to the market, I pass an old man pushing a wooden wagon full of avocados down the center of the street. The cars and taxis are flowing around him like water around a boulder in a river, without a honk or a second glance. I cautiously step into the traffic, stop the man and select two ripe avocados to add to my backpack.

I'm closing in on the market now, but I see a young girl sitting on the sidewalk in front of a miniature fold-out table covered in blueberries – I know they are grown in the nearby town of Caraz so I pick up a box of fresh, sweet berries.

I eventually reach the market and throw myself into the chaos. As I'm swept into the tide of people, I duck and dodge to avoid the metal posts sticking horizontally out from each stall into the narrow aisles, directly at my eye-height – this place is not set up for tall people like me! The vendors shout their prices incessantly and loudly, as I visit one stand to buy fruit, another to pick up fresh cheese, another for toilet paper – there's no such thing as a one-stop-shop here.

My last stop is the meat section. It's a swarm of buzzing flies, shouting people, and body parts hanging from metal hooks. I wait my turn to order while standing directly next to a full cow's head that is hanging at my head level. Its empty eye is directed at me, as if daring me to order beef. I add chicken legs to my now bulging backpack.

When I finally start back toward home, I have talked to at least 10 different people, and I know that all the money I spent is going directly to local farmers and vendors. It would be a frustratingly slow way to shop in my old, rushed life, but now it is delightfully entertaining.

These small towns like their fiestas. Somehow we run into three different parades while we are in Huaraz. We go out for dinner one evening and a parade passes us by – we simply sit down on the curb and watch people dance by, stamping their feet and swirling their bodies. The next day we see a larger, more organized version of the same parade, and we wonder if maybe the prior night was a rehearsal? But then the following day – yet another parade! I think these people just love to party in the streets – my kinda people.

Every time we go to Huaraz, in between our various mountain adventures in this area, we camp outside a climber hostel called the Monkey Wasi. I love hanging out with climbers for the first time in years. So many nationalities and languages all in one tiny kitchen, but all obsessed by the same topic of conversation – which climb are you doing next? It is entertaining to watch a pair of stoned German climbers carefully and devotedly standing under Lilly, the only kid around, ready to catch her if she falls as she clambers around on the indoor climbing wall.

At the beginning of our month in this gorgeous region, the van started belching white smoke. We hoped it was just due to the altitude, but it got worse and worse, plus we started losing power on hills. We realize that we have to address it, even though we want to continue exploring the Cordillera, so we descend 14,000 feet over two days to get to Lima, the capital of Peru.

We go straight to an injection specialist shop, assuming that this must have something to do with our good times in Puyango, and they discover that one of the injectors is not seated correctly. I'm amazed John got the other seven injectors right, considering he did the job entirely by himself, outdoors parked on the side of a dirt road, in the blazing hot sun, after having barely slept for four days. Oh, and he figured out how to do it by watching YouTube videos.

The Puyango moment of this mechanic visit is during the diagnostic phase. To figure out whether the problem is in the left or right bank of injectors, the mechanic takes off the exhaust manifold so he can see where the smoke comes from. This exposes two open pipes, both aiming squarely into the center of our home. So, I hold up a blanket in a feeble attempt to protect the freshly chopped vegetables I had just been preparing for lunch, and John turns the key.

A solid wall of gray-black smoke appears in front of me and then pours around the edges of my shield (blanket). Lilly starts coughing from up in the bed behind me, and our house immediately fills with thick smoke.

"Get out!" I shout to her. I struggle to spread the blanket as much as possible, while Lilly opens the door and jumps out. I hear a crash and a scream, and turn to see our little pink entrance step shattered into a thousand pieces sprayed across the mechanic's shop, and Lilly lying on the floor next to it, looking stunned. It's hard to laugh when your throat and eyes are full of black smoke, but I manage to do so in this particular instance.

Once we've identified, through this brute force methodology, that the right bank holds the offending injector, the mechanic removes all four right bank injectors. The injection technician identifies the bad injector, cleans it, replaces it, and we're back in business. What a difference to be in a large, modern city with fancy injector-testing machinery and experts who can diagnose our problem quickly, compared to Puyango.

My wise advice: if you're going to break down, do it in a big city.

We are now tempted to return to the Cordillera, but the impending rainy season and promise of more climbing and mountainous beauty in the south of Peru convinces us to continue south. It's tough to thread the needle between the various seasons in all these countries, but we hear that Bolivia is a disaster to drive through in the rainy season, so let's get a move on to check out southern Peru.

33

SAND, SAND, AND MORE SAND

This country is fast becoming our favorite in Latin America – the incredible mountain ranges, lively villages and diverse cities, fascinating culture and history across endless ruins.

However, the Peruvian coast is... how shall I put this? Cold, full of trash and dead animals, and bordered by endless dusty brown desert.

Perhaps we are just spoiled by our year of traveling through Central American tropical beaches, fringed by lush jungle and fascinating animals?

One exception to the Peruvian beaches is Paracas National Park – crumbling sandy cliffs of orange and red, framed by endless sand dunes on one side and ocean on the other – it's a highlight of the coast here. The national park entrance fee keeps down the number of visitors and, therefore, the trash. But it doesn't stop the dead animals from washing up on shore. Over the three days we camp here, we share our little section of beach with two dead seals and three dead turtles, plus the requisite carrion birds enjoying these free meals.

There is one paved road along the mainland that the tour buses take to various designated viewpoints. But the huge peninsula that juts out into the Pacific ocean is just one big flat expanse of hard-packed sand, with nary a road in sight. An overlanding paradise! We have a riot cruising around – following tracks, making our own, driving wherever we please. It is enticingly novel and silly to be able to spin the steering wheel any which way, knowing that there will be flat ground underneath your wheels and no cars in sight.

Turning east from Paracas, we drive through endless sand dunes punctuated by shantytowns – dozens of one-room shacks with corrugated metal roofs. Everything is covered in sand, giving the area a muted orange aura, like looking through dirty orange sunglass lenses. Trash piles up everywhere, perhaps deposited by locals with no trash removal service, or simply blown in by the ever-present winds through the sandy mountains. It's not a place I could imagine living.

Dwarfed by steep sand dunes on all sides, the tiny town of Huacachina calls itself an oasis due to the small lagoon in its center. It's basically a tourist trap, with almost no residents, only employees who come in from the nearby town of Ica to work the multitude of tour agencies and hostels. We enjoy a dune buggy ride at sunset over the never-ending sand dunes, and delight in renting skis to carve turns down some of the steeper dunes.

The landscape is so unique. Walking down the street to get dinner, I glance up in any direction and see sand towering above me on all sides. The dunes are so steep and so tall as to defy the physics of sand grains piled on top of one another. If you walk in any direction for more than five minutes you'll run into a solid wall of sand. Wouldn't this town be buried in a moment if there were a big sandstorm?

One morning while Lilly is still asleep in the van, I walk across the tiny town to approach the tallest of the dunes. I walk along the cement sidewalk until it dead-ends into a pile of orange sand. Looking up, I see a 200 foot high sand dune stretching into the sky in front of me. I take off my shoes and step up as high as my legs will allow. Walk two steps up, slide one step down, in the deep, cool, soft sand. It takes far longer than I anticipate to get to the summit.

From the crest, the views of sand dunes rise and fall in the distance as far as my eyes can see. It's such a unique perspective for me – accustomed to mountain vistas or beaches or cities – and I marvel at the similarity between the angular lines on the edges of each dune and the ridgelines on snowy mountains.

Running down is so fun! The pitch looks incredibly steep from where I'm standing at the top, but I can jog down as if I'm flying, with my feet sinking so deep into the sand with every step that there is no jarring on my poor old knees. I stop and look behind me and notice that my tracks are instantly gone. The pitch is so steep that the hole made by my leg is filled in by sand falling from above it as soon as I withdraw my foot.

The strangest thing is arriving back down at the edge of the town. There's a sidewalk that goes right into the sand – just disappears underneath it – so I step delicately from sand to concrete, back into my flip-flops, as if stepping from the beach onto a boardwalk.

It's a unique experience to live here a couple days, but feels somewhat stifling, like you're in a deep ditch with only one narrow road to escape. No wonder hardly anyone lives here.

Continuing south from the oasis town, we stop by a set of tombs in the desert that have been excavated for visitors to see. Online reviews say to be careful taking kids there because they might get scared, so I read one aloud to Lilly. She retorts, "But mama, I've seen lots of human bones," and starts listing off the places she's seen them already. Her upbringing is nothing if not unique.

So we park and walk out into the hot, dusty, brown desert. There are white painted stones marking a pathway that weaves between rectangular pits dug into the sand. Peering down into each hole in the ground, we see one or two mummies tied up in a sitting position, covered in shawls or blankets. Their eyeless skulls gape at each other, as if embarrassed by the few remaining strands of hair on their heads, and the ragtag state of their clothing after so many years. I frequently glance at Lilly to see if she's uncomfortable or scared (which means she'll be sleeping in our tiny bed tonight) but she seems totally blasé about the whole thing. (Even though she's still too scared to read Harry Potter #2!)

There are about a dozen tombs excavated for public viewing, but it's clear that there are many more still buried. We see mounds of sand interspersed between the open tombs, as well as stray bones sticking up out of the ground or just lying in the sand. Impromptu biology class time! We quiz Lilly, thankful that she's not yet at the eye-rolling teenager stage embarrassed by her parents in public, "What's that bone over there next to the skull?" or "Find a vertebra."

There is not much left inside the tombs besides the skeletons – this whole place has been looted of all valuables over the centuries, leaving me wondering... if our culture buried people with valuables, would our tombs also be raided? Imagine if everyone were buried with piles of $100 bills in their pockets. I'm sure we'd have looters just like they do here.

We consider sleeping at the Necropolis, but, denying any feelings of spookiness, we decide to travel a little further south to get closer to Arequipa where I'm keen to visit an old friend before she goes on vacation. Later in the afternoon, we turn off the paved road at an illegible sign and drive into the desert looking for a place to camp. John comments that the ground looks strange and feels different under our tires. We get out to investigate and find that we are driving on a solid sheet of tiny shells. But, we are miles away from the ocean! Lilly, in her eight-year-old wisdom, explains to me that this must have been an ocean many years ago.

A couple of miles later we are surprised to see a little cardboard sign on a post: *Museo* (museum). An older lady comes out of a one-room house made of grass and mud bricks. It's the only sign of life for miles around. We ask about the *Museo* sign and she explains that they found a fossilized whale skeleton here and that this whole area was ocean four million years ago. (Gold star for Lilly's science lessons!) She apologizes that she's in the middle of cooking dinner, but can go unlock the museum for us in just a minute. We thank her profusely, saying that we don't want to interrupt her dinner but would be grateful if we could just camp here for the night. "Of course," she replies enthusiastically, "you are welcome." We cook under a star-filled black sky, then sleep a peaceful night, dreaming of a four-million-year-old ocean under our wheels.

In the morning, the señora comes to the van to show us the one-room museum with a fossilized whale inside. She also points out another one a few hundred meters away, just lying in the sand outside. Then she locks the museum, walks away and we never see her again. There's nowhere to leave a donation, no response at the house we found her in yesterday, and we're left wondering: who maintains this place and how do they pay for it?

The desert is a unique experience for us, but it can get monotonous – I'm desperate to see some trees or flowers or color of any kind. Plus, I'm excited to get to Arequipa before a dear old friend there leaves town. So we skip Cusco for now, and beeline to the White City of Arequipa.

* * *

Late summer 1996, in a college dorm room in New Hampshire: two 19-year-olds decide they want to go to South America. Luckily, I was living with my super motivated and adventurous best friend Lee, who helped turn our crazy idea into reality.

I wrote to all the alumni of my university who were living in South America – all four of them – and got one response from James in Peru. He would hire me to work at his cotton farming business in Arequipa. Lee found another opportunity in Buenos Aires, Argentina. We wrote grant applications, got enough money for plane tickets, and off we went.

The job fell through before I'd even arrived, but James connected me to a large clothing manufacturer that needed a translator, and somehow I bluffed my way through the interview in Spanish to land the job. More importantly, James' neighbor Anita rented me a room in her house, and she and I became fast friends.

I returned to New Hampshire months later with an adopted Peruvian family, almost perfect fluency in Spanish, and dear friends whom I've stayed in touch with for the last 22 years. It was a significant chapter of my young life, one that I'll never forget.

Fast forward to September 2019: After two years on the road driving from California to Peru, we pull up in front of "my" house in

Arequipa. My Peruvian mama and sister come running out to greet us with hugs and tears, and they meet Lilly for the first time.

We walk into the very same house where I lived 22 years ago. It is surreal. So many memories! We have so much to catch up on. I haven't seen Anita since she came to our wedding in California in 2007. And my baby sister, who was 10 when I lived here, is now all grown up. I have so many questions – significant others, jobs, travels, school – tell me everything!

We talk for hours every evening in Anita's warm and inviting kitchen. I sit in the same chair at the same table as I did when I felt my first ever earthquake. I'll never forget that moment: I was chatting with Anita and her boyfriend, drinking rum and coke together, then just as I pushed back my chair and stood up, I felt really wobbly as if I were on a boat in the ocean.

"What? Am I that drunk?"

"No," Anita explained, "it's an earthquake."

Of course some things have changed. They've turned their house into a hotel, as the popularity of Arequipa has grown among tourists. The street in front used to be so quiet with cows walking by, but now there are cars and taxis buzzing by all day. And, unfortunately for me, most of my Peruvian friends from 1997 have moved away – to London, Germany, France, Canada – they turned out to be a really international bunch.

One of my closest friends, Pati, is still living here, now married to her then-boyfriend Aldo. We spend a raucous day at their house, trying out Aldo's many varieties of Pisco (the national Peruvian alcohol), laughing at everything, and reminiscing about our younger days dancing until dawn.

It's wonderful to be with "family" and friends for the first time in so long on this trip, and we are sad to eventually say good-bye. It's one thing that I miss about constant travel – the deep relationships that are impossible to foster when we're never in the same place for more than a few days or weeks.

One unfortunate outcome of our visit to Arequipa is that John somehow got a nasty throat infection. It gets so bad that he can barely stand up and he has a high fever, so we decide to go to an urgent care doctor for the first time on this trip. Here's how it goes:

Step One: Walk in and join a queue to pay S/15 – about $4.

Step Two: Go to another queue where a nurse takes John's blood pressure and asks his weight and height. We know his height in inches, but this is meaningless anywhere outside of the US. I pull out my phone to translate into meters, but the nurse gets impatient due to the line of people waiting behind us, so puts him on the scale. She notes down his weight in kilos, but then realizes she can't reach up high enough to see his height. I look up from my phone to tell her I know his height in meters now, but she leaves the room, returning a moment later with a tall man who looks up at the marks on the wall above John for her.

Finally she has the numbers she needs, but now glances at her notes with a confused look on her face, "I must have written it down wrong, please get back on the scale." (Cue murmurs of increasingly impatient people behind us.) She measures again, then studies the numbers again on her chart and looks up, concerned, "He's impossibly thin for his height." I assure her this is normal for us weird gringos and she sends us to the next queue.

Step Three: We wait outside a door behind two other people and eventually are invited into a doctor's office. Finally, we've made it to a doctor! I start trying to explain John's throat pain, but the doctor interrupts me, "How long has he been so skinny?" I hold back my snarky response of, "About 40 years," and instead try to explain that this is normal, but the doctor is sure that John's low weight is the source of whatever problem he's experiencing. He spends several minutes calculating John's body mass index and showing us a chart to demonstrate that we're clearly overlooking a serious problem, while I try to redirect him to John's throat. He finally looks into John's mouth, gasps, puts a mask over his own mouth, and writes a prescription for antibiotics.

Step Four: Go to a fourth queue to buy antibiotics and get outta there. (John recovered fully in a few days)

Although we're tired of the dusty, hot desert, we can't miss the deepest canyon in the world! So we make a short detour to Colca Canyon, only to find out that its neighbor Cotohuasi was recently measured as being 700 feet deeper. Regardless, it's still almost twice as deep as my reference point of the Grand Canyon in the US (11,000 feet vs 6,000 feet).

But depth isn't everything. I'm here to save you the trouble of hiking all the way to the bottom, like we did – the views are nowhere near as impressive as in the Grand Canyon. There are no steep rock walls and dramatic angles, it's mostly a gentle dusty bowl. Are our standards skewed because we just got back from the impressive Cordillera Blanca mountains up north? Perhaps, but I would declare Colca Canyon the second most underwhelming tourist site in Peru. (The most underwhelming was the Nazca lines.)

The condor sightings, however, are spectacular and well worth the detour to Colca. We camp two nights at a viewpoint above the canyon and enjoy close-up views of these astonishingly large creatures riding the air currents every morning. One flew directly over our heads – it was so close that I heard the whooshing sound from its wings displacing the air as it passed! Another flew right in front of my face, turning its head to look at me as it glided by – for one long moment it felt like we were looking directly into each other's eyes, evaluating each other's foreign species.

After all this time in the desert, we've had enough of the sand in our eyes, dust in our food, and dirt all over the floor of the van. We're ready for a change of scenery. Time to go to the jewel in the crown of Peru – Machu Picchu.

34

MACHU PICCHU AND ALL THAT

The Incas left lots of piles of rocks down here. Everywhere we look, every road we drive down, every trail we hike, we see signs of ancient buildings. Some are the famous sites that are protected and named and visited by thousands of tourists daily, but there are hundreds more that appear to be abandoned, or even still in use by modern-day people.

We join the crowds tramping through Machu Picchu, we camp alone at deserted ruins in the middle of nowhere, and we hike over mountain ranges past ancient rocky buildings. Where did it all come from?

About 600 years ago, Incan leaders united disparate communities of people from Ecuador all the way down to Chile. They managed to propagate one common language, religious practice, standard of writing, network of roads, and method of building... across 10 million people!

From hundreds of distinct languages emerged Quechua as the common tongue, which is still widely spoken today.

Written communication developed using knots on strings (*quipus*) to represent numbers and possibly words.

Ritual worship of the sun, moon, stars, and water became the norm, and many of these practices continue today in rural communities.

A system of mail was created using human runners (*chasquis*) who formed a human relay chain to get messages between kings and battle-fields over hundreds of miles in a matter of days.

A network of roads spread across the empire, many of which are still in use today.

Ok, so that was all very impressive. But most relevant to the modern-day tourist are the incredible stone structures still standing. We first started seeing Incan terraces around us in the Colca Canyon area, and we then toured the more famous ones at Pisaq and Moray in the Cusco area a few weeks later. The Incas transformed steep hillsides into steps of flat areas using thousands of stones and a lot of digging. The purpose was presumably to grow food and/or graze their animals. People are still using some of these very same terraces today for the same purpose!

Although no one can definitively state the purpose of the various Incan ruins – houses/religious temples/fortresses/holiday homes for royalty – we can all agree that the method of building was incredible. The most outstanding feature is the perfect alignment of enormous rocks on top of each other without any mortar or gaps. They carved each stone to mesh perfectly into the sides of the next one, like a gigantic jigsaw puzzle, using materials that could only be moved by a dozen men. Saqsaywaman is a great place to see this Incan trapezoidal architecture up close. At Ollantay-tambo we even saw it with narrow sections between rocks to allow gentle movement during earthquakes – yup, seismic engineering 600 years ago!

The location of these structures makes them even more impressive. At Pisaq, we hiked for an hour over a hilltop through pre-Incan ruins, only to find a perfect set of Incan walls hidden down in a canyon on the other side. On the way to Machu Picchu, we walked through the terraces and rooms of the WiñayWayna ruins high up on a steep slope near the top of a mountain. Standing at the top, looking down at the complex below, I had to wonder, *Why would anyone choose to build in such an inaccessible place?*

Machu Picchu is another great example of expansive ruins in a difficult location. Nowadays you can take a train to the base of the hill where it sits, and then a bus up to the ruins themselves. But not so back then. The famous Inca Trail purports to follow the original Inca road and enter Machu Picchu in the same way that the king would have entered. We walked for several hours to arrive at the sun gate, Inti Punku, and then down into the ruins of Machu Picchu, marveling at how they got these gigantic rocks up here.

I am also fascinated to see how these ruins are built into modern-day life. Why build a new rock wall to contain your alpacas when you can use one that's been there for hundreds of years? In a city, why tear down an ancient stone wall if it's still strong? Every time we walk around the town of Cusco, we come across Incan stonework that has been built into a restaurant or other modern-day locale.

Q'oricancha was one of the more intriguing sites for me within Cusco. It used to be a magnificent sun temple, whose walls were covered in sheets of gold and whose interior was filled with solid gold figurines. The Spanish melted down all the gold and built a Christian church around the remains of the building, leaving today's tourists with a surprising contrast – turn this way and see a panel worshipping the sun god, turn that way and see Jesus on his cross, all within the same church. Interestingly, the mind-boggling Incan trapezoidal walls have withstood multiple earthquakes over the past 600 years while much of the colonial building has fallen down.

It's eye-opening for me, raised as a Catholic, to learn a little about the ancient religious practices here. People worship the sun god *Inti* and mother Earth *Pachamama*. They bury coca leaves in the earth, or push them into crevices in a rock face as an offering to Pachamama. They will pour *chicha* (local drink) onto the earth as a thank-you before consuming any themselves. They also revere the different mountains around them, calling them *Apus*. They point to and call by name each one around them, as a sign of respect or gratitude. One logical difference we notice when we get to the Lake Titicaca area later is that they talk more about Mamacocha (water) than Pachamama (earth).

These may be ancient beliefs, but I can relate whole-heartedly to the idea. Regardless of how you believe the Earth was created, there's no debating that we'd be nothing without the sun and water and land, so it makes sense to appreciate these aspects of our life. I think at heart I am a sun-worshipper.

One question that keeps surfacing in my mind is: how has this pre-European history survived until the present day? The Aztecs and Mayans in Mexico and Guatemala, and the Incas down here, had such a strong influence that the effect is still felt and seen today. People still speak languages other than Spanish in spite of 300 years of Spanish rule, there are ruins of impressive temples and road networks still standing today, and people wear traditional clothing like a uniform that identifies them as part of a particular area. Why don't I see this else-where in the Americas?

The clothing and physical characteristics of the people really stand out – we haven't seen these differences since Guatemala, where we'd remark upon a passing elderly woman who was the same height as Lilly! Most of the indigenous ladies we see here in Peru are about half as tall as John and twice as broad. Their hair is always very long and black, worn in braids that are typically woven together at the ends, with decorations hanging from the bottom that indicate whether they are married or single. For example, black means married. They tell me that they've never cut their hair in their life! They explain that they undo the braids every now and then to wash their hair, but never cut it. This partly explains their curiosity about Lilly, since she currently has very short hair.

They typically carry a bright multi-colored woven shawl on their back, usually with a baby's head or feet poking out of the top or bottom, or full of hidden goods going to or coming from the market. They wear wide, layered skirts with stockings, and some unique larger-than-life hat that indicates where they're from. Some of the hats are so outrageous it looks like a Mardi Gras costume. Picture it: here's an elderly woman hunched over, carrying a heavy load in her shawl, wearing well-worn clothes, but with this enormous bright yellow hat on her head embroidered with colorful flowers and glittering silver beads. The hat is so incongruous to the rest of the person! Each town seems to have its own hat uniform – sometimes it's just a brown floppy hat, sometimes a prim black bowler hat, and oftentimes the bright glittery wide-brimmed style.

Similarly, the Quechua language is proudly and widely spoken. How did it survive hundreds of years of being outlawed? I'm told that as recently as the 1970s it was forbidden to speak it at school! Everyone up here tells me that Quechua is their mother tongue and they're more comfortable speaking it, but they also learn Spanish in school and can speak it well. The further away we get from cities, the stronger the accent I hear when locals speak Spanish. Quechua is a tough language for our foreign tongues to pronounce correctly, but we learn some basic phrases to greet the locals.

So why has so much of the Incan culture survived while others have not? I guess it comes down to how strong of an identity was present when the Europeans arrived. The Incas pulled together a civilization of about 10 million people extending from Ecuador to Chile, with strong societal norms around dress and religion, traditions like weaving and spoken language passed through generations of families, and of course physical evidence in buildings and roads. Other countries were perhaps more fragmented with smaller societies each having their own religious beliefs and dress and language, but not extensive enough to survive the generations after the Spanish.

It's intriguing to spend so much time in a country with such different cultures of people living together. I find myself more fascinated by my conversations with local people about their traditions than by the ancient buildings themselves. But we've seen enough piles of ancient rocks to last a lifetime. We Yosemite monkeys are more interested in still-intact rocks, aka mountains, so it's time to head south in search of climbing.

35

EVEN THINNER AIR,
AND LAST DAYS IN PERU

There is so much potential for rock climbing here. We see vertical rock faces all around us as we're driving or hiking around. The Cordillera Blanca up north was also rich in climbing areas, but there we found a community of climbers and even purchased a guidebook. Here, there's almost nothing.

So we dip our toes in the baby pool, climbing at one of the few established areas that has some route maps, Ch'acco Hayllascca. It's tucked away above the mountain town of Pitumarca at 4,130 m (13,500 feet), but we don't even notice the elevation while we're camped there – we've been spending so much time in the 4,000 m range lately that it has become normal! We camp with another overlanding family who we met back in Huaraz, so Lilly spends her days playing with the other kids while John and I climb. We're not going to push her to climb unless she really wants to.

I also find another multi-day trek for us, again in the donkey+chef style that we so enjoyed up north. Unfortunately, this time I can't find another family crazy enough to join us, so we buy lots of candy to help coax Lilly along. Everything I read about this hike says that it's one of the most demanding in Peru, but I rationalize that it's because of the elevation, to which we're already accustomed, so we should be fine.

There's also the small matter of the impending rainy season, but we spot a few dry days in the forecast and go for it.

The first day of the trek, we start hiking under very gray skies. We can see the bottom of a big mountain looming ahead of us; evidently this is Ausungate but it's enveloped in thick clouds so we see almost nothing of it. We put on another layer of clothing. Then another. We realize that Lilly's sweater somehow got left behind in the van. We walk faster. I feel wet drops hit my upper lip and try to pretend I don't notice them. Somehow it feels different than rain... uh oh, it's snowing!

A few minutes later, I see a perfectly round ball of white ice bounce off the ground in front of me. Within minutes, there are white micro-balls hitting the ground all around us. John and I look at each other. We are walking away from civilization, deep into the mountains at a higher elevation than we've ever been before, on a hike that no one takes kids on, and it's hailing. Is this a bad idea? We decide to push on to the first campsite and re-evaluate in the morning.

Lucky for us, the next day breaks with clear blue skies and sunshine, and stays that way. We enjoy magnificent views of glaciers, snowy peaks, rocky summits, and alpine lakes over the next three days. Lilly spots chinchillas, John studies routes up icy mountain faces, and I'm most fascinated by the people we see living out here. We're a day's walk from any other humans. We're over 15,000 feet elevation. It is literally freezing as soon as the sun goes down. But people live out here in simple shelters with their families. How do they do it?

They plant potatoes for food and trade, and raise llamas and alpacas for meat and wool. They make thread and garments from the wool and sell or trade it for things they can't produce themselves. I express surprise at such a limited diet of potato and alpaca meat, and our guide protests, "But they grow several *different kinds* of potato," as if this makes it a totally easy lifestyle, ha!

Throughout this central Andes region, we always see llamas and alpacas on the hillsides with people herding them. It's intriguing to think about thousands of people still living such a simple life. According to Wikipedia, "The region...constitutes one of the few remaining pastoralist societies in the world." Or quoting my preferred source of wisdom, my husband, "Whenever you see a herd of animals, just scan your eyes across the landscape and eventually you'll see a bowler hat attached to a lady tending her animals."

Every time someone passes close enough to realize we have a child hiking with us, they are delighted and curious. They are intrigued by Lilly's hair, her skin, her size. I guess we do look very different, and they rarely see a non-local kid out here.

On the second afternoon of our hike, we take a break from walking to have some snacks beside the trail. A couple approaches us, wearing the colorful local dress and trailed by their herd of alpacas. I didn't think the lady's welcoming grin could get any bigger, but then I prompt Lilly to greet her in Quechua instead of in Spanish.

"Ay yee yan chu?" Lilly says hesitantly. (My phonetic spelling.)

The lady's eyes grow wide in surprise and her grin broadens to show all her black teeth. "Ay yee yam eh," she replies. She turns to me and switches to Spanish, "How old is she?"

I give my usual response when adults assume Lilly can't speak for herself, "Ask her."

Lilly cuts in, "Tengo ocho años." (I'm eight.)

"What is her name?" The lady again directs the question to me, even though she has to lean across Lilly.

And Lilly cuts in again, "Me llamo Lilly."

Then with two arms outstretched in eager anticipation, the lady asks, "Can I touch her?"

Lilly is a bit uncomfortable, but allows the woman to touch her face and stroke her hair. Then the man reaches out similarly, but Lilly has had enough and crawls into my lap to escape. "You never have to let someone touch you if you don't want," I whisper in her ear.

In general on this van trip, ladies have been enamored with Lilly, and even more so here in southern Peru. When we walk past women on the street they smile and point, commenting on how beautiful Lilly is, "Que linda!" If we stop to talk to them, they want to touch her hair and face. They call out to their friends to come look at the *gringita* (little gringo) as if she's an animal in a zoo. Lilly always smiles but generally turns away, unaccustomed to being manhandled by strange ladies sporting big smiles full of black teeth.

This particular lady we've bumped into on the trail, having gotten her fill of examining Lilly, is now turning a clump of alpaca fur into thread. She sits down next to Lilly on the high alpine grass to encourage her to try it. She shows us how she pulls on the bundle of fur, plucking out dirt and sticks, then spins it on itself using a wooden reel to make the thread stronger. Once she deems the thread sturdy enough for weaving, she wraps it around the reel to use later. She keeps pushing the reel into Lilly's hands, prompting her to try it, amused and surprised that an eight-year-old female wouldn't already be an expert at this. (Good thing she didn't ask me!)

We see this weaving on display in a little store the following week, where a friendly family shows us how they dye their alpaca wool different colors. I'm impressed by the variety of colors they create by boiling the wool with natural sources like flowers and leaves, but the most surprising color source is red: The woman shows us a large green cactus leaf and points to dozens of white dots sprinkled across it, explaining that they are small insects that live on the cactus. She plucks one off and squishes it between her fingers, creating a red smear of blood on the palm of her hand, then puts the blood into a small bowl of water to make red dye – genius!

Although I haven't picked up a new weaving habit from the Peruvians, we have adopted the custom of drinking coca tea. At first I was hesitant – aren't coca leaves somehow associated with cocaine? But the leaves are many stages removed from cocaine, and it's a tasty tea that locals swear will help with altitude adjustment. We now have a thermos in the van – which was given to us by a random guy in Colombia, of course, friendliest country of the trip to date – and a bag of loose coca leaves that we use to make hot tea multiple times a day. I can't say whether it's helping with our acclimatization or our energy levels, but it definitely helps to warm up our bodies on these cold days.

With or without coca, I am loving the feeling of doing something physically challenging day after day on this trek. My body feels so deliciously worn out. Every evening we fall asleep so quickly and so early. Every morning I wake up with my body deeply rested and stretching. Reminds me how much I love daily physical challenge and how good I think it is for my body, but how hard it's been to keep it in my life since Lilly was born. It's wonderful that she's now getting big enough to be an adventure partner.

The afternoon of the third day on our hike we are surrounded by rainbow striped mountains and various bright red peaks and valleys. How has the color of the hillsides changed so much since yesterday's white glaciers and gray rock faces? It is spectacular!

That night we camp at 5,000 m (16,400 feet). Now we're getting into some seriously high altitudes. As soon as the sun goes down, the temperature plummets. It's too cold to even brush our teeth. We are in bed at 6.30 p.m. and wear all our layers of clothes inside our sleeping bags.

I start to worry as I lie down to sleep. Will the elevation hurt us? It's one thing to hike over a 5,000 m pass and down again, but it's entirely different to sleep the whole night up here. We keep asking Lilly how she feels, but, as usual, she is the least affected of us. In fact, she pulls off her socks and coat, complaining that she's too hot inside her sleeping bag. We are very well acclimatized, having been in the 4,000 m range for several weeks now, and we have no problems. I do wake up gasping for air several times in the night, but only because I've pulled the sleeping bag over my head for warmth, and there's no margin for error in getting oxygen into your lungs up here!

We wake up the fourth morning to freezing temperatures and thick clouds. Lilly is so cold that she wears all her clothes plus John's heavy coat which hangs down past her knees. She struggles to walk the final few miles, breaking down in tears from the intense cold on her tiny body, but she makes it. We wrap her in bear hugs and feed her candy, feeling so proud of the tough little kid she is becoming. We finish up at Rainbow Mountain parking lot in a sudden swarm of tourists and buses, always a surprise when you've been away from civilization for a few days, and collapse into a bus to return to Cusco.

It turns out to be one of the best hikes I've ever done – walking around the glaciated mountain with endlessly impressive views, and then over the 5,000 m pass to enter the rainbow wonderland of colorful peaks all around. If it weren't for the impending rainy season, we'd probably sign up for another multi-day trek. But we're feeling the urgency of the seasons changing, so we head to Lake Titicaca to visit the floating reed islands and cross the remote border there, bidding farewell to Peru.

I now finally have an answer when people ask my favorite country of the trip. The jaw-dropping mountain scenery with accessible hiking trails, the friendly and unique villages ever-welcoming to us foreigners, and the rich culture and history omnipresent in language and dress and ancient sites – Peru is officially the winner of our trip so far!

Lilly making friends with the locals

Pueblo de los Muertos - can you believe they let tourists up here?

Yet another wiggly mountain road in northern Peru

Cruising around the Paracas peninsula

Peering down into an old tomb with skeletons mostly still intact

BOLIVIA

We drove 940 miles over 3.5 weeks in Bolivia.
October to November, 2019.

36

LIVING THROUGH THE
BOLIVIAN REVOLUTION

L et's go see real dinosaur footprints! Rock climb in Sucre! Go down into the silver mines in Potosi! I eagerly draw out a route across this country on our map, weaving through the highlights I've read about.

But it wasn't meant to be.

Road blocks. Threats of border closures. Police in riot gear patrolling the streets.

Checking the news every hour. Stocking up on food and water and fuel. An emergency trip back to Peru. This was our unexpected Bolivia experience.

Background

Evo Morales is in his third term as President in Bolivia, so isn't allowed to run again. In 2016 he issued a referendum to the Bolivians asking if they'd approve his running for another term – 51% voted no. But he had the court declare that it would be against his human rights to forbid him to run, and put his name on the ballot anyway.

Fast forward to the election on October 20th, 2019. We are camped on the shore of Lake Titicaca (the border with Peru) carefully watching the news, hesitant to enter Bolivia in case there's a problem.

The election appears to go off without a hitch, and the results are reported live over the course of the day. Evo isn't going to get the required minimum to win outright, so there will be a runoff election on December 15th.

Ok, that gives us six weeks of peace – let's drive in. Goodbye Peru!

We cross the border and wild camp on the Bolivia side of Lake Titicaca and have no phone reception. The next day we approach the capital city, La Paz, and learn that things have become complicated: the election results stopped updating for 24 hours with no explanation, and when they were re-published, Evo was suddenly on track to win outright. Many Bolivians are not buying this story, and protests erupt across the country. We pull into a small camping area hosted by a lovely Bolivian family on the outskirts of La Paz, and end up staying there two weeks, watching the mayhem unfold.

One Small Complication

In our last days in Peru, John discovered a pair of leaking high pressure hoses in the van and ordered replacements from the US to be mailed to us in Bolivia. Once we got to La Paz, he realized the leak was serious, and we ideally wouldn't drive again until we got the new hoses, in case they broke entirely and we became stranded somewhere. After Puyango, we are much more cautious about potential mechanical issues.

No problem. The parts get from the US to Bolivia within a day of us arriving in La Paz, so we just have to wait for them to clear customs (there are no issues with shipping car parts here, unlike in Peru). Easy peasy, right?

Nope. Not when the entire country shuts down.

While we're waiting for the hoses to show up, John drives the van downtown to a turbo mechanic for a checkup – he's always wondered if it got damaged during our Puyango fiasco – while Lilly and I stay at the campsite for the day. Later in the afternoon he calls to say it's taking longer than expected and so he'll spend the night to avoid driving home in the dark. Marcos, the campground host, says that Lilly and I can sleep in his spare room.

But at 7 p.m. Marcos' wife comes to find me, "They're announcing road blocks starting at 6 a.m. tomorrow all over La Paz – your husband needs to come back NOW or else he'll be stuck."

What?! This is an entirely new experience for me. Is it more dangerous for John to drive across the city in the night by himself in this volatile climate? Or more dangerous for him to get stuck down-town behind roadblocks?

I call John to tell him the news, and of course he decides to drive back immediately. Marcos says he is *pendiente* (ready) if John gets stuck somewhere to go help him.

It's all a bit scary. It's very different to read about this kind of thing on the news than to experience it firsthand. Lilly can sense my stress and constantly asks me, "When will Papa get home?"

It's a huge relief when John drives through the gate, late that night. We discuss the idea of packing up immediately and driving across the country through the night to escape to Chile or Argentina. Once the road blocks are in place tomorrow, we have no idea what will happen.

Lilly starts crying. She's been homeless (vanless) all day, worried about her Papa all evening, and now is hearing her parents use words like "escape" and "trapped" – it's all a bit much. We talk to our resident expert Marcos who assures us that road blocks aren't a big deal in this country – he's experienced them dozens of times in his life – and he expects there'll be no danger.

So we hole up for a few days waiting for our hoses to arrive, watching the news and the streets.

The next day, roadblocks are set up at most major intersections and there are peaceful protests in the streets. It's an inconvenience but not a danger. The protesters usually have Bolivian flags wrapped around their bodies, and the people greet each other with smiles and hand-shakes. It feels more festive than tense. I go to the grocery store every day to stock up on food, just in case, but there is always plenty. I start following all the major Bolivian news outlets, and join various Facebook groups to get up-to-date information.

The road blocks are very simple – a rope, a car parked sideways, some tires, or just a few people. Once we even saw a washing machine standing proudly in the center of the intersection, holding up a rope across the road!

We check in with our parts importer daily, but he says our hoses are still sitting in the airport in Santa Cruz (major city in Bolivia). That city is totally shut down by protests and no one is working – including the customs officers – meaning that our parts cannot get out.

Thursday Oct 24: Evo announces that the vote count is complete and that he won the election fair and square. There will be no run-off in December. He is President for five more years.

The people revolt. Now the protests become more intense. When we walk past, they are chanting, "We're not Venezuela! We're not Cuba!" or "Evo Dictator!" The schools are all closed and people don't go to work. Lilly plays with Marcos' kids who are now home all day.

We get a tiny inkling of what it might be like to live in a war-torn country. Every day I go to the markets and buy all the food I can carry. Just in case. We can't go visit any of the usual tourist sights in Bolivia. To get downtown, we walk until we reach the first roadblock, cross through the crowds of people chanting and waving flags until we find a taxi driver on the other side, ask him how far until the next roadblock and if he can take us part way to town, then either hop in or keep walking – we never know if we'll be walking three miles or three minutes!

Every evening around 9 p.m. the sound of banging pots echoes all around us from the windows and balconies of the neighboring houses – apparently it's a common way to anonymously protest down here. It's a nightly reminder, as we're getting ready for bed in the van, that all is not well.

John and I endlessly analyze our situation, debating what we should do. Could the country run out of food? Could things get violent? We decide to wait it out because we know we can always get on an airplane, abandoning Vancito, if things get really ugly.

But a week later, the airport is blocked. Escape is no longer an option!

Tuesday Oct 29: Marcos tells us that he saw a video on the news of truckers surrounding the Santa Cruz airport customs office and wrapping chains around the building. That's where our parts are sitting waiting for customs clearance. We're never going to see them!

I ask various locals, "Could this last for weeks?" And they generally reply, "It could last for months."

Ok, that's it! We're not waiting one more day for our parts to get out of that building.

We kick off Operation Escape From Bolivia. Marcos thinks if we leave early in the morning, we should be able to skirt around the roadblocks. We consider driving away without replacing these hoses, but, by some stroke of luck, a friend of a friend is flying from the US to Cusco (Peru) in three days. If we can ship the parts to her in the US then she'll mule them for us, and I can fly to Cusco to pick them up. It's worth waiting only three more days, so John reorders the same hoses that are already sitting in customs right here in Bolivia, and I book flights to Peru for November first.

I am slightly nervous about this plan. My worst-case scenario planning brain goes into overdrive:

What if the borders close while I am gone so I can't get back to my family?

And all cell networks go down so we can't communicate?

And zombies climb out of the graveyards?

We come up with a Plan Z that I'm sure we won't need to enact – I would take a bus from Cusco to the border of Bolivia, and John would make his way somehow someway to that same border on the other side, and I'd sneak over to rejoin my family.

This is not quite how I envisioned our Bolivia tour going.

. . .

Wednesday Oct 30: News outlets report that there are threats to cut off the water supply to La Paz if the residents continue with the road-blocks. Marcos says don't worry about it, "They always threaten that but never do. Well," he pauses, "ok they did once, but that was a long time ago."

I fill up our water tank and every bottle I can get my hands on.

Thursday Oct 31: The president announces that his supporters will "siege the cities." He says he's bringing out the miners and they'll use dynamite to break up the blockades.

John sees first-hand the reality of this announcement when he walks downtown to do our shopping that day: There are armed guards outside the storefront for the first time since we've been here. And when he steps out of the store half an hour later, carrying his bags full of groceries, he watches in amazement as thousands of miners and farmers march down the road in front of him. The miners are in helmets and matching backpacks, and many have something slung over their shoulder. John watches in surprise and fear as one of the miners reaches into his shoulder sling, pulls out a stick of dynamite, lights it and tosses it away from the procession. This happens every few minutes, causing an almighty BOOM that shakes the street and sets off car alarms. John says it felt like he was watching a militia march into town. He gets home that afternoon visibly shaken and ready to get outta here.

Meanwhile, I help Lilly carve a watermelon for a Halloween pump-kin, and take her trick-or-treating at Marcos' house. Not quite the fun of Dia de Muertos in Mexico, but it's a learning experience for all three of us to live through this chaos. For her writing school this week I make her pretend she's a journalist and she writes a news article about what's happening in Bolivia.

Friday Nov 1: Today's the day I fly to Peru.

I wake up and read on the news that two people were killed in

Santa Cruz (the town where our parts are stuck) from gunfire during protests yesterday. They are the first deaths of this situation. I don't think Santa Cruz is going to be worrying about opening their customs office anytime soon.

I hug John and Lilly goodbye and walk out of the campground with a small, mostly empty backpack on my back. I walk through several roadblocks, catch a minibus, ride the teleferique, catch a taxi, and get to the La Paz airport without incident.

I fly to Cusco and hang out with overlanding friends that evening. It's so relaxing to be wandering around the city amid throngs of tourists, gaping at architecture, talking about something other than the political situation in Bolivia for once. I'm surprised when I see police officers walking around alone and wearing a simple uniform – in La Paz they are always in groups, wearing helmets and protective armor.

Saturday Nov 2: Early morning, I meet our hero friend-of-a-friend at the airport and transfer the hoses from her bag into mine. (These parts are so small that she had no issues with Peruvian customs.)

The airplane back to Bolivia is so empty, it's unreal – most of the rows don't have a single person in them. Bolivia is not a particularly popular destination right now! I fly back with the parts, feeling like a nervous drug smuggler as I walk through customs, remembering John's ordeal in Peru six months ago, but no one bats an eyelid.

Trying to get home from the airport, I discover that the road blocks have multiplied across the city since yesterday and I'll have to walk over an hour through the car-less streets. But halfway home, John shows up on a motorcycle borrowed from Marcos, and I hop on for a quick ride up the hill.

Saturday evening there are two announcements:

1) Evo says if the road blocks don't stop then he's bringing in the military in 48 hours.

2) Anti-Evo social leaders give him an ultimatum – he has to resign in 48 hours, or else... (they don't say or else what).

Conclusion: we need to leave in 48 hours!

. . .

Sunday Nov 3: John spends the day working on the van to replace the high pressure hoses. As I'm making dinner in the camp kitchen that evening, I hear cries of anguish from the van, and run over expecting to see a severed hand or gaping eye socket. John over-torqued a bolt and stripped it, and it's buried way down in the engine making it impossible to fix. I've never seen him so distraught.

Monday Nov 4: John and Marcos try a longer bolt and it holds up to the torque specifications required, because only part of the hole was stripped – we lost one day, but we're back on track.

7 p.m. One of the opposition social leaders, Luis Camacho, stands under the Jesus Christ statue in Santa Cruz in front of an enormous crowd of supporters. He announces that the 48 hour ultimatum has passed without the President resigning. He's written a resignation letter for Evo and will fly to La Paz the next day to personally deliver it for him to sign! This seems audacious. More concerning for us is when I hear Camacho shout into his loudspeaker to the cheering crowd, "Can we close the borders?" and everyone yells back in wild excitement, "Si!"

What the...?! Can they do that? I know that protesters in Ecuador did it just a few weeks ago. Will we be able to leave now?

Tuesday Nov 5: Camacho arrives in La Paz to deliver his promised resignation letter to Evo. We watch live video of La Paz airport filled and surrounded by protesters. They are carrying home-made weapons and are marching through the airport. I just landed there three days ago! When I go out for my daily grocery store visit I see a pickup truck full of police with all their riot gear on, right on our street. Things are heating up.

Meanwhile, John and Marcos go for a successful test drive and return to the campsite to put the van back together, while I research if and how we can leave tomorrow. Marcos says we are welcome to stay as long as we want, but he thinks things are going to get worse before they get better. There's a super remote land border we can cross that he thinks no one would bother to block, so we decide to go for it early tomorrow morning before the blockades are set up.

Wednesday Nov 6: I mess up the alarm and we don't drive away until 6 a.m. Idiot!

Fifteen minutes down the road John realizes he left his phone behind. Double idiot! We are back at Marcos' at 6:30 a.m. We don't have keys anymore so I climb over the gate, sprint to the bathroom, grab John's phone, and sprint back to the van.

6:35 a.m. we're off again. At every intersection we see groups of protesters amassing with their flags and tires and ropes to start setting up the road blocks. We also see large groups of police in vehicles with riot gear, preparing for their part in the day's activities. It is very intimidating. Why are we out here driving around when we should be tucked away safely indoors somewhere?

At 6:59 a.m. we approach the last big intersection we need to cross before we're out of the city. In front of us, there's a big crowd of people starting to string up the rope. John hesitates – do we slow down or speed up? A guy holding one end of the rope starting to block the road sees us and makes a split-second decision based on I-don't-know-what and waves us through.

"Did we escape?" Lilly looks up from her Kindle. Yes, I think we've escaped. We all breathe a sigh of relief.

The only other town between us and the Chilean border is Oruro. I've been researching the past two days trying to find out if there are roadblocks or not. We can make a multi-hour detour to avoid the town entirely, but the toll booth operator and gas station attendant both say it's clear. So we approach.

Why are cars driving toward us the wrong way on a one-way road? Not a good sign. We get to the first intersection to see an 18-wheeler truck parked perfectly across the roundabout entrance, preventing any passage. We park and I cautiously walk over to talk to the people at the roadblock, acting as calm and friendly as I can. They direct us around on side streets and we pass by with barely a five minute delay.

The next hurdle is one we've been warned about for months already, and totally unrelated to the protests. Buying gas without a Bolivian ID. The gas pump attendant looks at our foreign faces and license plate with concern. He goes inside the little building to hide. We try to call him over. He pretends not to see us. Finally we manage to engage him and he mumbles something about foreigners. He takes me to his computer to show me the price of 3.7 bolivianos per liter for nationals and 8.9 for foreigners. I'm more concerned with escaping this country than with saving a few bolivianos, so ask simply, "What price do we need to pay?" He says without hesitation that we can pay something in-between if we don't get a receipt so that he can keep the difference. Ok, 5 bolivianos it is!

We make it to the Salar de Uyuni, the largest salt flat in the world. There is no sign of political unrest. Well, unless you count the fact that every store I walk into has the news playing on their TV and the shopkeepers' eyes are glued to it. Usually there is some drivel game show or soap opera playing, so this is a very noticeable change.

After two nights adventuring and relaxing on the Salar, we emerge and head south to exit Bolivia. We get to an intersection and have to decide – do we escape to the border of Chile or Argentina?

If we turn left, we head toward Argentina: We'd have to pass through a big city which everyone tells us will be impassable due to road blocks. Plus, there is still talk of closing the borders so we could be prevented from driving out.

If we turn right, we head toward Chile: They are having violent protests of their own, and this route requires driving 300 km on a high-elevation dirt road. But, that border crossing is so incredibly remote that no one would bother to block it.

We turn right.

Between our days on the Salar, and then four days on this remote dirt road to the border, we have no connection to the outside world for almost a week. We are dying of suspense.

So what happened?

Friday Nov 8: While we're camped on the Salar de Uyuni, the police forces in major cities announce mutiny against their own government! Videos show the police standing on rooftops cheering and throwing fireworks.

Saturday Nov 9: While we're driving on the remote dirt road toward Chile, the official audit by the Organization of American States finds "clear manipulation" and calls for the election results to be annulled. The chief of the armed forces chimes in, urging Evo to step down.

Sunday Nov 10: While we are watching flamingos and vicuñas cavort in the altiplano, Evo resigns! We assume this means things will calm down, but no. It simply means that the protesters change sides – before it was the anti-Evo contingent and now it's the pro-Evo contingent building roadblocks and marching down the streets.

Monday Nov 11: Evo flees to Mexico (then later moves to Argentina).

Tuesday Nov 12: The U.S. Department of State lists Bolivia at level four, the highest danger level available, putting it in the same category as such fun-loving places as Syria, Afghanistan, and Iraq. They start evacuating government employees and their families, and announce: "U.S. citizens in Bolivia should depart as soon as they safely can."

Thursday Nov 14: we cross the border out of Bolivia into Chile.

Marcos tells us that we left just in time. The roadblocks, that used to go up at 7 a.m., are now 24 hours a day. It's impossible for anyone to get in or out. The military is patrolling on the very street where we camped – Marcos sends a photo of a military truck parked in front of the wall where we slept. He's no longer able to buy fuel for driving. We see photos on the news of people queuing up to get propane for cooking. There's no more fresh food available. Schools are still closed.

An Unexpected Civics Lesson

I never thought about how important it is to have the freedom to protest peacefully in the streets and for the media to be able to report on the truth of what's happening. We have that privilege in the US, and the people of Bolivia seem to also be able to exercise that right. We keep hearing Bolivians say Evo is a dictator, but at least he didn't prevent the protests from happening or the media from showing what was happening. (Whether that was due to lack of desire or lack of ability, I have no idea.)

It is quite an education for us to see how people down here take to the streets and entirely stop the flow of business when they don't like what is happening in the government. The schools have been closed for over three weeks, people aren't able to work, major roads are closed through big cities, and they are starting to run out of food and fuel – they are causing significant and organized disruption in the hopes that the government won't be able to ignore them. This is not just a march down the street at a published time, pre-arranged with police escort, then return to work on Monday, like I've often seen in the US.

Ecuador recently endured 10 days of standstill because the government removed the fuel subsidy there. The people took to the streets and stopped everything. Our family in Cuenca said they couldn't go to work, the kids couldn't go to school, and the town started to run out of food and fuel – they told me that they had to wait in a queue for nine hours to get a new bottle of propane for cooking! Then, the government brought back the fuel subsidy and everything immediately returned to normal.

What would happen if protestors in the US started blocking major roads to stop the flow of food, fuel, and people? I think the police would immediately disperse them, and we know that, thus we don't do it. Or perhaps we just don't have an issue that we care enough about to systematically stop day-to-day life until the government addresses it?

Every new experience on this trip prompts new discussions between John and me. I don't have any answers, but I hope I'll come out of this more open-minded about different ways to solve problems.

The Fun Stuff

Although we didn't get to see most of the sights in Bolivia, we did experience two of the highlights – the Salar de Uyuni and the Lagunas off-road route.

The Salar de Uyuni is the world's largest salt flat, with 12,000 square kilometers of endless white salt. It is such a unique place to visit! I keep thinking we're on snow. Or white sand. Or the moon! We can drive in any direction at any speed for any length of time, and not run into anything. John rides on the hood, we all take a turn riding on the roof, Lilly roller blades in front of the van – the endless silliness is a wonderful change from the stress of the past two weeks.

We decide it's a great place for Lilly to have her first solo drive. She's sat on John's lap before and helped steer, but now she's on her own in the driver's seat. It starts as a joke, and John and I crouch at her elbows ready to grab the wheel, but ends up with her driving solo for 30 minutes while John plays guitar in the back and I look out the window. Occasionally I look over and remind her to keep it under 40 mph. You simply can't screw it up when you're driving on an infinite flat surface with no one around!

Choosing a spot to set up camp here is pretty straightforward – we simply stop driving and park, wherever we are. It feels so wild and free to be here in the middle of white nothing-ness. Seems like John needs the mental break – I'm sitting outside at our table chopping vegetables for dinner when suddenly the door of the van flings open and John runs out naked and goes sprinting away into the distance. I see him on the horizon standing with hands on hips, wearing just a hat and shoes. Lilly is busy with John's axe hacking into the ground to get some salt for our dinner, but when she sees her crazy papa, she runs off after him in fits of giggles. We're all unwinding after the intensity of La Paz.

We've been hearing about the infamous Lagunas Route from other travelers for the past two years. It's somewhat notorious as a terrible dirt track, but with breath-taking views. Literally breathtaking – it passes over 5,000 m elevation (16,400 feet).

We bump along on dirt roads for four days, gaping out the window at stunning endless landscapes of lakes, colorful red mountains, and so many pink flamingos. It's hard to describe, and it's even tougher to photograph. The landscapes are impossibly broad, stretching from horizon to horizon, with so many horizontal layers squeezed into the frame that we simply can't capture it.

First is the foreground of dirt flecked by white salt streaks here and there, then the inevitable lagoon with a layer of pink dots – flamingos – and many different colors of water, then the red/orange/brown/yellow hillsides behind the lagoon, larger mountains beyond that, and finally the bright blue sky stretching to infinity behind it.

On our last night, we park on the shore of yet another colorful lake full of flamingos, but this time with a convenient hot spring on the edge. It's certainly the most unique and picturesque swim I've had – a hot infinity pool looking out over flamingos in an incredible backdrop of layered lakes and mountains. That night, we are treated to an impressive lightning storm in the far horizon over the lake. The three of us sit upstairs in bed together watching through the window. Lilly keeps bouncing up and down, yelling "BOOM!" and "Wow, did you see that one?"

Our last few days in Bolivia are spectacular, but unfortunately will be all we know of this country.

Political Postscript: Evo, his Vice President, and several others in his cabinet fled to Mexico together, leaving a woman several layers down the chain of command as the interim President. New elections were scheduled for May, but then COVID struck. After several delays, new elections were finally held in October 2020 and received record voter turnout of 88%. Evo's successor, Luis Arce, won in a landslide and Evo immediately returned to Bolivia, after 11 months in exile.

Endless white of the Uyuni Salt Flats

Natural hot tub backed by flamingos and mountains on the Lagunas Route

ARGENTINA

We drove 11,120 miles over 16 months in Argentina.
November, 2019 to March, 2021 (including one week in Chile).

37

A BIG DECISION IN
NORTHERN ARGENTINA

F
or over two years now, I've been telling everyone we meet, "We're driving to Argentina!" It's been this vague goal I throw out as an explanation for our trip, the rationale that explains our crazy life choices. So my emotions jump between excitement and trepidation when we finally cross the border to this much-talked-about country – is this the beginning of the end? We want to drive all the way to the southern tip of Argentina, but then what? We have no plan for after. I'm nervous to think about the huge question mark that lies in wait for us after we finish this road trip.

After escaping Bolivia, we first spent a few days in northern Chile in the Atacama desert. But Chile was in turmoil following an increase in public transport fares which triggered mass protests about the cost of living and general inequality. Over a million Chileans took to the streets in violent protests that left many people dead. Rather than constantly monitor the news and attempt to explore while avoiding political danger, we chose to bail out to Argentina immediately. After our experience in Bolivia, we are ready for some peace and stability.

Entering Argentina is like stepping through a magic portal from Latin America to Europe. The people are taller, whiter, and have a somewhat Italian accent. Everyone greets each other with a kiss on the cheek, rather than the handshake we've experienced so far. Restaurants have pizza and pasta, and I'm shocked when I sit down at a small, simple restaurant and am served bread while waiting for my food – that hasn't happened since we left California.

The best change for us is that we are often mistaken for locals. If we're not sitting by our obviously foreign van, then we look just like many of the people here. Someone will talk to Lilly, then express surprise to hear her accent when she responds, having assumed she's Argentine. It's a wonderful change to be able to walk around without being stared at, after two years of standing out like bright neon signs!

The hardest change for us is that everything shuts down in the middle of the day for a multi-hour siesta, and restaurants don't open up for dinner until 8:30 p.m. or so. Our very first night in Argentina we asked a restaurant if we could camp behind their building (yes, no problem) and get dinner, "Well, we have some lunch leftovers, but the kitchen won't open for dinner until 9:30 p.m." I was gobsmacked! We swiftly moved onto another restaurant, which generously planned to open at 9 p.m. I think we are not going to eat dinner out very often in this country!

There's often a slight change in accent when we change countries, but Argentine Spanish has a dramatically different pronunciation and even conjugates their verbs differently, so it takes me longer to adjust. The names of basic items also tend to change from country to country in South America, and Argentina is no exception.

On our first morning here, I approach someone to ask if they have a faucet we can use to fill our water tank, and find myself with three different words on the tip of my tongue, from the last few countries we've been in. I wonder which one they use here in Argentina? I rattle off all three back-to-back, hoping that I'm not speaking nonsense, "Tienes un grifo / caño / llave?" But the person just looks at me blankly and I have to explain, eventually learning that here it has yet another name, *canilla*. Not to mention, they conjugate the "you" part of the verb differently here, so my "tienes" was also incorrect.

Most language differences just make for short-lived confusion, but there's one that I have to be extra careful about. In every other country on this trip the word *coger* means to grab or take something. It's very commonly used. But here, I discover it means "fuck." Yes, seriously. I get a lot of horrified looks when I accidentally use it. "Can you *coger* that banana for me please?" What the coger?!

Exploring northern Argentina we enjoy a national park full of dinosaur fossils, remote hot spring camps, and multicolored mountains reminiscent of Peru. We endure the capital city chaos of Santiago, Chile to buy a new climbing rope, and even get to rock climb in the Andes, although Lilly prefers to sit and read at the base of the rock while John and I climb, so we only stay one night. One of my favorite stops is a rocky river canyon where we end up camping for three days. I'm so impressed by Lilly's fearlessness as we leap off boulders into deep, dark pools of water, and swim between steep vertical cliff faces together – she may still be battling her fear of heights, but she sure shows her bravery in the water.

We spend three days over Christmas wild camping on a river, living like feral hippies and loving it. It's particularly fun to reminisce about our first Christmas of the trip two years ago on the remote island in Belize when Lilly was sure that she saw reindeer footprints in the sand, and last year's van Christmas working at the monkey preserve in Ecuador when I got mugged by a squirrel monkey. We've now perfected our home-made paper Christmas tree stuck on the wall of the van, and Lilly is totally accustomed to getting just a few, small presents.

John is delighted to have his baby (Vancito, not Lilly) running smoothly again after all the trouble in Bolivia and Peru. His confidence is up, which means we explore more remote areas again. Aiming for an obscure camp down a dirt road one afternoon, we come to a river with a bridge across it. There is tape strung loosely across the road and we see that the bridge has fallen into the water. John's been waiting for this Dukes of Hazzard moment all his life.

"Looks like the bridge is out, Luke, we're gonna have to jump it!" I convince him that jumping it might not end well, and find a possible detour on the map, but he's already wading across the river next to the fallen-in bridge, eyeing his options. "I think we can make it. Hold my beer." (Ok, maybe I made up the beer part.) He locks the 4WD hubs on the van, points at the river and starts slowly motoring down the sandy bank. I wade into the water so I can... um, give the five-ton van a little push when it gets stuck? But, although John has to give it a couple of tries, he gets through without too much trouble. He almost seems disappointed, "I thought I'd at least have to use the sand rails, if not the winch, on that one." This is what happens when we go a whole week without having to repair the van!

So, as if on cue, a few days later Vancito decides to go on strike again. We've had a mysterious diesel leak ever since Puyango, and John was tightening a fuel hose in an attempt to fix the problem, but the hose broke off. It wouldn't be a big issue, except that we're camped on a remote lake bed in the middle of nowhere with no reception. So I walk down the beach and find a vacationing family who gives John a ride to the village a few miles away. There he finds a mechanic who says he can fabricate the part and that his buddy will tow us in the morning.

That evening, watching the sunset over the lake while Lilly plays in the water, an older couple walks over to investigate our van. Noemi and Kike live in the nearby village and go for a walk along the beach every day at sunset. They are fascinated by the van and our story, and talk to us for hours, only departing once we promise to visit them the following day when we get to their town.

After breakfast the next morning, a quiet man with a pickup truck appears at the lake bed and tows us a couple miles to Boris the mechanic's house. There, John is invited into the garage where a large pile of loose parts lies spread across the floor in disarray. He kneels down and starts rifling through, looking for something that could replace our broken part, when I hear someone shouting from the street. I go investigate and find Kike, the friendly older man from last night at the lake.

"I'm here to take you to my house. Noemi is cooking lunch for us. Let's go!" This is obviously one of those tiny towns where everyone knows everyone, so when a large, foreign van appears on a side street, everyone hears about it. I promise we'll come as soon as we're done and note down his address, politely declining his offer to take Lilly with him to play.

John and Boris are able to fabricate the part we need fairly easily and the van is up and running again in no time. But when we try to pay, Boris refuses, saying it's such a trivial repair that we don't owe him anything. We try to insist we at least pay for his time and materials, but he keeps saying no. Then we ask how to pay his friend who towed us from the lakebed, but he simply says that if we see him around town we can offer him some money. Finally, John presses a 500 peso note into his hand and he reluctantly accepts it. This trip is constantly teaching us about generosity to strangers.

Leaving Boris's house, we are feeling a little bummed out and not in the mood for socializing, after this latest in the string of never-ending van problems we've had since Puyango. But I point out it would be rude not to visit Kike and Noemi at least for a few minutes, so we detour a few blocks to their house on our way out of town. We park in a flat dirt area behind the house and are immediately swept into a happy, lively family. They live in a small house with concrete floors and walls, a dirt backyard, and lots of kids and constant laughter. They usher Lilly into a kiddie pool to play with their grandkids, and offer us showers and watermelon, both of which we gratefully accept.

While I'm showering, John asks if he can wash his diesel-covered shorts somewhere, and Noemi replies that she'll show me (Mary) where the bucket and faucet are once I'm out of the shower. John wonders if he misunderstood and explains himself again, to which Noemi replies in astonishment, "You're going to wash your own shorts?" John told me later that the whole family watched intently as he filled the bucket with soap and water, unable to believe that a man would wash his own clothes when he has a perfectly good wife to do so.

Due to our late arrival, the lunch invitation turns into a dinner invitation turns into a sleepover. Yet again, we find ourselves part of a family who welcomes us in with open arms and an open house. My discomfort in these situations hasn't subsided over the past two years – I hate to impose on someone when I know I probably won't ever see them again to pay them back – but this has happened enough times now that I'm starting to embrace it.

I walk to the local store to buy wine and supplies to make a salad, and I help Noemi make dinner. John helping in the kitchen is simply not an option. They graciously eat dinner "early" at 9:30 p.m. for us weird North Americans, and we chat for hours afterwards about everything – history, politics, travel, anthropology.

Kike dominates the conversation most of the evening. He is a hilarious character! He has a huge rectangle of a tummy that he absentmindedly rubs, especially while eating, as if encouraging it to grow larger to fit more meat in. I don't know how he eats so much meat, because he only has one tooth left in his mouth! When he roars with laughter, which is often, you see his empty mouth and one lonely tooth on the side. He's also partly deaf, so anytime I speak to him, he lunges his head close to mine and cups his hand around his ear with a quizzical look on his face. He explains that he used to have a hearing aid but lost it and doesn't have the money for a new one. And he continues, "If I did have the money, I should probably spend it on new teeth!" He opens his mouth in uproarious laughter, pointing out the vacancy. After an evening with Kike, you can't help but have an aching belly from eating and laughing so much.

Finally around midnight, with Lilly falling asleep at the table and John and me stifling yawns, we give our thanks and make our apologies for leaving so "early," and retreat to the van to sleep. Living in a van, basically camping, we typically go to sleep early and wake up early, but we are quickly learning that is not going to fly in Argentina.

The next morning is one of those surreal moments that frequently occur when you're living in a van changing location every day.

My brain turns on before my eyes open. Where am I? I don't hear the ocean or river or birds, but nor do I hear city noises. It's hot out, but Central America was many months ago. I hear someone outside moving things around and peer out my window to see a young man loading up a small boat right next to the van.

Oh yes, of course! We broke down on a lake bed in Argentina and ended up camped in a family's backyard in a nearby village, and John agreed last night to go fishing with them early this morning. I love the unpredictability of vanlife.

John gets up and disappears with Kike, his son and grandson, while I leave Lilly sleeping soundly in the van and go make breakfast with Noemi. She and I sit together and chat on their small patio at the front of the house, sharing the special tea-like drink that Argentines adore – *mate*, pronounced mah-tay – and feeding Lilly and the various grand-children who come by over the course of the morning.

It's a peaceful couple of hours that affords me yet another window into someone else's life. Almost every person who passes by on the street stops to wave or chat to Noemi, and I can't help but notice what a wonderful thing it is to be surrounded by family and friends. When I meet people who've lived in the same town their entire lives, and have lots of children and grandchildren, I feel envious of that feeling of security and love. But I recognize that my love of adventure and change makes that lifestyle mostly unattainable for me.

I thank Noemi for welcoming us into her home, and say that we'll be moving on when John gets back from fishing, but she says that Kike has invited their other kids, grandkids, and more neighbors over for a BBQ lunch to see us off! So when the fishermen return with their big catch, I help Noemi prepare the fish and John helps Kike's son chop wood to get the BBQ started. I walk to the store again to buy supplies to make a salad and a peach pie. We haven't seen peaches in two years, but they are in season down here and partly make up for the lack of papayas and mangoes.

The family borrows tables and chairs from their neighbors and packs over a dozen people into their modest backyard. When the fire dies down to coals, they start roasting enormous slabs of beef, serving endless platefuls to all of us. I look around this enormous table full of friendly strangers to see Lilly squeezed between two other kids, eating meat with her fingers and jumping up to play every few minutes. We are, yet again, part of someone else's family whom we've only just met. It's a heart-warming and belly-filling feast.

When we load up the van to leave after lunch, we are called to the front patio where Kike and two friends pull out guitars and start singing. I am overwhelmed when I listen to the words and realize they've written an impromptu song about us! Lilly stands right next to Kike's friend, staring at his lips, entranced to hear words coming out about her. The hugs and kisses and blessings are endless when we finally make our departure that afternoon.

This latest van debacle, although it ended with a wonderful experience, underscores the fact that we have not fully recovered from the Puyango disaster. The van has been leaking oil and fuel ever since the Puyango mechanic hacks dug around in our engine – is it sensible to drive into remote Patagonia with the van in this state?

At the same time, John's neck pain from his Costa Rica surfing days is resurfacing with a vengeance, likely exacerbated by all the time spent craning his neck into the engine doing repairs. The lake bed break-down event turns out to be the final straw, not just because the van stranded us again, but because John's right arm was so numb and painful the next morning that he couldn't cast his fishing line.

We need to take this seriously. We can't pop into a random doctor here and there and hope it's going to resolve itself. So we decide we need to be stable for at least a few months to properly address both issues.

The problem is the timing. We want to explore Patagonia – the southernmost part of Chile and Argentina – but that needs to happen during their summer, December to March. It's January now, so if we stop for a few months then we'll miss the season and will have to wait until next December to go down there.

What?! We're committing to being stable for almost a year? It's not what we'd planned, but it just doesn't make sense to drive thousands of miles through remote Patagonia when John's neck is killing him and the van might break down at any moment.

But where should we stop?

Do you remember our first and favorite overlander friends, Argentine Vicky and Canadian Brad and their little son Tai, whom we met swimming with whale sharks way back in Baja at the start of our trip? They got to Argentina long before we did and settled down in the small mountain town of Capilla del Monte. We detoured from our drive down the Andes to visit them just before Christmas and loved the area, but wanted to get to Patagonia for summer so moved on. But now we decide to turn around and head back to Capilla del Monte.

The Argentine school year is March to December, so it works out perfectly: Lilly will attend a local school for a full year, while John works on his neck and the van, and I concentrate on freelancing to refill our bank account. We rent a house, enroll Lilly in a bilingual school, set up osteopath appointments for John, and I start working again for the friend who hired me back in Ecuador.

I feel disappointed about not getting to Patagonia for another year, but I'm excited about a year of socializing regularly with friends and not having to homeschool.

This year is going to be great! What difference could it possibly make if we visit Patagonia in January 2020 or January 2021?

As it turns out, all the difference in the world...

38

LOCKED DOWN

Vanlife is about constant change. Over the past two-and-a-half years, I've woken up in a different place almost every morning. Sometimes I fall asleep to the sound of ocean waves crashing just a few feet from my bed, other times I'm subjected to the constant barrage of city traffic or dogs barking all night, and often I'm surrounded by that incredible silence that can only be found at high elevation in the mountains. Each day we talk to new people, navigate different roads, and explore unfamiliar towns. It's endlessly stimulating, and sometimes exhausting.

So, going from vanlife to lockdown is a big change.

Not only are we trapped in one place, we're also prohibited from exploring our surroundings or from talking to people around us. I didn't realize how much I thrive on change, social interaction, and physical adventure – all things that we experienced daily when living in a van – until it was taken away.

So, what's happening here in Argentina?

On March 20th, 2020, we had only 100 cases of COVID in the entire country, and President Fernandez shut everything down. Argentina enacted one of the stricter quarantines in the world.

You could only leave home on designated days based on the last digit of your ID number. My passport ends in an odd number, so I was only allowed to leave the house on odd-numbered dates of the month.

Only one person per household was allowed out, only for essential purchases, and only within a 500-meter radius of home.

No kids were allowed out, ever. Yup, I didn't lay eyes on another child for almost two months! Lilly was literally climbing the walls from boredom – we hung pieces of old garden hose from the roof of our balcony for her to swing and climb on.

Most shops were shuttered. Biking down the main street, it looked like a ghost town. Except, that is, for the long queues outside each grocery store and bank – essential stores could open for just a few hours, and only one person could enter at a time. Normally I hate lining up for anything, but I came to appreciate those rare moments that I could speak to another human face to face.

They enacted a 4 p.m. curfew in our town. A siren would ring at 3 p.m. as a warning, then again at 4 p.m. to signal curfew. After that, the only sound I'd hear was the occasional police car cruising around looking for curfew-breakers. I was reminded of movie reels from the Great Depression or WW1, where everyone is lining up for food rations and hiding in their homes in the evening while the police patrol.

Borders were closed. No one could enter or leave the country.

They also locked down travel within the country. We couldn't even go to the next town 15 minutes away without a special permit, which was impossible to get without an Argentine ID.

Our ATM cards stopped working in the banks and the Western Union in our town stopped processing international transactions, leaving us carefully counting our pesos and digging into our safe for our emergency stash of US dollars.

From my snippets of conversation while out shopping or on the phone, I found that people were mostly positive and accepting of the sudden changes. Friends pointed out that Argentines have had to deal with much worse in their country's history. Our neighborhood self-organized to identify at-risk people and set up a system for delivering groceries to them. We had no shortage of food or toilet paper like we saw in the US, and I gained a new appreciation for the geographic scope of Argentina – this country stretches from tropical rainforest to snowy peaks to the ocean, so we get diverse foods here without importation.

Like most people across the world in March and April 2020, I read the news fanatically, trying to analyze the limited information available. John and I debated endlessly what to do.

A small town in a developing country is a great place to be if you're trying to avoid COVID, but it's a terrible place to be if you contract COVID and become seriously ill. It was a huge relief when the news reported that children are mostly immune, but I had nightmares about John being taken away in an ambulance to some foreign hospital by himself.

In April, the Argentine President announced he'd allow repatriation flights for US citizens over the following week, and that there may not be any more flights until September! You can imagine that piece of news caused a stir in our household. We had to commit to staying six months in this foreign place during this period of extreme uncertainty, or leave immediately. John and I spent the day researching online and calling doctor friends, trying to analyze our way to a logical answer.

The overlander groups were abuzz with people attempting desperate drives across the country to get to Buenos Aires, the only functioning airport, to get the "last flight out." The government was only allowing one airline to operate and tickets were thousands of dollars each, yet they sold out within minutes of being posted.

Each province in Argentina demanded different paperwork from travelers to pass through – a letter from your embassy proving you had a repatriation flight, a doctor's note saying you were healthy, something from the police – the list was constantly changing. Some overlanders were turned around, while others were stopped and taken to a forced quarantine in hotel rooms shared with other travelers. Those who made it to Buenos Aires were only allowed into city limits if they could prove they had a flight out within 24 hours – that left no time to sell/import/ship their camper vans.

The prospect of trying to buy three elusive tickets, travel 500 miles over land to Buenos Aires, potentially abandon our van, and then subject ourselves to a dozen-plus hours of travel with hundreds of other people just didn't seem like a smart idea when trying to avoid a contagious disease. Plus, our home countries (US and UK) had far more COVID cases than Argentina due to much more relaxed quarantines.

On the other hand, I feel vaguely uneasy to live through such a significant world event in a foreign country. I struggle to understand the official decrees about ever-changing quarantine rules in Spanish. We don't know how the healthcare system works, or how we'd be treated as foreigners if we have to go to hospital. We don't have a network of friends and family to lean on. Our legal status is unclear – our visa and van importation expired in April but we can't get to a city to extend them.

And, fundamentally, we are less free here than we would be in the US. The news regularly reports the number of people arrested or fined for breaking quarantine – not wearing a mask or going for a bike ride too far from their house. While this feels foreign and terrifying for Americans like us, used to our inalienable rights, it is the reason Argentina has so many fewer cases than the US, so we try to look at it as a good thing.

Ultimately, we've decided to stay put, keeping a careful eye on the news and ready to change plans.

April and May were hard months of uncertainty and confinement, but in June the President started relaxing the quarantine. Curfew was abolished, outdoor activities and social gatherings permitted, non-essential stores like restaurants opened, and I started to fall in love with our new hometown.

From our back door, we can hike into the mountains or bike on the web of dirt roads that make up much of the town and surrounding area. It's a short ride to several rivers which provide delightful rock-hopping and swimming through natural pools or under waterfalls, and there are lakes for fishing or boating or just enjoying a picnic with friends on the shore. The views from our house are amazing – sitting on our front porch we watch the rock-covered mountain faces turn alpenglow red at sunset, or on a cold day I watch the sunset over the lake from my bedroom window.

It's an incredible luxury for me to have such easy access to the outdoors. In our old lives in California, we drove at least three hours for our favorite outdoor activities, and this typically came with crowds of people and a high cost of living. Here, I can walk directly out my back door onto trails into the mountains, usually seeing more condors than people.

Best of all, we start going regularly to the two local climbing areas and finally start to meet other climbers. (It's not easy to meet new people during a nationwide quarantine!) Both areas are so picturesque, running along river canyons and surrounded by colorful trees, and I am so happy to be getting out on the rock again.

The people here are really into exercise, healthy food, and looking out for the environment and each other. I might not identify as hippie, but these are all things I value highly, so we try to embrace some of their "hippie" habits. We start reusing jars that I would normally toss into the recycling bin – why buy a plastic bag of rice if I can reuse an old glass honey jar to buy rice from the bulk store instead? We can't buy pre-made tahini or hummus, so we buy sesame seeds and dry garbanzos and make it ourselves, consuming less preservatives and packaging. There's no Amazon delivery here, so when we want something, we get creative – we turn milk cartons into a bird feeder, a pencil holder, and a toothbrush stand. The Argentines are incredibly resourceful and I hope we can bring some of their low-waste habits back to the US with us.

The pro-environment attitude here resonates with us, but the anti-science beliefs are harder to understand, especially in relation to COVID. At first I debate their disbelief in news coming from the government health officials, but then I discover that this lack of trust is well deserved. Our friends tell us about the time 20 years ago when the government suddenly blocked millions of people's bank accounts. Can you imagine waking up one morning to find that you can no longer access your savings because the government has commandeered it? It's no surprise that people here bury their money in their back yard, or drive to Uruguay to use the bank system there, rather than trust the Argentine banks.

Similarly, we hear comical but shocking true stories of buying a house here. One friend transferred her foreign-held dollars to a stranger's US account and then met them in a cafe where they surreptitiously handed her the cash in a plastic bag. Another made a dozen consecutive day trips to Uruguay to smuggle her money into Argentina in her underwear. I kid you not! Large transactions have to happen in US dollars and in cash, because no one trusts the banking system, so people get creative.

On top of the financial mess, looking further back in history but still very much alive in Argentine memory, is the "Dirty War" in the early 1980s. Tens of thousands of people were kidnapped by the military dictatorship, and most of them are still missing today. So I really can't blame Argentines for not trusting their government, given the examples they've experienced in their lifetime.

But the result is that people mostly ignore the government's COVID rules after the first few months. John and I find ourselves the most strict parents among Lilly's group of friends, declining invitations to sleepovers but letting her attend outdoor pool parties. When I go climbing, my friends still share their *mate* drink, which I decline, and kiss everyone hello and goodbye, which I do while holding my breath! The most comical is when I see someone enter a store and recognize a friend inside – they both pull off their masks to kiss each other hello and then put them back on to continue shopping. Argentine culture does not fit well with social distancing!

So what's *mate*? "Let's share mate" is akin to "Let's get a coffee," except that everyone takes turns sipping the same drink from a shared straw and cup, rather than ordering their own personal favorite. Argentines never leave home without a thermos of hot water under their arm and a bag of tea leaves, along with a cute little cup and special straw for sharing. It's an indispensable part of Argentine social life, and a small nod to their strong sense of community and solidarity. It makes me feel even more foreign to decline the *mate* cup when it's passed to me, but it just doesn't seem like a good idea during COVID.

The other indomitable Argentine custom that we've struggled to adopt is the late night schedule. Imagine dropping off your four-year-old son at an art class at 6 p.m., then picking him up at 10 p.m. and returning home to start cooking dinner – it's perfectly normal! We endure several evenings of starvation before we learn our lesson: always eat dinner at home before you go to someone's house for dinner. They won't usually even start the fire for cooking until 10 p.m. I am forever impressed by the tenacity of the Argentine stomach.

What we lack in social interaction, we make up for in animal loving, being adopted by three strays in the first few months.

A tiny black cat was living in a tree next to our house and approached our deck one morning meowing pitifully with hunger. We poured her some milk and opened a can of tuna, which she cautiously approached and then rapidly devoured. She gradually got more comfortable with us, and eventually we took her to the vet to get checked out and spayed. Lilly named her Midnight and they've become very close, always snuggled up together on the couch or running around on the roof of the house together.

Not long after Midnight adopted us, a large black male dog wandered nervously by our porch, his ribs visible against his tick-covered skin. So we gave him some of Midnight's cat food. He returned with a dog buddy (sister?) who was even more skittish. We started to feed them twice a day, sneaking tick medicine into their food monthly, and watched their skin start to shine and their muscles grow strong. Now, a few months later, Frida flips onto her back to get her tummy rubbed when she sees us, and Jim lays his head in our laps – this from two dogs who used to run away if I so much as stretched my hand out toward them!

Now every morning when I open our front door, I laugh at the stampede of 12 black furry legs and two furiously wagging tails shoving their way into the house for snuggles and breakfast. We are falling head over heels in love with all three animals, and I know it will be terrible when we have to ultimately leave, but how could we ignore them?

My primary disappointment of the year 2020 is that Lilly won't get a year of normal school. After two-and-a-half years of homeschooling, it's time for her to experience groups of kids, teachers, peer pressure –

all the good and bad that come with school. She attended school here for only two weeks before COVID shut them down.

I was so proud of her on the first day! There were hundreds of kids and parents in a huge courtyard, most of whom already knew each other and were chatting away in slangy Argentine Spanish. They had a flag raising ceremony, people made long speeches, and then everyone sang the national anthem – of course we didn't know it so we just mumbled along, trying to fit in. Then they grouped up the kids into their respective classrooms and marched them away. Lilly ran back to give me a tight hug with a slightly worried look in her eyes, then turned around and joined her class. I had tears in my eyes. She is one incredible girl.

But, alas, two weeks later the schools closed. Now, we are torn between doing the homework sent by the school so Lilly will be ready to return if they re-open, versus continuing with our own home-schooling to match California standards. She can't read very well in Spanish, so I sit beside her every morning to help with the homework from the school, and it takes hours. Eventually we stop doing our English language school entirely because it's just too much, but of course that leaves me worried that we're letting her fall behind in English writing just so she can learn to read Spanish. Is that the right decision?

* * *

The wilderness access and friendly people make for a mostly happy year in Capilla del Monte, but there is a constant shadow over our lives from COVID. Of course we have the same worries as anyone else in the world about potentially getting seriously ill, but we also have the permanent question mark of our legal status.

Argentine Immigration decreed that all foreigners and their vehicles can stay as long as the country is in quarantine, but when the quarantine ends we'll have to leave within 20 days. But the quarantine is only announced in two-week increments, so we never know if we might have to leave in two weeks. It's endlessly frustrating not being in control of your own destiny. Big decisions like the right way to educate Lilly or how much ownership we should take of the dogs and cat, as well as smaller decisions like should we buy a washing machine or a couch – everything depends on whether we'll be living here for a year or flying out of the country in two weeks.

For the first time, after living together in a tiny home for over two years, John and I start arguing over trivial things like washing the dishes. We talk openly about it, wondering why we've had no trouble handling stressful situations before – like the Bolivian revolution or being stranded in Puyango, or being lost and hungry on top of a climb in Yosemite together – but now living in a comfortable house in safety we are squabbling?

We recognize that we're not angry with each other, we're feeling frustrated by our sudden lack of purpose. We're no longer able to travel because all borders are closed, so we may never accomplish our goal of driving to Patagonia. John can't see medical professionals for his neck problem because they're only handling emergencies, nor can he order parts to do van repairs because the borders are closed. I worry that we're making the wrong decisions about Lilly's education, plus there's no demand for my freelancing work due to COVID. We both feel directionless. If we only knew how long this situation would continue, then we could make a decision and a plan, but now we're waiting. Just like the rest of the world.

Ultimately, we recognize that we are so much better off than so many others this year. We are healthy and live with our delightfully cheerful little girl and three adorable animals. John helps me appreciate the little things that make me happy, pushing me to go climb with a friend or go for a bike ride while he watches Lilly, and I return exhausted and happy. Likewise, I cover homeschooling while he does online physical therapy for his neck and takes guitar-making lessons from a luthier he met in town here, invigorating him mentally and physically. This is just one more experience to chalk up in our varied history together, learning how best to support each other and thrive in this lockdown situation.

* * *

After surviving the uncertainty of COVID during winter in the Southern Hemisphere, and entering springtime in November, we are happy to be on the home stretch to a more free life. But now we're entering fire season in this drought-stricken part of Argentina.

One morning we wake up to see a significant column of smoke to the north of us. The town mobilizes quickly. By the time I've eaten breakfast there are already several groups self-organizing to deliver meals to the volunteer firefighters and collect equipment donations. My group chats are going crazy with messages – identifying elderly people who need help evacuating, posting offers of places to stay for those most affected, sharing trailers to move large animals out of harm's way. For someone who has lived in a big city with government-run emergency services most of my life, it's amazing to see this solidarity and self-initiative.

By late afternoon, we hear that the volunteer firefighters are evacuating people who live at the north end of our town. Friends who live south of us call and tell us to go stay with them. I pack our bags just in case and tell Lilly that we might have a sleepover.

By sheer bad luck, John had chosen this week to work on the fuel filtration system on the van, meaning that the engine is entirely dismantled. He quickly works to put the engine back together as the skies get darker with smoke over the course of the day. The sunset is an eerie bright red in a smoke-filled sky. I deliver him dinner at the van, and he pauses work to look at the horizon where there's now an obvious red glow from the approaching fire. He works late into the night by flashlight to get it ready in case we have to drive away the next day.

He laments, "Last time I was working on the van, there was a political revolution exploding all around us, and now I'm working against the clock of an approaching wildfire!"

That night we set our alarm to go off every two hours so we can look out the window and evacuate if the fire gets closer. Luckily, the wind changes direction and the firefighters are able to get the fire under control.

But a few weeks later, it's deja vu. The smoke-filled skies, the eerie red light, the ash falling on our heads. At least this time the van is not in the middle of a repair.

Around 4 p.m. we get the notification: our neighborhood is being evacuated.

GULP. I've never experienced this before. Stay calm.

We pack the van with anything irreplaceable and try to get the animals in. Midnight is easy to grab, but the dogs are panicked and skittish. We realize they've probably never been inside of a vehicle before! It takes almost an hour but we finally manage to force them into the van. But then, when I open the front door to get in myself, the cat runs off!

Lilly and I chase after her. The wind is really picking up now, blowing loudly through the trees and knocking over the smaller plant pots on our patio. Ash is raining onto my hair, mixing with the dust that is flying around in the wind. It all feels very apocalyptic. Lilly and I search for Midnight but I know there's no way we'll find her if she doesn't want to be found. Around us, everyone is driving away and it's getting dark even though it's early afternoon. We can now see the red glow of the fire at the top of the hill and John says we have to leave. We drive down the hill with heavy hearts. Lilly won't stop crying.

We go to a friend's house downtown and watch the fire as it crests the mountain near our house. As it starts to move downwards, it picks up speed until it looks like lava cascading down a volcano in the black sky. We know our neighborhood will burn up in the next few minutes. It's an incredible but terrifying sight.

But then, BOOM! Lightning cracks, thunder booms, and rain starts falling. The timing is unbelievable. We tell Lilly that Midnight will be fine, hoping that we're not lying, and we set up our beds in Vancito, falling asleep to the sound of rain hammering on the roof above our heads.

The next morning driving back to our house is intense. The mountain that we've stared at every day for the past eight months is burned to ash. There are black fingers reaching down in several places almost touching the houses. A few more minutes and the houses would have burned.

But the best part of our return is Midnight sitting casually on our ash-covered doormat meowing as if to ask, "What was the big deal, and why is my breakfast late?"

39

PATAGONIA AND THE END OF THE ROAD

D riving toward the jagged peaks of Fitz Roy and Cerro Torre feels momentous and surreal. This is the Patagonia that we have heard about for so many years. This is the true ending of our epic road trip that we've been planning and living for so long. It's hard to believe, after so many obstacles, that we've made it all the way down here.

I keep staring at John in disbelief, saying, "You drove this van from California to Patagonia! You're amazing!"

After ten months of COVID lock-down in a rental house in central Argentina, we finally get to move back into the van. In December 2020, the Argentine government announces that they'll allow limited travel within the country for the summer – that's January and February down here – so we decide to risk driving down to Patagonia.

There is a great deal of uncertainty – rumors that the country will lock down again on January 15th and constantly changing rules about what paperwork is required to enter each province – so this mini-trip feels very different from the freedom we had before COVID. We worry that we could get stuck down in Patagonia during their severe winter if there's another lockdown, so we always have one eye on the news and the road back north.

Also in December, the Argentine government changed their COVID policy for foreign vehicles. Throughout most of 2020, they kept extending the temporary importation for foreign vehicles, but at the end of the year they tossed that out. We manage to get a three-month extension, but Argentine customs officials tell us we must drive out of the country before that expires or Vancito will be *secuestrado* (confiscated)! But, in the same breath they tell us that all borders are closed so we can't drive out. Bureaucracy at its finest!

It's hard to make decisions about anything when you're not sure if you may be kicked out of the country in the next two months, so this uncertainty casts a small, constant shadow over our enjoyment of the trip. It gives me just a hint of appreciation for how undocumented immigrants might feel. Although, we have a safe country to return to if we do get thrown out of Argentina, which many immigrants do not.

Another downside to traveling during COVID is the lack of social interaction. One of my favorite aspects of vanlife is that we're always meeting new people and Lilly usually has playmates at every campsite. Now with COVID, we no longer stop to pick up hitch-hikers (of which there are many in Argentina), we don't invite people into the van for tours (which used to happen all the time), and conversations with strangers happen briefly and at an antisocial distance.

At the same time, however, we are drawing even more attention than usual. The borders have been closed since March 2020, and almost all foreigners evacuated back to their countries long ago, so we are a rare breed. When we get to campgrounds, the owners frequently comment, "You're the first foreigners I've seen in nine months!" Talking to each other in English in a supermarket draws lots of confused, and sometimes suspicious, stares from people around us. Almost every interaction prompts the question, "But how did you get here?"

Most towns are open for tourism with masks and social distancing, so we are surprised at the much stricter rules we find in the southern-most province of Santa Cruz. We approach the first town past the province border checkpoint, thinking we can stop for a shower and to buy groceries, but at the entrance there is a barrier and police waving us to stop. They interrogate us through our window then make us follow an escort car through town to the other side, whereupon they close that barrier behind us. They say we can only go to the gas station, and only under escort, but nowhere else inside the town limits. I get out and approach a man to ask if we can buy groceries, but he starts backing away from me as I get closer, as if I'm a dangerous person! It's unsettling. I want to shout, "We've been alone in our van for three weeks, we can't possibly have COVID!" but instead we depart feeling like unwanted refugees. What a difference from the welcome we received throughout Latin America prior to COVID.

In spite of the COVID-related stresses, or perhaps because of them, we greatly appreciate our two months of Patagonia adventuring. We enjoy countless amazing hikes around El Chalten and Bariloche, and Lilly proves herself time and again to be just as strong a hiker as John and me. This nine-year-old has walked farther than most adults! The sharp, jagged mountain ranges down in the far south of Patagonia are astounding, as is the wind that can literally knock you off your feet when you step outside of the van. We delight in the unique monkey puzzle and alerce trees, visit the outlaw Butch Cassidy's house where he hid for several years, and we blow out the first tire of the whole trip. But primarily my memories are dominated by countless picnics with magnificent views on our way to yet another lake or peak or volcano or waterfall.

Due to the border closure with Chile, we cannot get to Ushuaia, the "southernmost city in the world," which is disappointing, but we take El Calafate as a decent second-place prize. Its Perito Moreno glacier makes for a good spontaneous science lesson. The three of us stand at the viewing platform, huddled together in our thickest down jackets, enjoying the regular cracking and booming noise as enormous chunks of ice flake off and crash into the lake.

* * *

For years now, I've struggled to contain my disappointment that Lilly is so afraid of heights. She loves climbing trees, boulders, and onto the roof of the house or van, but when she's tied into a rope on a vertical rock wall and gets high off the ground, she starts shaking in fear and crying. We tell her it's no big deal, and let her sit at the base of the rock reading a book while we climb without her, or we just go hiking together instead of climbing. But it's hard not to feel jealous when I see other kids climbing fearlessly, and it makes me sad to push away my dreams of doing family ascents of peaks together one day.

So imagine my surprise at Piedra Parada climbing area when I begin to pull down a rope from a route I have just climbed and Lilly stops me, "Wait! I want to try it."

John and I exchange nervous glances. We really don't want to put her in a position of being terrified for the hundredth time. I tell her this route is hard and if she's really excited to climb then I'll find an easier one for her to do. She insists, so I hesitantly let her tie in and start climbing. She cruises up about 15 feet, gets to the hard part and hangs there, swinging around on the rope looking for a way up, unable to pass. I am amazed at how relaxed she appears to be. I ask if she'd like to do an easier route and she comes down, enthusiastic. John and I try not to overreact, but it's hard to contain our surprise and excitement.

We find an 80-foot climb that's easier. I climb up to the top and belay from up there, and John ties Lilly into the rope. She cruises up, pausing a couple times at hard spots, but never showing signs of distress. Periodically she leans back on the rope, as comfortable as though she's reclining in a chair, to call up to me, "Hi Mama!" with a huge grin on her face. Tears start streaming down my face. I've been imagining this moment for nine years! I don't know what has changed – maybe she just grew out of her fear – but I'm overjoyed.

After this success, we also climb down south in El Chalten and then revisit our favorite climbing area in Argentina back up near Mendoza – Arenales. Last time we were here, we climbed only a little because we felt bad leaving Lilly at the base by herself. This time, we climb a 700-foot multi-pitch route up a spire! Lilly gets scared in two tough spots but she climbs to the top with a smile on her face. It's a day I'll never forget.

* * *

Returning to our home in Capilla del Monte, we are excited to be reunited with our cat and two dogs (who were being cared for by a friend while we were gone), and of course to see our friends. However, the problems with our visa are still not resolved. We spend two more weeks attempting to convince Argentine customs to let us stay longer, pointing out that the borders are closed so it's impossible to drive out of the country, while I also research how to export Vancito out in a shipping container, just in case.

I learn that it takes up to three weeks to get the van exported, so we make one final plea at customs on the day four weeks before our visa expires, but they turn us down again.

So... we have no other option. We're out!

What follows is seven days of total chaos.

Finding good homes for our three animals, selling/giving away our furniture, tools, and kitchen appliances, organizing the van shipment, saying good-bye to a year's worth of friends (while attempting to minimize hugging), and driving 500 miles to get to Buenos Aires with three weeks to spare for van exportation before the visa expires. Phew!

In Buenos Aires we clean and pack up Vancito, then drop it off at the port to be searched by drug dogs and, far more terrifying, reviewed by Argentine customs to see if they'll let it out. We buy surprisingly cheap flights to California and subject ourselves to COVID tests so that we'll be allowed on the plane. There is one heart-stopping moment at the check-in desk when the lady sees we've overstayed our visa by a year and says we need to get clearance from Immigration to leave the country. I explain that tourist visas were automatically extended due to COVID, she makes some phone calls to confirm, and eventually lets us go.

Finally, sitting in the boarding lounge, our negative COVID test results approved and our passports stamped out, it hits me that we are leaving. I haven't been outside of South America for two-and-a-half years, when we left Colombia to visit home for a few weeks!

My emotions are mixed. Partly I'm exhausted from the uncertainty and logistics of the past few weeks, partly I'm sad that our incredible van trip is coming to an end in such an abrupt way, and partly I'm confused about how I will answer the inevitable question that everyone will ask, "What next?" I'm certainly looking forward to living in a country where we have the right to stay as long as we want. It's tough making life decisions based on visa rules.

But, most importantly, I'm looking forward to visiting friends and family. These three-and-a-half years have been an incredible adventure that I'll never forget, but the one thing missing throughout was close relationships. So for now, I'll push aside my uncertainty and concerns about what we're going to do with our lives, and concentrate on the logistics of flying to California, retrieving the van from Texas, getting COVID vaccines, figuring out health insurance, and hopefully reuniting with friends and family.

California here we come... (I hope).

Lilly climbing at Piedra Parada

Mary rappelling down after climbing at Piedra Parada

John & Lilly hiking out to Cerro Torre

Mary, John & Lilly in front of Fitz Roy

40

RE-ENTRY

We land in California and immediately get in trouble with US customs because I have an Argentine apple in my bag. After dealing with so much bureaucracy in Latin America, this feels so easy. He speaks English! He can't kick us out of our own country! We are not a rare circumstance that no one knows how to deal with! I didn't realize, until this moment, how often on the trip I'd worried about what some official in a uniform might do to us. It's especially refreshing when I decide to just sit down and let John handle the whole thing – he speaks the language here!

Within 24 hours of landing, we're offered two empty homes, two extra cars, several boxes of hand-me-down clothes and books – but no hugs – from various friends. It's wonderful to feel so loved after being mostly on our own the past several years. But it's also surreal to finally be with people whom I've known for ages and feel so close to, yet they stand 10 feet away from me with a mask on. In Argentina, even total strangers kissed me hello at any meeting.

Within two days of landing, we're both vaccinated against COVID. Back in Argentina, they are piecing together a vaccination plan with small batches being delivered from China and Russia, but not even the elderly can get one yet. I read about wealthy Argentines flying to Miami to get vaccinated.

Within two weeks of landing, Lilly is enrolled in the local public school near our Yosemite cabin. All the kids wear masks, but the school is otherwise entirely open, with all teachers vaccinated. Back in Argentina, the schools open briefly but then close down again as a new wave of COVID hits.

Within three weeks of landing, John and I get our second COVID shots and we start spending weekends with vaccinated friends, as if COVID never happened. Back in Argentina, the President announces a return to full lock-down, as cases hit new record highs and the hospitals are maxed out. COVID is now sweeping through our old hometown of Capilla, and many of our friends have it. A friend in Buenos Aires tells us two of her friends have died from COVID in the weeks since we left her apartment.

I've never experienced such an obvious contrast between the developing and the developed world. This is an international disaster that hits people equally regardless of their nationality, yet we are now almost entirely free and clear of it simply due to where we were born. Maybe I should thank Argentine customs for forcing us out of the country when they did.

Once we get through the initial chaos and logistics of our return, I fall into a temporary post-trip depression. For over four years now I've been either planning or living this incredible life dream. The thought of living in a normal house and finding a stable job and doing the same thing day after day for years on end... just doesn't inspire me.

John's excited about a new business idea to reduce carbon in our atmosphere. Lilly says she misses living in the van and cried the first week at her new school, but by the second week has made friends and is happy as can be. She's an amazingly flexible and positive kid.

But I find myself dreaming about the next adventure. I want to get on bicycles and explore Europe, even possibly make it to Asia under our own pedal-power! We may only have a couple more years of Lilly being such a sweet kid who loves to be with her parents. But with COVID right now it's not the time to travel, plus John needs to finally have extended time dedicated to healing his neck. So I tell myself that it's normal to feel down after a huge exciting event, and that I'll throw myself happily into a new community once I find one to love. Our mountain cabin is a wonderful place to wait for the van to arrive, but it's too remote and does not have a good school for long-term living.

So, I turn my energy to finding a new place to call home, and focus on the life learnings from our trip that are suddenly so relevant to this next, undefined stage of our lives...

I've amassed an incredible collection of personal experiences with diverse individuals, which teach me that there are so many ways to live a happy life on this planet. From Joe, the 71-year-old backpacker with the frostbitten toes who wanted nothing more than to live outside enjoying nature; to Rita, who made corn tortillas to feed her granddaughter in rural Guatemala but was full of joy in her simple life after surviving the violent years; to Kike, the jolly Argentine who couldn't afford false teeth but spent his weekends eating BBQ meat and laughing with his family. I want to be open-minded to new ways to live, and not get immediately sucked back into the life I had before. And I want to echo the kindness and generosity that we experienced so often in Latin America.

After living in so many different places in the last few years, I've realized I should be worrying less about *where* to live, and more about *how* to live. Educating our daughter among what community of peers? Sustaining ourselves financially in what way? Nourishing our bodies through what food and exercise? I've seen that it's so important to surround yourself with the kind of people you want to be, because their attitudes and habits will rub off on you. When you live in a hippie town in Argentina, you start reusing everything and appreciating mother nature more; when people around you are exceedingly generous like in Colombia, you notice your daughter starting to share her toys more; when people are unfailingly loving and polite like in Ecuador, you take the time to greet everyone you meet and it makes you feel good; when you notice people appreciating their simple life in Guatemala, you start to realize how happy you can feel when you simplify your own life. The community I live in will affect my happiness and how I feel about myself, perhaps more than the location itself.

And perhaps my biggest take-away is that it's the simplest things in life that make me happy. I'm often asked about my favorite country or experience from the trip, and I'm surprised to realize which moments stand out most to me. Sure, I'll never forget the wild beach camping in Baja, the unique friendships we forged while teaching in Guatemala, the multitude of generosity we experienced in Colombia, volunteering with the goofy spider monkeys in Ecuador, being welcomed into the tiny villages at ruins in Northern Peru... and yet... the strongest memories for me are the simple evenings in the van parked somewhere remote and quiet, just the three of us:

Snuggling with Lilly in bed reading an adventure story while enveloped by darkness outside our windows, listening to the foreign sounds of ocean waves crashing or monkeys howling, as she gasps in wonder or giggles in delight at the story.

Or the three of us dancing and singing in our tiny kitchen together – Lilly and I drumming on the counter with our hands while John plays guitar, all of us singing at the tops of our lungs, dancing in the five feet of floor space available to us.

Or the three of us tucked around our tiny table together, legs intertwined and plates alternating in the little table space available, eating our simple dinner that we cooked on the camp stove outside.

It's the collection of these hundreds of small moments that are my favorite memories of this trip. It makes me wonder: why did we need to quit our jobs and entirely drop out of normal life to have those experiences? Surely in our big house in a safe neighborhood with a comfy couch and more books than I can count, we could have those moments? But, somehow it felt impossible. Too busy with work and school, and getting caught up in the whirlwind of activity that comes with living in a city of overachieving people. It's hard to enjoy the present when I'm constantly planning for some future event or I always feel the need to be productive. I need to recognize the value of simple, seemingly unimportant moments.

Similarly, as I learned when we returned from the Galapagos, it is far more effective to make a small improvement in your daily life than to plan a big one-off event like a holiday. So I'll try to set up my life now to have joy in each day – whether it's a bike commute to Lilly's school or a fulfilling job that pays less but makes me feel good about what I'm doing – rather than dreaming about the next big one-off adventure.

It's impossible to summarize the past three-and-a-half years except to emphasize the constant change. We lived with monkeys and swam with whale sharks, we taught English to local kids and talked our way out of police searches, we picked lice out of Lilly's hair and washed our bodies in waterfalls, we befriended Venezuelan refugees and lived through a revolution. Vanlife means new experiences every day, and I love that. We have no idea what the future holds, but this trip has taught me that a simpler life can be far richer than our traditional lives before this. So whether it's in a van, or on bicycles, or putting down roots in a new community in the US, we'll be trying to embrace that simplicity wherever we are.

EPILOGUE

Mary, John & Lilly are now living in Salt Lake City, Utah – a city that fulfilled their criteria of friends, climbing, skiing, and a good school.

John has started a business to capture carbon from the atmosphere, in the hopes that his grandchildren can explore the same beautiful and healthy planet that he got to see during this trip. Lilly is making friends at the public bilingual school, settling into yet another new lifestyle with nary a complaint. Mary is attempting to make a career out of writing, although she recognizes it's not much more profitable than volunteering at a monkey preserve, which was her first choice of career. They all enjoy the nearby rock climbing and mountain biking, and look forward to skiing this winter for the first time in four years.

Vancito spent three weeks with a team of specialist diesel mechanics getting the full spa treatment it deserved after Puyango and so many bumpy dirt roads. It miraculously passed the Utah smog test and is now a weekend adventure wagon, brimming with memories each time it gets transformed into a house again.

And, Mary is not-so-secretly plotting the next family adventure – fly to London, buy bicycles, and pedal east across Europe. Stay tuned!

NOTE TO READER

Thank you so much for reading my book. It has been a labor of love to write and publish – so much more work than I ever imagined – but it's all worth it, if it made you smile, cry, learn, or feel inspired!

If you enjoyed it, I would be so grateful if you could leave a review for me at Amazon. (It doesn't matter if you purchased it at Amazon or not.) I'm an independently published author, which means that Amazon reviews are the best way to get my book noticed and hopefully end up in more people's hands. You can find the direct review link on my website, or you can go to Amazon and find my book then scroll down to the reviews section to add yours.

Thank you so much for your support!

I'm also happy to hear from readers with your suggestions for future adventures we monkeys should pursue, or stories of your own crazy family road trips, or just to say hi.

You can reach me at our website: www.monkeysontheroad.com or by email at: mary@monkeysontheroad.com.

ACKNOWLEDGMENTS

Thank you to John's mum, Peggy, who generously accepted the job of being our mailing address while we were gone. Although I swore that I'd changed all our mail to be email delivery only, she patiently texted us photos of the endless paper mail that still made its way to us, and helped us deal with everything remotely. It's only because of her that Vancito's registration was still valid when we got back to the US!

Thank you to my mum, Susan, who flew across the Atlantic by herself multiple times to visit us in far-flung places, delivering home-school textbooks and van parts that were impossible to get locally, not to mention grandmotherly hugs. Mum, I hope I'll be as adventurous as you when I'm your age!

I am eternally grateful to have been blessed with such an easy-going daughter. She is so open-minded to new adventures and lifestyles, just as long as we are together and she can bring her Kindle and stuffed animals! Her positive energy and love for vanlife was contagious and made this experience that much more fun for all of us.

And of course, thank you to my husband John. Whether he's driving the van on terrifying roads, dealing with the never-ending engine problems, or just holding my hand while I negotiate with border guards, his endless optimism and patience is priceless and makes life so much more enjoyable. He always listens to my never-ending supply of crazy ideas and just smiles, saying, "Will you be there? Ok then, I'll pack."

And the biggest thank-you is one that probably won't be read by its recipients: to those hundreds of people who welcomed us into their homes, shared their food, helped us fix the van, looked out for Lilly, or simply waved and smiled as we drove by. The places we visited were beautiful and memorable, but it's the local people who made us feel so at home on the road.

ABOUT THE AUTHOR

Mary is passionate about travel and the outdoors. Originally from England, she moved to California for its rock climbing and sunshine, worked a season on the Yosemite Search and Rescue team, but then ended up climbing the corporate ladder at Google for a decade to fund her travel obsession.

She has bicycled across Central America, motorcycled across Mexico, driven the length of Australia, and backpacked around Europe, S.E. Asia, and Africa – all as a prelude to the epic drive through the Americas that is the subject of this book. She's written for travel, climbing, and retirement magazines, and this is her first foray into a full-length book.

https://www.monkeysontheroad.com

Made in the USA
Coppell, TX
29 November 2021

66704678R00194